RACE AND POLITICS

PARTNERSHIP IN THE FEDERATION OF
RHODESIA AND NYASALAND

RACE AND POLITICS

PARTNERSHIP IN THE FEDERATION OF
RHODESIA AND NYASALAND

MARSHALL

EDWARD CLEGG

LAMAR UNIVERSITY LIBRARY

GREENWOOD PRESS, PUBLISHERS
WESTPORT, CONNECTICUT

Library of Congress Cataloging in Publication Data

Clegg, Edward Marshall.
   Race and politics.

   Reprint of the ed. published by Oxford University
Press, London.
   Includes bibliographical references and index.
   1.   Rhodesia and Nyasaland--Politics and govern-
ment.   2.   Rhodesia and Nyasaland--Native races.
I.   Title.
[DT856.C58 1975]   968.9'03   75-3731
ISBN 0-8371-8061-9

To Adriana

THE spring is wound up tight. It will uncoil of itself. That is what is so convenient in tragedy. Anything will set it going. . . . The rest is automatic. The machine is in perfect order; it has been oiled ever since time began, and it runs without friction. . . . In a tragedy, nothing is in doubt and everyone's destiny is known. . . . He who kills is as innocent as he who gets killed; it's all a matter of what part you are playing. . . . There is no temptation to escape, argument is gratuitous. . . .

Chorus. *Antigone*, Jean Anouilh
(translated by Lewis Galantière).

Methuen and Co., Ltd., Modern Classics, 1957.

PREFACE

MY first contact with the multiracial societies of Central Africa was in a way accidental, for it was by chance that I was posted to Northern Rhodesia—a soil scientist in the Colonial Research Service. To that extent too, this book was unpremeditated. But in the field of race relations—and in Northern Rhodesia all else is subservient to race relations—the ability to make quick and decisive judgements, so easy in the first few days, quickly disappeared. Instead of being clear cut and simple, the racial problem became every day more complex, more baffling. And in like measure, the stereotyped justifications and accusations continually advanced, both in the Rhodesias and the United Kingdom, became ever more disturbing, for the fundamentals of the problem appeared to have become buried under an edifice of generalizations and irrelevancies. Increasingly I felt that an attempt was being made to grapple with a problem without actually knowing what basically constituted it.

This book is essentially an explanation therefore. It is not an exhaustive history of Northern Rhodesia; indeed, it does not fit into any specific academic niche because there is no single branch of learning which in itself can adequately explain the intricacies and complexities of the problems arising from the contact of White and Black men in Central Africa. Anthropology and history are intermixed; a knowledge of the technicalities of agricultural development in this type of environment is essential; so is an appreciation of the problems it poses for a European—an appreciation of which can only come from having lived and worked there. In this respect I was perhaps fortunate. The three years I spent in Northern Rhodesia—1951 to 1954—were particularly significant. I was able to travel extensively in the Territory and also in Nyasaland and Southern Rhodesia; I lived in the remote bush and on the Copperbelt; on a European farm and on government stations. When I worked with a gang of African labourers in the field it was not as a student of anthropology but as an employer seeking an efficient day's work.

I could not have collected much of the material used in this work, however, had I not been employed by the Institute of Race Relations in London in connexion with studies undertaken by the Institute and financed by the Rockefeller Foundation, which enabled me to revisit the two Rhodesias in 1956, and I am glad of this opportunity of thanking both the Institute and the Foundation. I should also like to thank Mr. Philip Mason, the Director of the Institute, for his help and kindness.

My final—and most important—acknowledgement is to my wife, for her patience and continual encouragement over the years this manuscript has been in preparation. Indeed, without these and her help, it would never have been finished, for she has read and re-read the innumerable manuscripts, made invaluable suggestions, listened to interminable arguments, and performed admirably the tiresome task of typing.

6 March 1960

CONTENTS

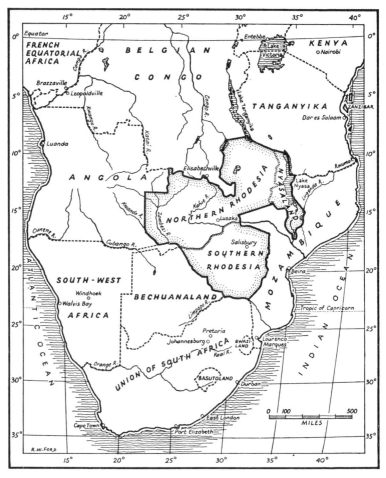

The Federation in relation to Central and Southern Africa

CHAPTER 1

INTRODUCTION

ONE of the most perplexing yet important problems in the world today is the friction and conflict arising from the close contact of two or more communities, each with differing cultural patterns, within the same political entity. Where these are associated with the indelible stamp of differing physical characteristics, notably of skin colour, the associated problems are incomparably more complex. In this context, the contact of peoples of European stock with the Coloured peoples of the world is unquestionably the most fruitful of trouble. Moreover, in certain instances, the European, by virtue of his technological superiority, has established a monopoly of economic and political power, and consequently an administrative and social structure which limits the contact of the two races and the opportunities of the non-European majority. Such racial repression is, in view of prevailing world trends, certain to have an ever-increasing impact on international affairs.

In the eighteenth and nineteenth centuries large areas of the world inhabited by the technically backward Coloured peoples were also brought under the control of the powerful states of Western Europe. But the conditions under which these Empires were established, in particular, Western Europe's monopoly of world power, are no longer operative, and many of the states formerly governed by Colonial Administrations, particularly in South-East Asia, have achieved political independence. This in itself has generated a fierce desire among those non-European peoples who remain subject to the authority of a Colonial Power to press for political independence. Likewise it has brought to the world's councils an ever-increasing number of nations who are particularly sensitive to instances of racial repression or discrimination, actual or implied. And with the present division of the world into two opposed blocs led by the United States of America, on the one hand, and the Union of Soviet Socialist Republics, on the other, these newly independent nations have been swept to a position of unprecedented prominence and influence, as each bloc attempts to coax them into their respective spheres of influence.

These associated problems occur *par excellence* in the continent of Africa south of the Sahara. Over the greater part of the area, European Colonial Administrations are still responsible for the government of the peoples living therein. Nevertheless, the trend by which political power passes into the hands of the indigenous African people has already begun. In the British sphere, the Gold Coast achieved independence as Ghana in 1956, the first African-peopled state to emerge from dependent status. And Nigeria is about to follow in her footsteps. These events are a magnet attracting the attention of the whole of Africa, and, in particular, African political leaders throughout the still dependent portion of the African Continent. At the other geographical extremity, however, the Union of South Africa is also an independent state. But in this case political power is concentrated exclusively in the hands of a minority of European stock.

The Federation of Rhodesia and Nyasaland lies geographically between these two extremes. Furthermore, while it has the largest European population outside the Union of South Africa, in those territories south of the Sahara for which the British Government remains responsible, the British Government is also under solemn obligation in two of the constituent states, Northern Rhodesia and Nyasaland, which are British Protectorates, to safeguard African interests. Similarly, while the European communities, particularly in Northern and Southern Rhodesia, have achieved a substantial measure of power, likewise the African has made not unsubstantial political progress in the two Protectorates. And neither the Federal Government nor any constituent state government are as yet independent. Thus the Federation is literally balanced between the two lodestars of Africa, Ghana on the one hand, and South Africa on the other, and to accentuate this, the Federation was established on an official policy of inter-racial partnership.

The Federation was born, however, in the midst of a violent political controversy. The African communities in the Protectorates—and they were supported by a substantial section of public opinion in the United Kingdom—declared that the creation of the Federation was another step in the direction of establishing a White oligarchy, since the political union of the Protectorates and Southern Rhodesia weakened the ability of the British Government to protect African interests in the face of the more advanced and technically able European settler population. On the other hand, the European communities in the three constituent states broadly supported the creation of the Federation—and they too were upheld by a large section of British public opinion—their view being that the Federation would provide the key to multiracial living in Africa. During the short history of the Federation, there had been continuous political skirmishing along these lines, broadly between African and European in the Federation and between the Conservative and Labour Parties in the United Kingdom political arena. Consequently, the Federal Constitution review, to be held between seven and nine years after the Federation's inception, that is between 1960 and 1962, is certain to be the occasion of acute political controversy. Because of these contradictory views there is a pressing need for an objective assessment of the actual problems of the Federal states and of the policies being pursued therein.

To ascribe the problems of the Federation to European prejudice or African backwardness is a naïve simplification. The European communities in Central Africa broadly reflect, in their community life, the habits, characteristics, and standards of material well-being established in the United Kingdom. Indeed, many of them are recent immigrants from Britain, and to assert that a sea voyage and transposition to Central Africa necessarily entails a coincidental reversal of previously-held beliefs and attitudes is, to say the least, not plausible. But living in the Federation, and working in close contact with the African, quickly convinces a European of the difference not only between his living standards and those of the African but of the different attitudes each race has to a whole range of activities, from attitudes to and aptitudes for work, to punctuality, leisure, family relationships, and ambition. However, even with those Europeans living in close contact with the African, the reasons for these differences remain a closed book: to the overwhelming majority, the African is known only by his reactions in a European-dominated sphere, this 'knowledge' being supplemented by a wealth of amusing anecdotes, the African's foibles being a favourite conversational topic. Knowledge of his ways of living, whether in the towns or the African rural areas, is scanty to the point of ignorance.

The key to understanding African behaviour patterns lies within the tribal societies. All over the Federation of Rhodesia and Nyasaland, but particularly in Northern Rhodesia and Nyasaland, Africans still live and work within their framework; an overwhelming majority of those employed in the urban areas were born and reared in the tribal rural areas. What ambitions, attitudes to family relationships, and behaviour patterns does this impart? How have these been affected by the impact of European settlement, and in particular, industrialization and urbanization? To attempt an assessment for each of the multiplicity of African tribes in the Federation of Rhodesia and Nyasaland would constitute a monumental study. Fortunately, it is not necessary. The Federation is not a unitary state: substantial powers remain with each of the Territorial Governments, and while each state faces essentially the same racial problems, the pattern of race relations differs according to the degree of industrialization, the nature and extent of European settlement, and the policies followed by the individual governments. Thus a study of one constituent state, providing there has been both a substantial degree of European settlement and industrialization, will furnish the essential background from which to examine the central problem of their impact on African tribal life. The field can thus be narrowed to Northern and Southern Rhodesia. It is of particular importance, however, to assess the role of the British Government, both in the past and at present, especially its influence with regard to the forthcoming Federal constitutional review. In view of all these factors, the study can be further narrowed to Northern Rhodesia, which in many ways is the key to the Federation. It is a Protectorate; but the European settler community has already achieved a substantial measure of power. It contains the largest industrial enterprise in the Federal state, namely the copper-mining industry, of vital import to the economy of the entire area. Moreover, the industry was established at a comparatively early date, so that the impact of industrialization and urbanization on the African tribal societies was both sharper and had greater effects than comparable developments in Southern Rhodesia.

This, in brief outline, is both a justification of the following study and an explanation of its structure. The characteristics imparted to the African people by the tribal societies prior to the establishing of a British administration are examined, and then, by following the Territory's history, the impact of the administrative policies pursued and the influence of European settlement on both those policies, the tribal societies, and the African individual evaluated. Particular attention is paid to the relationship between the British Government, the Northern Rhodesian Government, the European settlers, and the African communities prior to the establishing of the Federation, and then in the light of trends and tendencies established, the achievements of the Federation of Rhodesia and Nyasaland are examined, both in relation to the policy of inter-racial partnership, the prospects for the Federal constitutional review, and the future.

CHAPTER 2

A GLIMPSE OF AFRICAN TRIBAL LIFE

PRECISELY when the first African peoples penetrated into what was subsequently to be Northern Rhodesia is not known. Its earliest inhabitants were primitive Bushmen, but these were decimated by waves of migrant Bantu-speaking peoples from the north, who, it is generally considered, had overrun the area by the year A.D. 1500. Thereafter the region was in a state of flux, new migrant tribes entering it and conquering others already established there, only to be conquered in turn by other newcomers.

As the first half of the nineteenth century drew to a close, four powerful warrior tribes had established themselves in dominant positions, the Lunda, Barotse, Bemba, and Ngoni. The exact routes by which the first three arrived, or their arrival dates, are not known precisely. The Bemba, an offshoot of the Luba tribe of the Katanga region of the Belgian Congo, are thought to have occupied their present homeland towards the end of the seventeenth century, crossing the Luapula river and passing to the north of the Bengweulu swamps before finally establishing the village of their Paramount Chief at the centre of the Tanganyika Plateau, not far from the site of the present government administrative post of Kasama in the Territory's Northern Province. Once established, they gradually extended their sphere of influence, driving weaker tribes, such as the Bisa, before them, until almost the whole of the district between the four lakes, Tanganyika, Nyasa, Mweru, and Bengweulu, was under their control.

The Lunda tribe also originated in the Belgian Congo, but farther to the north-west, across the Lualaba river. During the course of its migration, the tribe split, the two sons of the old chief Mwatayamvu each leading an army to conquer fresh lands. One of them, Kazembe, also crossed the Luapula, defeated the Ushi people in the vicinity of Lake Mweru, and settled in the Luapula Valley. Manuel Pereira, a Portuguese half-caste, and one of the first non-Africans to penetrate Central

Africa, visited his court in 1796, during an exploratory journey from Tete in Portuguese East Africa. The other son, Musokontanda, led his people south-west, and eventually they settled in the headwaters region of the Zambesi. The village of their chief, still known by the traditional name of Musokontanda, is now sited in the Belgian Congo.

Of the Barotse, inhabitants of the flood plain of the Zambesi upstream from the Victoria Falls, little is known of their early history, although they were the first tribe north of the Zambesi to be contacted by Livingstone, who, in his second exploratory journey, established friendly relations with Sebitoane, then ruler of Barotseland. Originally Sebitoane had been the chief of the Kalolo tribe, a branch of the Basuto people whose homeland was a thousand miles south of Barotseland. But defeat in battle had set him and his followers roving; eventually they crossed the Zambesi and settled in the Tonga plateau region of Northern Rhodesia. Following a civil war among the Barotse, Sebitoane and the Kalolo invaded Barotseland and conquered it. Thus Sebitoane became king of the Barotse, and the Kalolo privileged overlords. Such was the state of affairs when Livingstone first crossed the Zambesi. Sebitoane's death set in train another struggle for power, and ultimately the Barotse rebelled and annihilated their Kalolo overlords.

The Ngoni, last of the powerful warrior tribes to establish themselves in the area, journeyed northwards, like the Kalolo, from the southern part of the continent. When Zwide of the Ndandwe was defeated by Shaka, the Zulu chief, parties of Ndandwe refugees fled northward. At least two groups travelled as far as the Zambesi, and one, led by Zwangendaba, crossed the river on 19 November 1835, a date fixed by a coincidental eclipse of the sun, whose effects were incorporated into Ngoni—as the group was called eventually—tribal lore. Continuing north, they reached Lake Tanganyika, where Zwangendaba died. Following his death, the tribe split into different factions. Under a new leader each scattered, one group journeying as far north as Lake Victoria–Nyanza, another as far south as Central Nyasaland, while a third journeyed into what was to become Northern Rhodesia, brushing past the Bemba kingdom in a battle lasting several days, to settle eventually over what in later years was to be the Northern Rhodesia–Nyasaland border.

With the arrival of the Ngoni, the disposition of the principal tribes in Northern Rhodesia was broadly that found by the early European explorers and hunters. Each of these warrior tribes occupied a specific area, over which they maintained a more or less highly developed administration, though the boundaries were usually ill-defined. All of them sent raiding bands of warriors out into the country in between, to raid, pillage, and capture slaves. Thus the Tonga, prey to raids by the Barotse from the west and the Matabele from the south, were by 1890, 'a broken, beaten people, their cattle stolen, and many of their people enslaved in Barotseland or among the Matabele'.[1]

With this pattern of conquered and conquerors superimposed on a multiplicity of tribes, each with different institutions, traditions, and customs, any attempt to establish general characteristics typical of the tribal African and his society before the coming of the European would appear almost impossible. Lord Hailey has pointed out, however, that 'despite the great diversity of communities in Africa, there are certain salient characteristics which have differentiated African traditional institutions from those now associated with Western civilization'.[2] To illustrate these salient characteristics it is sufficient for our purpose to outline briefly the organization and structure of two of the more important Northern Rhodesian tribes, the Bemba and the Ngoni. Though both were warrior peoples, there were important differences between their modes of life. Moreover, both were subsequently affected to a considerable degree by demands for industrial labour.

The area of Bemba[3] domination, the high plateau between the great lakes, is an extensive tract of flattish country. Seen from the air, it has the appearance of a vast, camouflaged fabric patterned in green, the more extensive darker patches being woodland, and the long tongues of lighter hue, shallow, waterlogged depressions known locally as *damboes*. (Northern and Southern Rhodesia lie on the high African plateau, and as such,

---

[1] *Seven Tribes of British Central Africa*, ed. by Elizabeth Colson and Max Gluckman (London, 1951), p. 100.

[2] *An African Survey Revised*, Lord Hailey (London, 1956), p. 30.

[3] This account of Bemba tribal organization is taken from *Land, Labour and Diet in Northern Rhodesia: An Economic Study of the Bemba Tribe*, Dr. A. Richards (London, 1939). For Ngoni history, tribal organization, and custom, see *Politics in a Changing Society*, J. A. Barnes (Cape Town, 1954).

this landscape is characteristic over very wide areas.) Villages can be seen thinly scattered over the area, each a cluster of mud-walled, thatch-roofed huts set in circular bare patches, where the earth shows warmly red in contrast with the surrounding green. Stretching out around each village are cultivated areas, where the trees have been cut down and the land tilled, each being roughly circular and centred on the village. The entire countryside, irrespective of the presence of villages, appears to be covered with these pock-like marks. These manifestations of human activity apart, there is nothing to be seen on the vast, brooding plain. As a view, it has scarcely changed since the Bemba owned warrior sway over it.

The environment in which the Bemba lived was, from an agricultural point of view, harsh. There was a long period without rainfall, the soils were infertile, while tsetse fly prevented cattle being kept. To overcome these difficulties, the Bemba practised a primitive system of agriculture which in its way was well suited to these conditions. An area adjacent to a village was selected as a garden, the branches of the trees standing on it and the surrounding area were cut down, piled over the central portion, and then burnt. The resulting wood ash provided a seedbed for millet, the principal crop grown. Strictly speaking, the Bemba could scarcely be termed agriculturists; their main food-producing weapon was the axe, and their judgement of good agricultural land was based not on the soil but on the types of trees growing thereon. Up to twelve acres of woodland had to be devastated to produce an acre of *chitimene* garden.

Since the Bemba knew only this method of inducing fertility, they had to repeat this process continually. This involved extending the garden areas outwards from the village, so that after four or five years the new garden areas might be several miles from it. At this point the village migrated to a new area of fresh woodland, where an exactly similar cycle was begun. Thus each Bemba village shifted every five or six years, moving in its entirety to a new site, usually some five to six miles from the old one. Since the population density was extremely low and the land available unlimited, the long-term effects of this system were not serious. Sufficient time was allowed for the woodland to regenerate before a village returned to a former site, this allowing the fertility of the soil to be restored by natural processes.

This constant round of shifting naturally enforced certain limitations on the Bemba life pattern. Material possessions had necessarily to be few, since they had to be moved so frequently, for the Bemba had no transport animals. Houses were built in the knowledge that their maximum life would only be of the order of five or six years. Not only did this system impose a common poverty; it enforced a common mode of life. Bemba society was one in which everyone lived in the same type of hut, grew the same crops, and ate the same kinds of food; a society based on village life, on small, intimate communities. That the Bemba were likely, under such conditions, to have a totally different scale of values from those current in the more materialistic societies of Western Europe is readily apparent. According to Dr. Richards, the strongest ambition of the Bemba was the conquest of territory, the exacting of tribute from defeated and subjugated tribes. And if tribal ambition was to conquer, that of the individual centred on warriorhood, which as a consequence stood supreme in the eyes of the tribe. Even as late as 1930, when warriorhood was long a thing of the past, Bemba men, questioned as to what they considered their tribal characteristic *par excellence* before the coming of the White men, invariably replied *Ubukali* . . . fierceness, ruthlessness. Agricultural activities were despised—except for the dangerous task of lopping off tree branches for the *chitimene* gardens.

The most important measure of a man's wealth and status was the number of followers owing him allegiance. In the case of a chief, apart of course from his own family, his following consisted of the tribute labour provided by young men from the area for which he was the administrative head, together with slaves captured during raids and inter-tribal warfare. The greater their combined numbers, the more important a chief's status.[4] In order to maintain followers at his court, a chief had to feed them, for in Bemba society the giving of cooked food was

---

[4] Briefly the political system of the Bemba consisted of a Paramount Chief, the *Chitimukulu*, a hereditary ruler with a fixed title drawn from the Royal Clan, who ruled over his own district but was overlord to a number of territorial chiefs, who governed districts similar in size, and likewise succeeded to fixed titles and were drawn from the family of the Paramount Chief. Beneath the chiefs were headmen of villages, whom they appointed.

recognized as a reward for services rendered, in the same way as a European recognizes payment in cash. To some extent, therefore, the increase of wealth, in Bemba terms, involved an apparent contradiction. To augment his following a chief had to be able to distribute more food and beer, and increased production of food and beer demanded a larger number of followers. In reality, however, no such contradiction existed. A chief was assured of followers by virtue of his supernatural powers over the prosperity of the land and the welfare of his individual subjects. By his inheritance of the guardian spirits of the line of dead chiefs, his ancestors, and his possession of the sacred relics of the tribe, he was empowered to approach tribal deities and perform economic rites on which the people believed food production depended. If the rains failed or locust depredations became serious, the sole cause to the Bemba mind was that the ancestral spirits were displeased. Only by placating them, by restoring their well-being, could that of the tribe be reestablished. Thus the Paramount Chief, inheritor and guardian of the spirits of former Paramount Chiefs, supreme link between the spiritual and temporal worlds, was thought to hold tribal well-being completely in his hands. Should he refuse to intercede, or conduct himself in a manner offensive to his ancestors, the whole tribe was imperilled.

Similarly, each member of the tribe was responsible to his ancestral spirits, and each could bring, within his or her own sphere, a measure of disaster by not observing the correct tribal rituals, taboos, and traditions. On this integration of belief, tribal unity hung, for at each administrative level, allegiance was to the guardian of the ancestral spirits, to the village headman, regional chief, and finally, and most important of all, to the Paramount Chief. Consequently it was necessary to take elaborate precautions to see that tribal customs, taboos, and traditions were faithfully observed, and a special hierarchy of officials, the *Bakabilo*, many of them of royal descent, were entrusted with carrying out and organizing all the complex ceremonials in the life of the Paramount Chief, as well as acting as a council for the tribe as a whole.

In addition to their supernatural powers, the chiefs' authority was further enhanced by the physical forces they controlled in the shape of armed warriors. Consequently they had power

of life and death over their subjects, whom they could kill, enslave or sell, and in the case of women, bestow in marriage.
Their legal system gave them the right to mutilate those who
offended them, and put them in supreme charge of the poison
ordeal.[5] Tribute in labour and kind was exacted from all, and
the land theoretically belonged to them. No Bemba could reach
a high social status or obtain economic privileges unless he was
either related to the royal family or was a personal favourite.

As in the case of a chief, the wealth of a Bemba male commoner was also measured by the number of his followers, as distinct from his social status, which was entirely determined by a
man's relationship to the chief, whether by blood or otherwise.
Likewise, the accumulation of followers depended on a man's
ability to distribute food and beer. But a commoner could command no tribute labour. His economic strength, on the contrary, was rooted in the family structure. The nucleus of each
Bemba village was a matrilocal family consisting of the headman, his married daughters, their husbands and children, the
whole, depending to a degree on its size, functioning as an integrated economic unit. When a Bemba youth was betrothed he
moved to his fiancée's village, acknowledged her father as the
family head and director of the family pool of labour, of which
he was an integral part, for every Bemba father-in-law had a
legal right to the labour of his son-in-law. Moreover, during the
first years of marriage, a couple were not allowed a separate
domestic existence. The husband worked entirely under the
direction of his father-in-law, and the produce of their common
effort went into the family grain bins. These, in turn, were under
the mother's charge, for she was responsible for supervising the
feeding of the entire family. Her newly married daughter continued as she had before marriage, a helper, working under her
supervision.

Obviously there was a degree of luck in a man satisfying his
desire for a following, since the essential foundation was a high
percentage of daughters in his family. But if a man was so
favoured, sooner or later suitors would seek their hands. With
many sons-in-law, a man might then begin to distribute gifts of
food and beer, and so become recognized for generosity and good
sense. In time, the married daughters would have children, and

[5] Dr. A. Richards, op. cit., p. 25.

their daughters in turn would attract suitors. Eventually a man might have a sufficient number of relatives owing him allegiance for him to establish a village of his own: then other more distant relatives might be attracted to it. Thus was a Bemba village built up.

The most important occasion in the agricultural year for the Bemba was the lopping of tree branches in preparation for the planting season. But as a task, this occupied only one or two months of the year. In any case, a young man was not expected to excel in the work of gardening. First and foremost he was a warrior: prestige emanated from warriorhood, not ability to wield a hoe or an axe. After moving to his future bride's village, a man lived alone at first, although the young couple might be permitted to sleep together if the prospective husband proved respectful and diligent. Not until the approach of puberty, Bemba girls being betrothed between the ages of ten and twelve, was a marriage ceremony contemplated. Even then it was of less importance than the preceding ceremonial which marked the girl's initiation into adult life, for to become pregnant without initiation was to give mortal offence to the ancestral spirits. After the completion of these ceremonials, a girl was allowed to return to her husband's hut, but at any time during the first years of marriage she could be taken away, should he prove in any way unsatisfactory. Before initiation a marriage could be terminated with ease, should it not be prospering; afterwards, while such drastic action could still be taken, every effort was made by the girl's family to try to make it work, for a divorce after initiation inevitably meant that the girl's value as a bride was considerably reduced.

This situation, in which the bride was firmly part of a stable family group, protected and guided by her parents and relatives, while the husband was loosely attached to it, came to an end gradually by a series of definite and well-marked stages. It was a question of the husband becoming more absorbed, the wife a little less strongly attached. But the marriage was accepted by the family group as stable only after a period of years, the exact number depending on the quality of the husband and the number of children produced. The husband had in fact to demonstrate that physically and emotionally he could fit harmoniously into his wife's family and ensure its continuance. This process of adjustment coincided with a change in a man's ambitions, from being primarily a warrior to a 'settled' family man, anxious to achieve domestic independence and a following of his own. Once his marriage was finally accepted as stable, an occasion ceremoniously marked, the husband had the right to make his own gardens, and his wife to cook and handle her own supplies of grain.

Even after this final stage in the development of a Bemba marriage, the relation of husband and wife bore little resemblance to those of a happily married European couple, for in Bemba society men and women occupied separate watertight compartments which dissolved only at night and in old age. This was merely symptomatic of another characteristic of Bemba society: everyone fitted into a specific niche, the pattern of behaviour between different relatives, and the legal obligations binding them, being traditionally fixed and regulated by a complex code of etiquette. A young son-in-law, for instance, coming to live in his wife's village was an outsider, a stranger, and often the source of amusement and jokes. His wife could be taken from him should he not conform to his parents-in-law's requirements: he was surrounded by her family. Even so, he had to be treated with the correct courtesies. A son-in-law had the right to expect good and generous supplies of food, presented neatly in a covered basket. Should a man be dissatisfied with the food he received, he could go to the extreme length of breaking off the marriage, for to be ungenerous in supplying food was disrespectful. The strength of this code is well illustrated by a case recorded by Dr. Richards. An old Bemba woman, herself on the point of starvation, made up her last dish of food and sent it to her son-in-law, although he was a comparatively wealthy government clerk. Starvation was as nothing compared with the rightful dues of a son-in-law!

Bemba eating habits well illustrate this compartmenting within the tribe. The adults had only one meal each day, and that in the evening, for to eat more frequently was childish and immature. The main constituent of the meal was a thick porridge made of ground millet, which, while being the only part to count as food, was at the same time impossible to eat without a 'relish', preferably a kind of meat stew, although groundnuts, mushrooms, and caterpillars were also used according to the season. This evening meal came as the climax of the day, for in a society both formal and monotonously simple, food and drink assumed great importance. It was also a signal for a Bemba community to split into definite groups, the men into divisions based on age, kinship, and friendship, the elders eating together on one of the hut verandas and the young men sharing food baskets under the shelter specially built for them. The women belonged to no such fixed groupings, women of associated households eating together, as was convenient. Nobody ate alone; men and women never together in public.

Working functions were similarly divided between the sexes. Men undertook branch cutting, the repair of houses, the fencing round of gardens to prevent crops being damaged by wild animals, and some hoeing and gardening. The tasks of the women were more extensive and arduous. They had to fetch firewood and water, pound grain into flour using crude wooden pestles and mortars, collect the materials from which 'relish' was made, undertake crop harvest and grain storage, in addition to most of the hoeing and domestic chores in general. The division of function was all but absolute: while a man might cut branches for firewood, it was a woman's task to fetch it into the village. Women consequently bore the brunt of the village's domestic and agricultural work, and this occasionally had important repercussions.

The Bemba year was divided into two well-marked seasons, November to April being the time of the rains, broadly the season of planting and harvesting, and April to October the dry period, when gardens were prepared, tree branches lopped, and houses repaired. Thus about the time when the rains were ending, agricultural activity was at its height. Harvesting was in full swing; grain had to be carried from the gardens to the village granaries, often a long journey. Shortly afterwards, the tree-lopping season began, the work of the men *par excellence*. It was initiated by a rich ceremonial at the Paramount Chief's court and followed by a similar but simpler rite in every village in Bembaland, as headmen asked the ancestral spirits to ensure the safety of the men in their hazardous occupation and the success of their operations. Once the men had lopped down the branches, their duties were over. The remaining tasks, not so dangerous but nonetheless long and arduous, of dragging the branches to a central area and piling them prior to burning was the work of the women. These additional activities, augmenting the daily round associated with the collection and preparation of food, and following on harvesting, often meant that the womenfolk were overworked and tired during this period. The result was that on occasion no food was prepared. In the circumstances Bemba males could hardly complain. And indeed they never did. A man returning from his garden, or from hunting, never stayed about his hut. After leaving his axe or hoe there, he immediately went to the place where he habitually ate, and there stayed, talking to friends, until such time as food was brought to him. If it failed to arrive, the situation was accepted without complaint. Warriorhood had its logic as well as its pride.

This fatalism and acceptance of the inevitable was a marked feature of the Bemba character. It becomes manifest if the yearly life cycle of the tribe is examined. The beginning of the dry season was both the period of greatest agricultural activity and the season of plenty. The harvest was recently reaped; millet was available for porridge and beer-making. It was thus a time of enjoyment, of full stomachs, beer brewing, and dancing.[6] Abundance of beer was the glory of the commoner's hospitality, and from May to August, each village brewed beer at least once a week, the chore of brewing rotating round each of the 'independent' wives in a village.

After August, however, millet supplies became increasingly scarce. Despite the long training which preceded domestic independence, Bemba women were apparently unable to 'ration' supplies over the year. Immediately after the harvest, grain supplies disappeared quickly in the jollifications. With a shock, the women saw the low state of their grain reserves in relation to the long months before the next harvest. Beer brewing was curtailed; care began to be exercised. By the time of the first rains in November, brewing was only an occasional activity, for supplies of millet, the staple food, were becoming scarce. Of the cultivated sources of relish only groundnuts were still available. Women and children began scavenging the bush for wild mushrooms and caterpillars. By February and March scavenging was

[6] A brew of beer was usually made by one woman for an entire village, and since it was a complex and lengthy operation, tended further to dislocate the ordinary domestic routine.

at its height, the only crops available being gourds and occasional maize-cobs from the ripening crop. This was the period
of famine, the 'hunger months' as the Bemba called them, the
famine that afflicted the tribe to a greater or lesser extent every
year.

But just as the occasional absence of food during harvesting
and garden making was stoically accepted, so was this yearly
famine. Though soil fertility was low, there was plenty of land
available: experience, it was fair to suppose, would have quickly
taught a man how many acres had to be cultivated to provide
for the needs of a given number of people. And the juxtaposition
of plenty and famine as part of an annual cycle was seemingly a
sufficient incentive to learn. But in reality there was no relation
between the acreage cultivated and the amount of grain har-
vested to the Bemba mind. The land was held to be under the
influence of the supernatural, yielding or withholding its fruits
according to whether the tribe's ancestral spirits were contented
or offended. In like manner, any ill fortune affecting a family
had only one explanation: the failure of someone within the
group to respect the ancestral spirits.

With such an acute awareness of the power of the supernatural, it was inevitable that the Bemba should be a prey to
magic, which was extensively used, both offensively and de-
fensively. It played an important role in conditioning their attitude to food production, for the Bemba believed that the ability
of a supply of grain to last out the season or of cooked food to
satisfy the hunger of the eater depended upon special magical
properties which could be induced by human beings, should
they perform the necessary rites. Hence food, and particularly
millet, was especially subject to witchcraft. Wizards placed
horns in their granaries to attract other men's grain; black birds
were sent out at night on the same nefarious purpose. And for
protection against these silent, supernatural depredations, the
only safeguard was to utilize counter magic, one rite to keep the
granary full and another to make the food in a small eating pot
satisfy a family's hunger.

Inevitably magic was not confined to such activities as these.
It infiltrated every facet of Bemba life and activity, for if a man's
grain was prey to the wiles of a witch, so was his life, his wife,
and family. Magic was the curse of society, ravaging it with

fear. Bemba reasoning was always oriented towards the question 'why me?' Why did misfortune, disease, and accident afflict one man and not the next? Because a supernatural force, initiated by a particular individual with malevolent intent, had been directed specifically to that end. A tree branch crashing on a man's head was caused not by decay and the pull of gravity, but by a magic incantation which decreed that that particular branch should fall at that particular moment. Hence Bemba life was enmeshed in a frightening complex of suspicion and fear, of magic incantation and counter-measure.

Religious sanction operated in another fashion too to ensure that the Bemba did not attempt to increase their grain supplies by cultivating larger acreages. Tribal custom demanded that food be shared, that any member of a family who suffered misfortune must be sustained in adversity. Such practices were sufficiently common for them to be described by specific phrases, 'looking for porridge' or 'running from hunger'. Since it was impossible to hide the fact that one grain bin was full while others were empty in these small village societies, there was consequently little incentive to grow more crops. The inevitable result would be the arrival of relatives unwilling to work equally hard; and to refuse to share food with a relative was a crime of great seriousness, an offence against the ancestral spirits. Public opinion, mindful of the consequences, made certain therefore that the custom was followed. In any case, to be more successful than one's fellows was to stir suspicions that success hung on the pursuit of witchcraft.

These intertwined forces of social custom and supernatural sanction not only served to keep everyone at the same level of material well-being and to force everyone to live within a recurring cycle of famine and plenty; it bred a static society, where individualism, even curiosity in its wider sense, was suppressed. These factors naturally influenced Bemba attitudes to work. Hard, regular labour was quite unknown to the men, although the women, from sheer necessity, worked harder and longer. Dr. Richards, during her studies of the Bemba, timed some at work. In one village, during a slack season, the old men worked fourteen out of twenty days, the young men seven (the study was made in the early 1930s; hence the figure for young men was influenced by labour migrations). The average time spent working by the men was three hours: that of the women six. Even during the busier season, the men worked only four hours a day. Marriages, deaths, the departure of tribute labourers for the chief's village, the arrival of relatives on a visit, all were occasions bringing work to a stop. Some were sufficiently important to warrant celebrations. And a big celebration might last two days. In Dr. Richards's estimate, taking all Bemba activities into consideration, concentrating them together, and allowing for the slow rate of work, at least five months of the year were free from any kind of activity.

The tribal structure of the Ngoni, by virtue of their mode of life, inevitably showed considerable differences from that of the Bemba. Though the latter practised shifting agriculture, they were stabilized in the sense that as a nation they lived in a specific area. But when the Ngoni left their homeland, they were refugees; many of their women and cattle had been lost. The warriors had not only to find a new homeland, therefore: they had to rebuild the tribe, to re-create a viable social entity. For this they had only one asset, their warriorhood. Despite the defeat which precipitated their roving, the Ngoni were still more powerful than the majority of the tribes encountered on their northward march. Hence they began systematically to raid, to conquer, and enslave. Cattle were captured to replace those left behind; women of defeated tribes were forcibly absorbed into their ranks, to become wives and concubines, and thus begin the process of rebuilding the Ngoni nation. As its strength increased, so men as well as women were drafted into the ranks of the tribe.

By virtue of this mode of life and the need for rapid numerical expansion, the Ngoni tribal structure had necessarily to be adaptable and flexible. Important positions in the tribe's political structure were occupied by members of the royal lineage, their wives, the regional governors, and their lieutenants. Shortly before the British administration was established there were four important royal villages, each with several thousand inhabitants, three controlled by the wives of the Paramount Chief, Mpezeni I, and the other by his brother. Associated with the royal villages were several regional governors who were responsible for a group of smaller villages. Each village in turn was controlled by a headman. Every person of importance was helped by lieutenants; those of the Paramount Chief undertook general duties relating to the entire tribe or were responsible for looking after the villages of the Paramount Chief's wives and for securing their internal order. All these posts were inherited in the agnatic line.

The practice of polygamy was fundamental to the Ngoni mechanism for rapid expansion. An important man who had many wives divided them into groups each of some half dozen and allocated followers to them so that each of these divisions or segments within a village consisted of a senior wife, her junior co-wives, their sons, together with the dependants allocated to it, including those captured in battle. Within these divisions, sons and even quasi-related dependants could establish inferior segments of their own. Important persons in the royal lineage founded new royal villages by a similar process, a wife or a group of wives being allocated followers by recruitment from the man's own natal village. Thus the tribe, divided into a series of agnatic lineages, expanded by a process of constant snowballing and splitting, the pattern of residence coinciding with political allegiance. This pattern of expansion 'outward' from the focal point of tribal allegiance, the Paramount Chief, tended to weaken the tribe's cohesion, and this was partly offset by the practice of calling up all the young men in age-sets and drafting them into the warrior regiments. The latter also provided the Ngoni with an efficient fighting machine.

It is immediately apparent that the basic tribal organizations of the Ngoni and the Bemba were fundamentally different. The Ngoni were traditionally a patrilocal, patrilineal people; they traced descent through the male line, and on marriage Ngoni women went to live in the village of their husband's family. The Bemba, on the contrary, were a matrilocal, matrilineal people; a man was heir to his maternal grandfather or maternal uncle. The Bemba kept no cattle, whereas the Ngoni were pastoralists, for whom cattle were not only an important measure of wealth but essential for fulfilling social obligations, including the payment of 'brideprice'. Despite these differences, however, there was a surprising measure of similarity between the fundamental concepts of the two peoples—indeed, the manner in which the Ngoni nation was rebuilt demonstrates this compatibility between different tribal cultures. Most of the captives incorporated into the Ngoni nation came from matrilineal matrilocal tribes, for instance; nevertheless, they were successfully assimilated. No serious bars appear to have been raised against the advancement of captives either: 'men were enrolled into the age-set regiment appropriate to their age, and it was possible for them to rise to high positions in the state'.[7]

Thus both tribes regarded the attributes of warriorhood as supreme; both were primitive subsistence agriculturists, and in neither tribe were there social divisions based on material wealth. The Ngoni mode of life ensured that the tribe had no conception of individual land ownership; but neither had the Bemba. Land was a gift of nature, and all members of the tribe had the right to cultivate it and enjoy its fruits. If land 'belonged' at all, it was to the tribe as a whole, and in particular to the Paramount Chief, who was the trustee for his people. But there was no concept of his owning the land. There were, of course, certain rules regarding its use and allocation; a village headman indicated where an individual might cultivate. But in Bembaland no boundaries were ever marked, and apparently there were few disputes over the limits of the various garden areas, for to quarrel over land was a sign of ill-breeding.

Both tribes worshipped ancestral spirits; in each case it was the people's belief in and fear of the ancestral spirits of past Paramount Chiefs which was the root of their unity and the source of the Paramount's power. Both tribes were consequently acutely aware of the supernatural; both riddled with the use of magic. In both tribes there was a rigid division along the line of sex; both regarded consanguinity, rather than marriage, as the permanent bond. With a common level of poverty dictated by their lack of technical skills, the nature of the environment, and tribal belief and custom, both tribes lived primarily in the present. Neither Ngoni nor Bemba had a written language; nor had either tribe any experience of regular work.

[7] E. Colson and Max Gluckman, op. cit., p. 198.

CHAPTER 3

THE INITIAL COLLISION

In the second half of the nineteenth century new elements began to intrude into this pattern of African conquerors and conquered. Slave-traders reached the country, later to become Northern Rhodesia, from both the east and the west coasts; Arabs who crossed the Tanganyika plateau; the Yao, a Bantu people who had migrated to and settled in southern Nyasaland; Portuguese half-castes and their African followers, from the lower Zambesi valley in the east, and Angola in the west. Thrusting inland from Zanzibar and other centres on the east coast, the Arabs succeeded in establishing political dominion over the weaker African tribes lying athwart their slaving routes. With the stronger warrior peoples farther inland, such as the Bemba or the Lunda of the Luapula valley, they merely traded, exchanging guns and cloth for slaves and ivory. In terms of the existing structures of these warrior tribes, this trading had little effect. Indeed, it strengthened the power of the *Chitimukulu*, Paramount Chief of the Bemba, for he extended his traditional monopoly over ivory to a monopoly over guns. Moreover, the cloth traded by the Arabs was eagerly sought after, and by distributing it as a reward for exceptional services, the Paramount further consolidated his hold over the tribe. The demand for slaves, whether for sale in their own right or for transporting ivory down to the coast, coupled with the desire for cloth and guns, combined to extend the area, frequency, and ferocity of the warrior raids, and the consequent devastation and loss of life was fearful. Nevertheless, the slave-trade did not fundamentally change the relationships between the tribes of Northern Rhodesia: rather did it accentuate the salient features of the existing pattern, strengthening the warrior tribes and accelerating the decimation of the weaker, conquered peoples.

The coming of the missionaries was a different matter. Inspired by David Livingstone's epic journeys of exploration and his accounts of the horrors of the slave-trade and the barbarism of tribal Africa, missionaries of different Christian creeds and

nationalities began to penetrate the unknown continent. Un-
like the early European travellers, big-game hunters, and
traders, the missionaries were intent on establishing permanent
settlements among the African tribes, and were determined
actively to influence both their beliefs and ways of life. But
Livingstone appreciated that in itself Christianity would be unable to civilize Africa; the Dark Continent had also to be opened
to 'legitimate' commerce, and his descriptions of the economic
possibilities of the continent aroused considerable interest. But
it was the discovery of diamonds at Kimberley in the Cape Province, towards the end of the 1860s, that really focused attention
on the continent's economic potential; and interest was intensified by the discovery of gold on the Rand in the Transvaal.
Concession hunters, seeking mineral rights from African poten-
tates, began to follow in the missionaries' paths into the interior.

In 1889 John Cecil Rhodes, colossus of the gold and diamond
industries, formed the British South Africa Company to exploit
the concession he had gained from Lo Bengula, Paramount
Chief of the Matabele, and carry British interests north of the
Limpopo. A Royal Charter was granted to his company in
October 1889. By then Rhodes had purchased another con-
cession, obtained originally by Harry Ware from Lewanika,
Paramount Chief of the Barotse, whose lands lay north of the
Zambesi. In 1889 Mr. Harry Johnston was appointed British
Consul to Portuguese East Africa, and authorized by the For-
eign Office to travel inland and report on the trouble with the
Arabs and the Portuguese, and sign treaties with Native chiefs.
'Knowing that a great deal of ground would have to be covered
in treaty making and that I should be unable to reach all parts
of Central Africa myself,' Johnston wrote, 'I desired to engage
someone who might suitably represent me in such portions of
this territory as lay outside my route, especially in Central
Zambezia and the countries between Nyasaland and Barotse.' [1]

From the south, from the east, the net was closing. . . .

Settled in the region bounded by the Shire, Luangwa, and
Zambesi rivers, the Ngoni occupied a position of great importance, across the route taken by the Portuguese from Mozambique into the interior, which, with the expansion of British interests in Nyasaland, also lay between the British and Portuguese

[1] *British Central Africa*, Sir H. Johnston (London, 1897), p. 89.

spheres of influence. Moreover, Ngoniland was fertile, free from tsetse fly, and, being on the high plateau, had a cooler, pleasanter climate than the lower river valleys. It was thus well suited to White colonization, and like most of the powerful chiefs, Mpezeni, the Paramount of the Ngoni, had been visited by concession hunters. In November 1888 the Governor-General of Mozambique instructed Carl Weise, a German trader already in contact with Mpezeni, to lead a Portuguese expedition to his Court. Weise was well received and distributed Portuguese flags to the Paramount and his sons, a submissive gesture on the part of the Africans in Portuguese eyes. But in 1891 the Foreign Office granted the British South Africa Company permission to extend its operations north of the Zambesi; the western boundary of Nyasaland was proclaimed—it followed the watershed between the Zambesi and the Shire as had been decided at the Berlin West Africa Conference in 1885; and finally the Anglo-Portuguese agreement, signed on 11 June, delineated the boundary between the British and Portuguese spheres of influence. This agreement placed Mpezeni within the British sphere of influence; the defined western boundary of Nyasaland cut his people into two unequal parts, the larger lying to the west of the boundary.

Though Mpezeni's country fell within the British sphere of influence, Carl Weise had obtained a number of concessions from chiefs within the area dominated by Mpezeni before the signing of the Anglo-Portuguese agreement. Further, he claimed to have been given a concession by Mpezeni orally on 19 November 1886, and that this was subsequently ratified on 14 April 1891. In return for exclusive mineral, timber, water, railway, and other rights, Weise agreed to pay Mpezeni £200 annually and 1 per cent. of his profits. Johnston, in his dual capacity of Imperial Commissioner for Nyasaland and administrator for the domains of the Chartered Company—as the British South Africa Company was called—north of the Zambesi, had established a kind of land court where all concessions obtained from Native chiefs had to be registered, since they did not by themselves establish a clear right to title under British law. Weise saw Johnston and asked for his concessions to be registered, but Johnston refused to entertain the idea. Weise then journeyed to Europe and attempted to win support for his concessions. Ironically, he eventually found it in London, and in 1893 the Mozambique, Gold, Land, and Concessions Company Ltd., was formed to exploit the Weise concessions. Representatives of the company then approached the Foreign Office over the question of registration, but were told that application had to be made to the court in Nyasaland. When this was done, the Mozambique Company was informed that the British South Africa Company and the African Lakes Company, a trading enterprise founded originally in association with missionaries in Nyasaland to supply the mission stations around Lake Nyasa with goods from the coast and to trade with Africans, had presented treaties before the court in 1891, covering exactly the same area as the Weise concessions. In the absence of counter-claims, these had been registered, although it was not until September 1893 that Johnston issued a certificate of claim to the British South Africa Company 'entitling them to exercise mining and other rights throughout the greater part of what was to become North-Eastern Rhodesia, and including therein, the whole of Mpezeni's country outside Nyasaland'.[2] In support of their claim, the two companies produced treaties with six chiefs from the area, not including Mpezeni, though Dr. Barnes asserts that only one of the six chiefs' lands bordered the country dominated by the Ngoni.

In 1894 a representative of the Mozambique Company appeared in Nyasaland and again presented the Weise concessions before the land court. This time they were registered but not recognized. And when, in November 1894 the administrations of Nyasaland and the Chartered Company's territories north of the Zambesi were separated, the Foreign Office stipulated that the sanction for the treaties made by the British South Africa Company's agents was to be without prejudice to Weise's possible claims. Shortly afterwards negotiations were opened between the British South Africa Company and the Mozambique Company, and agreement was eventually reached. In return for renouncing all claims under the Weise concessions, the British South Africa Company granted the Mozambique Company land and mineral rights over 10,000 square miles of country in North-Eastern Rhodesia, country which included Ngoniland. A new company, the North Charterland Explora-

[2] *Politics in a Changing Society*, J. A. Barnes (London, 1954), p. 75.

tion, was formed to exploit the concession; the British South Africa Company had a financial interest in it.

Before the agreement was signed, the first party of Mozambique Company officials arrived at Tete in Portuguese East Africa on the way to North-Eastern Rhodesia. Since the British South Africa Company had not established an administration there—its administrative headquarters was still in Blantyre, Nyasaland—the first Europeans to enter Mpezeni's country on a permanent basis were representatives of a purely commercial concern. Initially they were well received by the Paramount. But it was only a question of time before friction developed. The Ngoni continued their cycle of raiding, enslaving, and looting the grain bins of their neighbours, activities which neither added to the Europeans' sense of security nor allowed them to trade satisfactorily. The Europeans, for their part, were constantly insulting men of importance in the Ngoni hierarchy, partly through ignorance of Ngoni custom, and partly because all Ngoni were considered primitive savages. Resentment and frustration mounted on both sides, particularly among the Ngoni warriors, for whom Nsingu, eldest son and heir to Mpezeni, became a figure-head. Subsequent to an incident in which Nsingu was involved, a section of the Ngoni rose, and hemmed a party of Europeans in a small fort. Imperial troops were dispatched from Nyasaland, and the rising was quickly quelled. Nsingu was captured, given a summary trial, and shot. A large number of villages were destroyed as a punitive measure while many thousands of head of Ngoni cattle were looted and taken to Nyasaland. To the old Ngoni, the coming of the Europeans and the date of their defeat are synonymous: 19 January 1898.

In the remainder of North-Eastern Rhodesia the Chartered Company's administration was established more easily. With the Arab slave routes cut by Johnston in Nyasaland and German activity in Tanganyika, those Arabs remaining in the north-east corner of the area were mopped up in a series of minor engagements between 1896 and 1899, while Kazembe of the Lunda yielded to an Imperial expedition from Nyasaland in 1899.

Events moved altogether more smoothly in the west. Lewanika, Paramount Chief of the Barotsę, signed a treaty with F.

Lochner, representing the Chartered Company, in 1890, largely through the influence of a French missionary, François Coillard, who had established the first permanent mission station north of the Zambesi in Barotseland in 1885. Thereafter, Lewanika pressed for a British resident to be sent to his domain, but because of the British South Africa Company's absorption with affairs in Southern Rhodesia, it was not until 1897 that one was appointed. In that year Robert Thorne Coryndon proceeded to Lealui, the Barotse capital, as British resident, his staff for administering North-Western Rhodesia—a sergeant, a corporal, and three troopers of the British South African Police. After lengthy negotiations, Lewanika was eventually persuaded to sign another treaty with the British South Africa Company, and several more were signed between 1898 and 1909. These resulted in the land rights in the whole of North-Western Rhodesia being given over to the Chartered Company, except in Barotseland itself, for Lewanika, realizing that he could no longer control events, was concerned only with keeping his own domain intact.[3] Moreover, the Chartered Company induced the Colonial Office to agree to the extension of the boundary included within North-Western Rhodesia and the Barotse treaty area from the Kafue river north to the narrow waist of Northern Rhodesia, between the Belgian Congo and Portuguese East Africa, the Company arguing that this region was too remote to be administered as part of North-Eastern Rhodesia and that there was a natural cleavage of tribes along the new boundary. In the circumstances there was little else the Colonial Office could do. As a result, however, the Company 'gained land rights over an area where no indigenous chief had made any treaty with its emissaries, and mineral rights greatly superior to those laid down in the original certificates of claim from H. Johnston.'[4] As Imperial Commissioner for Nyasaland Johnston had sanctioned the granting of mineral rights up to the Kafue river on the basis of the Lochner Treaty, though it was extremely doubtful whether the Barotse Paramount exerted any permanent influence over territory to the north of the Kafue. The Chartered Company thus placed their claim to

[3] *The Birth of a Plural Society: The Development of Northern Rhodesia under the British South African Company, 1894–1914*, L. H. Gann (Manchester, 1958), p. 135.
[4] L. H. Gann, op. cit., p. 136.

mineral rights in this area on a much stronger legal basis
—important in view of the mineral deposits known to exist
there.

Thus within a few years the area north of the Zambesi was
brought within the administrative orbit of the British South
Africa Company. In 1899 the new Administrator of North-
Eastern Rhodesia, Robert Codrington, moved his headquarters from Blantyre to the new post of Fort Jameson. Orders-
in-Council officially establishing the Administrations of North-
Eastern and North-Western Rhodesia were promulgated in
1899 and 1900 respectively. There was still only a handful of
administrators and missionaries in the two territories; nevertheless, a revolution had occurred north of the Zambesi. The pattern of African conquered and conquerors was no more; the
warrior power of the Ngoni had been smashed, and though
there had been no other clash on the same scale, the days of the
Bemba, Lunda, and Baroste warriors were also at an end. All
Africans, warriors and their former prey, were now equal, inferiors before their European masters.

Far reaching as these changes were, they were by no means
the last. The British South Africa Company was a commercial
concern, with shareholders expecting an adequate return on
their investments. When the first column of Pioneers crossed the
Limpopo and trekked into Mashonaland there was a general
expectation that riches similar to those unearthed at Kimberley
and on the Rand would soon be discovered in the new land.
Gold was discovered, but not on the same scale as south of the
Limpopo. Indeed, the new territory quickly became a financial
burden to the Company, with revenue scarcely balancing administrative expenses. The railway which the Company was
pushing north was a considerable expense, while the Mashona
and Matabele rebellions in Southern Rhodesia, in which many
European settlers were murdered, did not add to the Company's fortunes. In these circumstances it was anxious to limit
its expenditure and tap every source of revenue. The territories
north of the Zambesi were regarded as potentialities for the
future.

To increase its revenue, the Company imposed a poll tax of
3s. on each adult Native male, and each wife except the first, in
North-Eastern Rhodesia in 1900, and the impost was 'enforced

almost at once over most of the Territory'.[5] A similar measure was authorized for North-Eastern Rhodesia in the following year, but implementation was delayed until the administration was firmly established. When the tax was imposed the rate varied between 5s. and 10s., and was finally standardized at 10s. per head in 1914. The argument that the Native should make some contribution towards the cost of providing security and protection was not questioned either by the Imperial Government or the settlers—though the most recalcitrant tax-payers proved to be the scattered weak tribes who had gained most from the suppression of warriorhood. The effects of this imposition were far reaching. The poll tax had to be paid in cash. But the economies of the tribes were only at a subsistence level; money and its uses were entirely unknown. Taxation therefore forced the majority of African males into paid employment, and since there were comparatively few employment opportunities in the tribal areas, they had to migrate to where European enterprises had been established. Thus, while a poll tax was imposed as a means of defraying the cost to the Chartered Company of administering North-Western and North-Eastern Rhodesia, it also served the purpose of forcing Africans from their villages and into paid employment, particularly in Southern Rhodesia, where there was both greater employment opportunities and a shortage of labour.

In administering the tribes the Company was faced with many difficulties; the diversity of African languages, lack of knowledge of tribal custom and organization, shortage of money, and lack of skilled administrators. Consequently the Company utilized the existing tribal political structures for their own purposes, though the men they recognized as chiefs did not necessarily coincide with the leaders recognized by the tribes themselves. In the case of the Ngoni, for instance, some of the tribal leaders had been killed in the insurrection; others had fled. Of the remainder, some were not recognized because the Company was suspicious of them for the part they had played in the uprising. Eventually, the Administration recognized Mpezeni's grandson as the Paramount Chief, while a number of divisional headmen were appointed and made responsible for small areas. 'Some of these . . . were regional

[5] L. H. Gann, op. cit., p. 80.

governors, some lieutenants of Mpezeni I, some members of the royal lineage, and others were upstarts.' [6] Likewise, in Bembaland the Company recognized the *Chitimukulu* and other important chiefs; but not the traditional councillors who played an important part in the administration of the tribe. Conversely, with the weaker tribes, prominent men were selected and appointed as chiefs, even though in many cases no such institutions had previously existed. These differences and omissions, however, were no more than symbolic of the changed status of the chiefs under the Chartered Company. From being real leaders, they had become minor administrative officials recognized by the Company only in so far as their authority and privileges were not incompatible with the Company's requirements. [7]

Likewise, the chiefs were not allowed to exercise their former responsibilities in the administration of justice, again because of a fundamental conflict between the principles underlying customary tribal law and English common law. Broadly speaking, most tribal litigation was of a civil nature, and in adjudging wrong, a chief, together with his council of elders, sought to compensate the family offended against at the expense of both the wrongdoer and his family in such a way that its economic strength continued unimpaired. Thus a Bemba who had committed murder or damaged a family's gardens could be deprived of his liberty and given over to the offended family as a slave. In many tribes adultery was punished by death, while the poison ordeal was used by the chiefs to discover witches. Such punishments were considered to be contrary to 'natural justice'; consequently the administration of justice was taken over by European Native commissioners. In such a vast country, with a small, scattered population, it proved quite impossible for the Native commissioners to hear all Native litigation, and so the chiefs were left—and after a time encouraged—to handle minor civil cases, the Native commissioners dealing with criminal cases and offences against local legislation, such as breaches of labour contracts and non-payment of the poll tax.

In these early days missionaries were frequently in closer contact with the African tribes than the Administration, and they

---

[6] E. Colson and Max Gluckman, op. cit., p. 199.
[7] *Native Administration in the British African Territories, Part II*, Lord Hailey (H.M.S.O., London, 1950), p. 83.

were active in their attempts to spread Christianity and modify those facets of tribal life they found repugnant, from tribal religion and its ceremonial manifestations, polygamy and obscene dances, to the savage's nakedness. In addition, they introduced more advanced agricultural and building techniques into the tribal areas, as well as erecting schools in which Africans themselves began to be trained. The effect of all these forces was to halt the traditional rhythm of tribal life, on the one hand, and, on the other, to attempt to reorient those Native beliefs and customs repugnant to the European so that the African adopted those of the White man. No deliberate attempt was made to smash the tribal societies, however, and it is probably easy to overestimate the immediate impact of these forces and events on the African tribes. Over most of the country, Europeans were seen comparatively rarely; and circumstances were such that initially there was no flood of European settlers into the Territory. When the railway arrived at the Victoria Falls—a bridge was built across the gorge to enable travellers to see the magnificent spectacle that had stirred Rhodes's imagination—its northerly direction was controlled by the location of mineral deposits. Moreover, the route to the north, between the rugged escarpment marking the northern edge of the Zambesi valley and the flood plains of the Zambesi and Kafue to the west, passed between the areas dominated by the warrior tribes. A large-scale clash was thus avoided, both when the railway was constructed and when the first settlers crossed into North-Western Rhodesia in its wake.

Nevertheless, the extension of the British South African Company's administration north of the Zambesi brought two ways of life, two sets of values, two different civilizations into direct collision. The most immediately striking manifestation of this had been the clash between warriorhood and the Company's insistence on peace, on African submission. At the time, once the question of power and authority had been settled, the matter was left. But this did not resolve the problem of what was to become of the tribal societies. The aims and requirements of the Europeans were not only different from those characteristic of African tribal life; they were fundamentally opposed to them. Since the European wielded power and decreed conformity with his demands and the tribal societies were complex, integrated organizations, it followed that changes could not be made in one sector of their organization without other portions being affected, and that, furthermore, successful conformity with European requirements could only be achieved when a positive attempt was made to reorientate the whole basis of African life. While, for instance, the European settler wanted his African labourers to work hard, regularly, and efficiently, they could hardly be expected to do so as long as they were conditioned in a tribal system where those particular accomplishments were unknown. Neither could he expect thrift from the African when tribal society was organized on a basis in which materialism was non-existent. Clearly any attempt to transform African tribal life had to be centred on an economic revolution, for the ultimate bulwark on which the tribal way of life rested was the land, and the particular forms of agriculture practised. Until these were changed, there could be no dynamic movement away from the values of the tribe towards those which the European, whether settler, administrator, or missionary, wished to see instilled in the African.

These factors were not considered by the early European pioneers: the African was universally regarded as a savage, just rescued from the depths of barbarism. No anthropological studies in the structure of the varying tribes were undertaken; indeed, the practical uses of anthropology had still to be demonstrated. Even if they had been, the British South Africa Company merely wished to conserve the peace and induce a flow of labour to Southern Rhodesia. But a glimpse of things to come was soon seen in Ngoniland. The Ngoni of course had suffered more than any other tribe north of the Zambesi from contact with the European. Many of their cattle had been looted during the rebellion, and though several thousands were subsequently returned, within two years of the revolt the strength of the tribal herds fell from twelve to just over one thousand. For with the advent of peace, traders arrived in Ngoniland to set up stores filled with cheap baubles. And it was for these that the Ngoni sold their cattle, the cattle that had previously not only been a man's pride but the oil on which the smooth working of the Ngoni social organization depended. The coming of the stores opened a new field of delight for everyone: and more significantly introduced a completely new set of values, for the goods had to be purchased. While the Ngoni achieved this on a basis of barter, neither they nor the other tribes had a great deal to offer in this respect. Money was the obvious necessity, the bridge between the goods offered and the new tastes being stimulated. Thus demand for European consumer goods was in reality the only positive force directing the African away from the traditional values of the tribe towards those which the European wished, no matter how indirectly, to inculcate.

But economic development was thought of as being entirely in the hands of Europeans. They were creating a new world, their world. The African was needed as an instrument to help in that creation; he was not wanted as a permanent feature of it. His home was the tribal village. This attitude was not surprising. The African was a naked savage; his life bounded by the spear and primitive agriculture. To think of the differences between the races being bridged was to stretch human credulity unreasonably. And if the European thought in these terms, so did the African. At this early juncture the principal factor conditioning both races was fear, the European fearing an outbreak of Native violence, the African fearing the European because of his technical superiority. In any case, the African tribesman had never had ambitions associated with material possessions; consequently where desire for European consumer goods was generated it was not linked with the need for hard regular work, the essential requisite for satisfaction. And so those Africans who did journey to work attempted to return to their villages as quickly as possible.

Despite these contradictions, and the unawareness of both African and European of the long-term consequences arising from their contact, an irreversible process had begun. Provided the two races remained in contact, the seeds of decay sown within the tribal societies could only fructify, thereby accelerating the breakdown of the traditional structures. The African, both individually and collectively, had to achieve a new *modus vivendi* more in harmony with the changed circumstances created by the advent of the European. But this was not merely a problem for the African: the repercussions of this collision extended beyond the bounds of a withering in tribal tradition. In the case of the Ngoni, for instance, the tribal population density was far in excess of the numbers which the land could support in terms of Ngoni agricultural techniques. Consequently the tribe quickly devastated the area in which it was settled, removing the forest cover and inducing those inexorable concomitants, decline in soil fertility and erosion. Hitherto this problem had never disturbed the Ngoni; once the land—and their neighbours—were depleted, the tribe moved on across the broad face of the African continent. But the British South Africa Company stabilized the tribe in the area where it was residing at the time its administration was established over North-Eastern Rhodesia; and in addition there was the North Charterland concession covering the Ngoni area. Settlers began to arrive in Fort Jameson wanting to take up land in the concession area. And while Native labour was required, the settlers objected to the presence of Africans on 'their' land, since they naturally wished to own it on individual title, a concept totally foreign to tribal custom in Northern Rhodesia. They also took exception to the devastation caused by Ngoni agricultural practices. Those Natives resident in the concession area on land wanted by European settlers were consequently required to move. But it was explicitly stated in the North-Eastern Rhodesia Order-in-Council that when Natives were displaced, land of a similar type and suitable area had to be reserved for them. Since some 200 square miles were alienated for European settlement, and in view of the provisions of the Order-in-Council and the growing friction over land, a Land Commission was appointed in 1903 to investigate the need for Native reserves. Subsequently the first reserves were delineated, and those sections of the Native population living in the alienated zone moved therein. The letter of the law was thus obeyed, and the clash between European and African concepts of land tenure resolved.

It was but a question of time before the consequences implicit in breaking the old tribal rhythm of life forced themselves to the attention of the Administration. The breakdown of tribal social customs might be ignored; but the Chartered Company was a commercial concern and therefore vitally interested in maintaining its possessions, including the land, in good order. And as the Native population swelled, the natural resources of the Native reserves could only be progressively devastated unless and until the African population contained therein were taught improved agricultural techniques, and a new harmony between the area of land available, the population density, and the methods of cultivation practised was established. Since the European was responsible for the administration of the country and controlled the destiny of its African peoples, the responsibility for achieving this rested on his shoulders.

The Ngoni bore the full brunt of the impact with the European; hence these problems were heightened in the Fort Jameson area. Nevertheless, conditions there were but a reflection of those in the entire area of North-Eastern and North-Western Rhodesia. The only difference was one of degree, of time; the experiences and the problems posed by the Ngoni signposted the future.

CHAPTER 4

THE DEVELOPMENT OF THE COPPER-BELT—AN INDUSTRIAL REVOLUTION

No great change either in the strength or the nature of the forces unleashed against the tribal societies occurred for some time. The railway running from the small settlement of Livingstone, situated some seven miles north of the Victoria Falls, through Broken Hill to Bwana M'kubwa on the border of the Katanga Province of the Belgian Congo, was successfully completed, and the mines at the two townships brought into operation. Along the line of rail, land was alienated for the few Europeans who had migrated north of the Zambesi. Small townships began to spring up, usually coinciding with the sidings on the railway, containing a small hotel, an administrative post and store, a focal point for the scatter of Europeans living in the surrounding countryside.

Over to the east, the numbers of European farmers in the Fort Jameson district steadily increased. In 1912, one year after the administrations of North-Eastern and North-Western Rhodesia were merged, and a unitary state, Northern Rhodesia, created, tobacco growing was introduced into the area, and its initial success gave a further impetus to its expansion. This raised once again the question of land boundaries, and in 1913–14, six additional Native reserves were created in the Fort Jameson district, together with four in the Lundazi and nine in the Petauke districts. As yet, however, the Eastern District was the only portion of Northern Rhodesia where a fairly dense African population coincided with a specific European land concession. Along the line of rail, the density of the African population was low. Where a European wanted land it was simply alienated. In the majority of cases this did not result in the displacement of any Africans: where it did, they were merely pushed back beyond the boundaries of the European farm, which in any case were usually poorly defined. This did not cause the Africans any great inconvenience, since all practised shifting agriculture. And in any case there was land and to spare for all. That the contact between European and African was still slight can be seen from the European population figures, 1,500 in 1911, rising to 2,300 in 1914.

Even such a modest increase was not without significance. Each rise in the number of Europeans in Northern Rhodesia was reflected in a strengthening of the demand for African labour, with as a consequence, a heightening of the disruptive influences impinging on the tribal societies. Moreover, the building of the railway line brought about a distinct shift in the importance of the two gateways to the territory, the south gaining at the expense of the east. It was a change which was to have important repercussions in the future: for to the south, Southern Rhodesia and South Africa were not only more highly developed but, more significantly, had much larger European populations whose predominant political philosophy was the preservation of European standards, and consequently, the retention of political power in European hands.

This broad pattern continued until 1925, when an event occurred which was entirely to transform Northern Rhodesia. Sulphide deposits containing copper were discovered near Ndola close to the Belgian Congo border. Copper had, of course, been known to occur in the region for a considerable time, and the open-cast mine at Bwana M'kubwa had been in operation for a number of years. But the ore worked there was a surface oxide in which the copper content was so low that it could only be extracted economically when the world price was high. The discovery of sulphide deposits beneath the oxidized surface layer changed this position entirely, for the extractive process with the sulphide ore was neither complex nor expensive.

Interest in the region had been stimulated both by the success of the mines developed over the border in the Belgian Congo, by the high price of copper, and by a change of policy on the part of the British South Africa Company, which owned the entire mineral rights of Northern Rhodesia outside Barotseland (see Chapter 5, p. 52), whereby it granted prospecting rights to large companies over extensive areas, provided they undertook a specified amount of development work. Once the extent of the deposits was proved, development at four mines, the Roan Antelope (Luanshya), Rhokana (Kitwe), Mufulira, and

Nchanga (Chingola),[1] was begun. The railway only extended as far as Bwana M'kubwa, and consequently, the tremendous surge of development necessitated its extension to the new mines. Many experts doubted the success of the operation, for blackwater, dysentery, and malaria were endemic in the area. Waterlogged *damboes* had to be drained, and extensive operations undertaken against the scourge of malaria. Despite this, the erection of mine plant began at the Roan Antelope mine in October 1931, and the first copper was produced two years later. Thus this banana-shaped stretch of Northern Rhodesia was transformed from a thickly wooded, sparsely populated area, the home of the small Lala tribe, into a zone of heavy industry, the tranquil mantle of trees dwarfed by the shaft-head gear of the mines. Hundreds of Europeans flocked to the 'Copperbelt' as it was called; new towns were hastily constructed to house them. And if hundreds of Europeans were attracted, thousands of Africans were needed to supply the companies' labour requirements. The development of the Copperbelt had touched off a revolution.

Even prior to this, the number of Africans drawn from their village homes had been steadily increasing. By 1920, for instance, 5,500 Northern Rhodesian Africans were employed on the Katanga copper mines in the Belgian Congo, while no less than 24,000 were at work in Southern Rhodesia. Already the scale of migratory labour had changed radically from the early days of the British South Africa Company's administration. But these figures were dwarfed when the development of the Copperbelt began. In January 1927 the copper-mining companies were employing 8,500 Africans. By the end of the year the figure had risen to 11,000. One year later it was 16,000, and by December 1929, 22,000. In the following year, when construction was at its peak, there were also an estimated 48,000 Africans employed in Northern Rhodesia in occupations other than those connected with mining, while 38,000 Africans were employed outside the territory. In all therefore, some 102,000 able-bodied African males were in paid employment outside their traditional homes and occupations, some 37 per cent. of the estimated number in the whole of the territory.

[1] The names in brackets are the associated civil townships, in contradistinction to those controlled by the mining companies.

Neither were these migrations confined to the men. Early recruits to the mines in the Katanga were signed on a six-monthly
contract, after which they were compelled to return to their villages. In 1923, while continuing to recruit on a similar basis, the
Union Minière du Haut Katanga, the powerful mining group
controlling the Katanga copper mines, decided to allow African
labour recruits to bring their wives and families to the mining
townships if they wished, arguing that a man accompanied by
his wife was more likely to be contented and consequently a
better worker. Approximately one-fifth of the labourers are recorded as utilizing this concession. For the same reasons, the
copper-mining companies in Northern Rhodesia also allowed
African workers to bring their wives to the mine compounds.

What, in terms of the African tribal societies, did these
changes portend? In the first place it is important to note that
the development of the Copperbelt did not involve a clash with
any of the large Northern Rhodesian tribes. As with the railway
line originally, the Copperbelt lay between the areas of 'dense'
African population, and consequently the tribes affected were
small and easily moved from the areas of land leased to the
mining companies by the Crown (see Chapter 5, p. 52).
But because of this the African labour needed on the Copperbelt had to journey over long distances, since it was the large
tribes, and particularly the Bemba, which were the principal
sources of labour. Thus at one jump the African labourer left
his village and became an inhabitant of the large compounds
built by the mining companies to house them. To work on the
Copperbelt involved the same problems as did migrating to
Southern Rhodesia; but for the first time, the copper mines
provided extensive opportunities for paid employment within
the actual bounds of Northern Rhodesia.

In view of the fact that originally a hut tax had been needed
to force able-bodied Africans from their villages into employment, what new factor had emerged so that by 1930 almost 40
per cent. of the total number of able-bodied men in the territory
were in employment? The hut tax, or its equivalent, was still in
force, of course: and professional recruiters were employed on a
large scale to tempt the African into signing for a period of
work. But the new factor was the African's desire to own European goods, and particularly European clothing. According to

Dr. Richards, in the case of the Bemba this had, by the early 1930s, reached the proportions of a tribal obsession.[2] Since there was very little change in the economic opportunities within the tribal areas, satisfaction of these cravings could only be achieved by a period of paid employment with a European enterprise outside the tribal area. Not only did this new situation have far-reaching consequences in the rural areas; an urban problem was created too, particularly in view of the companies' decision to allow women and children to accompany their menfolk.

Let us consider in more detail the effects of this industrial revolution on the Bemba, since it was one of the main sources of labour for the Copperbelt. The mine compounds where the labourers lived were subdivided into single and married quarters, with an additional and rather less well-defined breakdown into areas reserved for specific tribes. While this might appear logical from an administrative point of view, it was revolutionary from that of the Bemba. In the compounds the Bemba labourers found not small villages of twenty or thirty huts, but vast agglomerations set out in neat lines in which the inhabitants were not close relatives and the traditional family circle, but strangers, many of whom did not even belong to the same tribe. Traditional enemies became neighbours and working-compatriots; strangers, bed-fellows; and if this was not revolutionary enough, the entire life and its tempo was controlled by the dictates of the mining industry, which in turn was controlled by Europeans.

For the men there was work every day, not the traditional tasks of lopping tree branches, or hunting in the bush, or repairing huts, but digging trenches, filling trucks, working among and handling strange pieces of equipment. It was not possible to stop and start at will as it was in the village. Each labour gang was supervised by a European, who shouted in an incomprehensible language whenever anything was wrong. Despite not understanding, each African quickly learnt that a White man's word was law; that in all things the European was the ultimate arbiter in their lives. For the women, the change was of even greater proportions. The world that had been theirs suddenly dissolved. From being a member of small communities where every woman was a working partner in the common task of pro-

[2] Dr. A. I. Richards, op. cit., p. 216.

viding the entire family with food, fuel, and drink, she was suddenly alone, an individual in foreign surroundings, with strangers as neighbours, solely responsible for cooking and pre-paring her husband's food. Heightening this physical and psychological isolation was the absence in the mining com-pounds of the familiar tasks, pounding grain into flour, collect-ing relish material, the thousand and one things that had filled women's lives every day for as long as they could remember.

Traditional food, with the grain already milled, was supplied by the mine authorities. But since eating remained a necessity, women, as in their villages, were called on to cook for their hus-bands. Such an ordinary seeming event had far-reaching reper-cussions. Individual responsibility for cooking marked a definite point in the progress of a Bemba marriage, a moment striven for both by husband and wife. It heralded independence, the end of a couple's economic dependence on the wife's family, and it was an occasion ceremonially marked and symbolized by the establishing of fire in a new and specially built hut. For the first time a husband was received into the full Bemba family of the living present and the dead past, the twin inter-related com-ponents of Bemba reality. In the mine compound a woman cer-tainly achieved independence; but in a manner completely con-trary to her tradition. No religious ceremonial was held; of necessity, her family, who was responsible for performing it, was absent. Because 'compound' independence was attained with-out the sanction and approval of the family's ancestral spirits, doubts arose which had to be assuaged. Consequently the com-pounds and locations of the urban areas brought into new prominence the dispensers of magic. Such men had always been present in Bemba village life—the tribe's acute fear of the supernatural ensured that it would be exploited. But while they and their arts were greatly feared, none the less, they operated in a sphere distinct from that of Bemba religion. In the towns the two began to intertwine, as the rigid, defined ways of tribal existence were adapted to totally different cir-cumstances.

Where possible village customs and habits were continued. Since a group of men from a village tended to journey to work together, there was usually a family grouping to which a man might belong. Consequently food supplies were often pooled and given to the wife of one of the men in the group to cook. With the day's work over, they would gather at his hut, squat on their haunches outside, and wait for the food to be brought to them. The huts might be of more substantial type than those of the village; but they were treated as was a hut in a village, a place in which to sleep or shelter from the sun or rain, not a home in the European sense. Likewise the tribal eating pattern continued. Squatting round the bowls of maize porridge and meat relish, each stretched out and took a handful of the thick dough-like mixture, fashioned it into a ball, dipped it into the relish, and quickly ate, silence and speed characterizing the meal. To be dilatory because of excessive talking while eating from a communal food basket was to consume less than a silent neighbour, and in a society accustomed to experiencing an annual food shortage, this was reason enough to compel speed and silence. In the location food came regularly from the mine authorities; but the silence of famine continued.

While the men naturally had a great deal more work to do than in their village, the women gained in leisure. No longer was it necessary to fetch water from a distant stream: it was in a nearby tap. There was no necessity to make gardens or to search for relish material. Women could sit and chatter in the sun—except that long-ingrained traditions did not die easily, since there was nothing to replace them. Consequently traditional activities were continued: women joined together and made gardens on land adjacent to the compounds, despite there being no necessity to grow food and the fact that it was not possible to make true *chitimene* gardens, since most of the trees had been felled for fuel. Such adjustments were comparatively easy. Cooking food and preparing gardens in 'traditional' form infringed none of the new rules of living. But the continuance of other habits definitely did. Women were the brewers of village society, and though many things were altered in the compounds, women's skill and men's thirsts were not among them. But conditions in the compounds were quite different from those of the village. There, shortage of grain, overwork at the time when it was plentiful, social obligations, and the manner of distribution all combined to limit both the quantity of beer that could be brewed and the volume available to each individual. In the compounds, however, grain could be purchased all the year round, water was conveniently and continuously provided in taps, and women had time and to spare. Moreover, there was no family present, no definite etiquette to govern the distribution of the beer brewed. Consequently, brewing became a widespread activity, and with abundance of beer, there was likewise abundance of participation. But excessive beer drinking brought in its train inevitable consequences, brawls, hangovers, and absenteeism, consequences to which the mine authorities took strong exception. At a village beer-drinking session, when a man consumed sufficient to produce a hangover the following morning, a state picturesquely described as 'beer before the eyes', he rested until well again. No complex industrial machine depended on his attendance, and the village had time enough to achieve its productive purpose without paying very much attention to a day lost through rest. And it was by this standard that the African behaved and judged behaviour in the urban compound.

To the European compound manager beer was his greatest enemy, the cause of industrial inefficiency and the breaking of the peace. Naturally he took steps to prevent it being brewed and to punish those he caught brewing. Women were issued with rations in the form of grain instead of meal, so that more of their time was taken up by the traditional method of pounding. A system of licensing private brewing was introduced, whereby individuals were given permission to brew small quantities of beer with which to entertain a few friends at the weekend. Unlicensed brewing was made an offence, and compound police instructed to keep a strict look-out for offenders, who were fined and even dismissed when caught. But brewing on an ever-increasing scale continued, since it was not imbued with the sanction of wrong, beer in a Bemba village being something more than a sign of generosity; it was a necessity for the fulfilment of certain social obligations and customs, the medium for making gifts, signs of respect, to elders and chiefs. And so the Africans in the urban areas indulged in what was an all too limited a luxury in their villages with little on their consciences. A further factor entrenching brewing in the urban communities was that in a society avaricious for money, brewing provided another, or at least an alternative, income, one which offered a greater reward more quickly and easily than did working for the European. Brewing produced more than pleasure: it was good business.

Both the effort and the failure to curb were fruitful sources of irritation to European and African alike. Unfortunately it was but one of many. The fundamental cause of each was the same: the clash of values, each the result of differing backgrounds, social organizations, and ambitions, which the juxtaposition of the African and European within a common industrial and urban framework produced. An urban environment and the discipline of regular work was normal for the majority of Europeans; but an African employed on the mine worked merely to gain specific objectives which contact with the European had stimulated. His ambitions were still couched largely in tribal terms; so was the rhythm of his life. The mining companies were prepared for a large turnover in their labour force: the very fact that recruited labour—and this constituted the greater proportion—was engaged only for a year at a time ensured this. What caused so much irritation was the irregularity of labour attendance, the desertions, and absenteeism which occurred—from the European's point of view—without rhyme or reason. Systems of attendance bonuses were introduced to induce greater regularity, and labour paid on the completion of a 'ticket', commonly thirty working shifts, and not at the end of the week, in order to obtain a minimum stability in the labour force. All workers lived in tied houses: once they ceased to be in employment on a mine they were ejected from their accommodation.

Despite these various temptations and pressures, however, little progress was made in obtaining regular working attendance. The tightening of the beer-brewing regulations in the official compounds brought into prominence African villages beyond the boundaries of the mining properties. These had been concentrated there initially when the African population had been removed from the land granted to the mining companies when development on the Copperbelt began. Outside the companies' jurisdiction, they quickly began to meet those desires of the African labourers discouraged in the compounds, becoming centres of brewing, gambling, and prostitution, as well as havens for those ejected from the official compounds. Even in the compounds, the companies' measures were easily circumvented. The detection of brewing depended to a large extent on the African compound police employed by the mines. Yet these very Africans were equally fond of beer and regarded brewing in no different light from the people they were supposed to apprehend. Though their value in this context was therefore limited, the compound police had a great deal of power and were widely feared, because they used it not to enforce company regulations but to blackmail offenders.

Payment by ticket might ensure regularity over thirty working days. But payment opened avenues to participation and satisfaction, and since these were the reasons why Africans journeyed to work, the labourers indulged themselves in satisfying pent-up desires, only returning to work when their pay was gone. And by being forced to work for a longer period the labourers had both more money to spend and a greater desire to relax. Neither did the threat of losing both a job and accommodation have a great deal of force. In the villages it was incumbent on a Bemba to succour and help another member of his family who was in distress or need. While this system imposed a common level of activity and material well-being, it also provided a comprehensive system of social security, so that no one could suffer privation in greater measure than that of the family as a whole. Backed by supernatural sanction—for to refuse to succour a family member was to offend his spirit, and should this lead to suffering or even death, the spirit was certain to wreak its vengeance on the wrongdoer—this custom was invoked in an urban context: a man dismissed from employment and therefore from his home simply went to a 'brother' and asked for hospitality, which by virtue of the pregnant fear of the supernatural, was granted. This naturally largely negatived the threat implicit in the tied cottage. Each of the official compounds were full of men who had been dismissed and who, according to company regulations, should have left. Naturally, steps were taken to weed them out, for the 'loafers', as they were called, were a source of potential and actual trouble. But once again the spearhead for discovering them was the African compound policeman! In any case a raid was soon widely advertised: the 'loafers' merely slipped out of the compound into the surrounding bush until it was over and then came back.

The large increase in the numbers of migrant labourers naturally had tremendous repercussions on village and tribal life. In the case of the Bemba, for instance, the absence of such large numbers of able-bodied men lowered once again the power and prestige of the chiefs. With warriorhood a thing of the past, the glory of serving a chief had already greatly declined, and while it was still incumbent on the young men to serve their chiefs as tribute labourers, it was impossible for a man to work on the mines and at the same time cultivate in the chief's gardens. Since the towns offered the greater attraction, men went there, and inevitably, the numbers at a chief's village steadily declined. For the same reason, Bemba economic production was considerably weakened. Cultivation of the *chitimene* gardens depended on men lopping tree branches, and since so many were away, fewer gardens were made. Consequently the annual cycle of famine became even more pronounced. Moreover, the annual food shortage was heightened by two additional factors. Men from a village often migrated to employment as a group, so that in many the male absentee rate rose far above the territorial average, often approaching 60–70 per cent.; and the decrease in the numbers of the old, the women and children living in the villages was comparatively small. Hence, while economic production was seriously reduced, the number of mouths to be fed did not decrease in anything like the same proportion.

From the African's point of view, town and village were entirely separated worlds, not only because the differences between them were so marked but also because the village was home and, comparatively speaking, unchanged. Economic activity continued to be shifting agriculture. Men and women might eat together in the compounds; water might come from turning a tap; there might be beer all the year round. But that was in the European's town. Regret for the compound's freedom from tribal discipline might linger in a man's mind; but so did the memories of police raids, the European supervisor's shouting, and most of all, the hard physical work which constituted the basis of life there. In the villages, on the other hand, a man was at home, among his people, living by the customs and in the way of life with which he was familiar, the life to which he had been conditioned since childhood.

When a young Bemba whose marriage had not been finally

declared stable returned home he was still legally part of his father-in-law's economic team, and had to work on such projects as his father-in-law directed. The latter had traditional custom on his side. But the young man considered his return primarily as a period of rest and recuperation from the toils of the mine, and consequently objected to working in his father-in-law's economic team. Again, it was common custom to pay respect to the village elders and important personages by small gifts, traditionally of beer. Now, caught by the new craze to own European clothes, the elders and wives left behind in the villages looked on the return of their brothers and husbands as heralding gifts bought in the urban stores. And a son-in-law, having given his father-in-law a substantial present, regarded it as absolving him from working in his gardens. Conditioned by an exchange economy in the compounds, the returning African measured his duties by the size of his gift.

The absence of large numbers of men naturally affected marriage customs. Before the coming of the European, adultery had been a serious offence in the Bemba tribe and was severely punished. Since it was the custom for a husband to go and live in a bride's village among her family, adultery was easily detected. But mass male migrations produced a man-starved land: adultery consequently became more commonplace and less severely punished. Wives demanded to be allowed to accompany their husbands to the distant compounds. In the event of a woman accompanying her husband to the town before their marriage was recognized as stable, it was deemed better to grant the couple 'independence' before they went, no matter what stage their marriage had reached on the traditional evolutionary scale. Not only was this done to cement more firmly the bonds between husband and wife; it also circumvented any possible annoyance to the family's ancestral spirits. Since the traditional marriage ceremonial was of great complexity and took a considerable time to perform, it was necessary to simplify and shorten it.

Such ceremonials as were held in Bembaland before beginning the tree pollarding season were similarly affected. Tree pollarding had previously been initiated by a rich ceremony held at the village of the Paramount Chief, which was followed by similar ceremonies on a smaller scale in every village in

Bembaland, the village headman leading the celebrations and initiating the work by himself lopping the first branch. With so many men absent from their homes, however, it was no longer possible to wait for and follow the lead of the headman. Work began as and when there were men in the villages to undertake it; hence it was merely a question of time before the ceremonies died out.

There was naturally a certain response from within the tribal societies to these changed circumstances. In Bembaland where there was a shortage of men in a particular village, women pooled their grain supplies and brewed beer, inviting such men as were in neighbouring villages to work in their gardens, rewarding them with 'gifts' of beer. Though there was an immediate reaction on the part of the village elders to hasten the granting of marriage independence, it was quickly discovered that this in itself did little to solve the basic problem. By having a shortened and simplified marriage ceremonial to mark the achievement of independence, the ancestral spirits might be placated. But a wife who went to the compounds still left behind all the traditional safeguards erected to protect and stabilize her marriage. Moreover, from living within the two all but watertight compartments which separated men and women in village society, husbands and wives were forced together as individual couples in the mining compounds, under conditions where none of the social customs which had conditioned their attitudes one to another were applicable. These changes inevitably strengthened the power of a husband. In the compound his wife's family was absent, and he was solely responsible for providing his family with food; their occupancy of a hut depended on his continued employment. Perhaps most important of all, it was only through him that material ambitions could be satisfied. The inevitable result was a rapid increase in the number of broken marriages. Husbands abandoned their wives; wives, tempted by the offer of envied goods, deserted their husbands. While there was a marked rise in prostitution, which had been unknown in tribal societies before the advent of the European, there was a greater increase in the casual exchange of wives as between a series of husbands, each keeping them for such time as they found convenient, whether in terms of diminished affection or of their leaving the compounds.

Parents and elders, the traditional guardians of marriage stability, became loath to allow women to leave the villages, hoping that by keeping them there, within the family, a husband would be forced to return from the towns, while his wife would be kept out of harm's way. New marriage safeguards also began to appear, arising out of traditional custom but linked with the values that came from contact with Europeans. Before the arrival of the White man, it was customary for a Bemba male on his betrothal to make a small gift to his bride's parents, such as a piece of bark cloth which he had made himself. In money terms its value was low: it was essentially a gift of respect, the procurement of which had involved some effort on his part. In the circumstances created by extensive migrations, parents began to demand betrothal gifts which had to be bought in the urban stores. Those with comely daughters considered they warranted more expensive gifts. In one sense this was merely another aspect of the universal demand for European consumer goods; but the Bemba also thought that by making a husband aware of the value of his bride in terms of the weariness of working for a European, he might be less willing to maltreat or abandon her. For if the marriage failed because of his misdemeanours, he would lose both the gift and his wife. But the demand for more expensive gifts forced the men to stay away from the villages for longer periods—and everyone looked to a man returning from the towns for gifts in any case. Thus this adapted marriage safeguard did not function as an effective measure but contributed directly to the further weakening of the tribal structure.

CHAPTER 5

EUROPEAN POLITICAL AMBITIONS CRYSTALLIZE

IN the very early days of the British South Africa Company's administration there was a strongly developed community bond between all the Europeans in its domains north of the Zambesi. All were pioneers into the unknown, welded together by isolation, the strangeness of the environment, and perhaps most of all by their common cultural heritage in the face of the surrounding sea of African backwardness. With the passing of the years, however, dissension developed between the settlers, on the one hand, and the missionaries and the Chartered Company, on the other, corresponding with the differences in the objectives each pursued. Dissension between the settlers and the missionaries centred primarily on the latter's treatment of the Natives, particularly in the field of education. As a single instance, many mission stations introduced technical education for Africans at an early date, if for no other reason than that the erection and maintenance of the mission buildings depended largely on Native artisans. But some of the mission-trained workers inevitably drifted away, and, in certain cases, were employed by the Administration. This angered the settler community, and while Codrington, when he was Administrator, overruled their protests, his successor, L. A. Wallace, agreed not to employ African carpenters and bricklayers.[1]

Dissension between the settlers and the Chartered Company did not arise so much from disagreement over the Company's Native policy as from the dual role of the Company itself, at once administering authority and commercial concern. In the settlers' opinion many of the dues which the Company levied were not designed to help the development of Northern Rhodesia but to satisfy the financial interests of distant shareholders who had little knowledge of or interest in the Territory. To meet settler dissatisfaction, the Chartered Company instituted

[1] L. H. Gann, op. cit., p. 161.

an Advisory Council in 1918, on which sat four members elected from North-Western Rhodesia and one from North-Eastern Rhodesia. The franchise was limited to male British subjects of European descent who were over twenty-one, who were in receipt of a salary of not less than £150 a year, or who occupied premises of no less value. Since the Council had neither legislative nor executive functions it failed to satisfy the settlers, and their representatives quickly demanded the right to veto finance bills. Settler dissatisfaction finally came to a head when the Company announced its intention of levying an income tax, and in 1921 the settlers petitioned the Imperial Government to tighten the control they exercised on the Chartered Company.[2]

There was also dissatisfaction with Company rule in Southern Rhodesia, although there was no agreement, either north or south of the Zambesi, as to what should replace it. The Company itself favoured the creation of a unified administration for both Southern and Northern Rhodesia, while South Africa wished Southern Rhodesia to become the fifth state of the Union. The then Secretary of State for the Colonies in the Imperial Government, Mr. Winston Churchill, consequently appointed a Commission under the chairmanship of Lord Buxton to inquire into their future. It recommended the granting of independence to Southern Rhodesia, subject to a referendum being held, and the incorporation of Northern Rhodesia into the British Colonial Empire as a Protectorate with a Crown Colony form of government. The agreement—after the referendum in Southern Rhodesia had favoured independence—covering both Territories was signed in London on 29 September 1923.

Thus ended thirty years of Company rule. It was a burden the Chartered Company was by no means loath to have removed, for Northern Rhodesia had in many ways proved a white elephant, there having been an average annual deficit of £130,000 on its administration. By the time the Imperial Government accepted responsibility for it, the total amounted to £1,250,000. With an eye to the future which subsequent events have proved shrewd, the transfer agreement contained

[2] 'Company Days', *The African Observer*, Kenneth Bradley, Vol. 85, October 1936, p. 63.

clauses whereby the Chartered Company was to receive one-half of all the net revenue arising from the sale or lease of land in North-Western Rhodesia for forty years, while the mineral rights were to belong to the Company in perpetuity. Land rights, except those areas the Chartered Company had granted in freehold title, or gazetted as Native Reserves, or were covered by the treaty with the Barotse Government, passed to the Crown.

Immediately the transfer of power took place in 1924, the British Government replaced the Advisory Council with a local Legislative Council which consisted of the Governor, who was president, the Chief Secretary, Attorney-General, Financial Secretary, and Secretary for Native Affairs, four other officials nominated by the Governor, and five elected Europeans representing the local settler community, soon to be known as the 'Unofficials'. The Legislature had the form of a Parliament; but executive power was concentrated in the hands of the Governor, who represented and was responsible to the Crown. Though assisted in his duties by an Executive Council, of which he was chairman, the Governor was not compelled to follow its advice. In the field of general policies nothing which could be considered revolutionary arose from the transfer of power. The Chartered Company had based its policies on the encouragement of European immigration and thereby of the economic development of the Territory, the maintaining of peace, and an adequate supply of African labour, all by means of the most economical methods of administration. These policy strands continued unbroken under the Colonial Office: indeed, in the circumstances prevailing in Northern Rhodesia the British Government had no alternative but to continue them. The territory was desperately poor, and since European immigrants brought new skills, energy, and capital into it, they could hardly be discouraged. For the same reason the African poll tax continued to be levied, for not only was it necessary to ensure an adequate supply of labour to further economic development, in these early years it supplied a not inconsiderable part of the total territorial revenue. For the year ending 31 March 1925, for instance, out of a total revenue of £309,000, Native poll tax contributed £101,400 and income tax £41,600.

Certain aspects of the established policies were clarified and consolidated. In 1924 a Native Reserves Commission was appointed to investigate the need for further reserved areas for the indigenous population, more especially in those districts adjacent to European occupied land along the line of rail. A new Government policy for African education was introduced. Under the Chartered Company, African education had been left entirely in the hands of missionaries, and the new policy proposed by the Government was simply one of co-ordination and supervision, together with a certain amount of financial assistance to those missions undertaking educational work. The aims of African education were defined as 'a training which will fit them [the Africans] to make better use of their opportunities, and of the land which they occupy; to teach them a certain amount of handicrafts, and to train them in the principles and methods of hygiene and generally to train them to become happier and more useful citizens than they could hope to become without some sort of educational help'.[3] The sum of £4,496 was voted for African education in the financial year 1925/6—the figure for European education was £13,325. The estimated populations in 1926 were 1,170,000 Africans and 5,100 Europeans. Paltry as was the expenditure on African education, it was nevertheless an advance. Previously no public funds had been expended in this field.

Settler representatives in the Legislature were immediately suspicious. Indeed, in the light of subsequent events, the Northern Rhodesian settler community's preference for a Crown Colony form of government appears inexplicable. At the time, however, amalgamation of the two Rhodesias was unpopular both north and south of the Zambesi. Europeans in Southern Rhodesia voted against it because they did not want to be saddled with the 'Black North', while the settlers in the North feared that Amalgamation would result in the more highly developed southern territory absorbing Northern Rhodesia without trace, a possibility distasteful to their growing sense of national consciousness. Moreover, Northern Rhodesia appeared to be on the verge of a considerable economic expansion. The output of minerals in 1920 had been only £347,000; three years later it had risen to £3,000,000, largely due to increased production from the lead–zinc mine at Broken Hill.

[3] Hansard, 21 May 1925, col. 127.

Acceptance of some form of Crown Colony type of government thus offered a period of tutelage during which the Imperial Government would supply trained personnel and ensure stable government while the natural resources of the territory could be developed and the European population greatly enlarged. When both these factors had reached a level commensurate with maintaining a stable, independent state, the settlers believed they would be granted responsible government, as had occurred in Southern Rhodesia.

But developments had not proceeded entirely according to the settlers' expectations. The Governor and his Officials were responsible not to local interests, but to distant 'Whitehall'; promotion within the Colonial Service entailed a constant movement from one post of the Empire to another, and the settlers feared that officials might not have a deep attachment for or a great interest in the territory to which they had been temporarily posted. In particular, they might not agree with the settlers' concept of the Native's place in society. The first Governor of Northern Rhodesia, Sir Herbert Stanley, touched their Achilles heel in his inaugural presidential address to the Legislative Council. 'It is hardly necessary for me to emphasize,' he pointed out, 'that a council such as ours is not a parliament in the generally accepted sense of that term. It is constituted on a different basis, which obviously places the Government in a position to exercise effective control.' [4] The settler representatives—five had been nominated so that the Governor could hear their views on the legislation to establish a franchise and five constituencies—took an entirely different view. Mr. Leopold Moore, an outspoken man who had founded the Territory's first newspaper, the *Livingstone Mail*, declared that 'the differences between a parliament and this council are small and . . . should not be emphasized. We are to all intents and purposes a parliament and likely to become a parliament.' [5]

When the franchise proposals were published the settlers found that men of any race and creed were to be allowed to qualify for the vote, in contrast with the franchise governing election to the former Advisory Council. During the debate in

[4] Hansard, 23 May 1924, col. 3.
[5] Hansard, 20 May 1925, cols. 102–3.

the Legislature, settler views were expressed bluntly. Mr. Ellis pointed out that it seemed to him a well-established fact that only people of European stock were capable of exercising the right of election, and that non-Europeans could be represented satisfactorily only by nominating Europeans to do so. 'No one would suggest that non-Europeans should not be represented at all,' Mr. Ellis continued, 'and I regret that better provision was not made in the Order-in-Council for nominating representatives of the non-European peoples in this Territory as asked for by the settlers a few years ago in their humble petition to His Majesty.' But Mr. Ellis went on to say: 'The position of the European settlers in this country is such that they must take unusual care to protect themselves, and must also adopt a parental and protective attitude towards the mass of uncivilized and ignorant Natives among whom they dwell. As the powers of the present government will eventually be handed over to an elected government, I consider that it is most important that we should make one now so that when the time comes, the elected government will be such that it is capable of protecting the civilized European population as well as the backward Native population. If we decide that all races who may happen to be British subjects are to be entitled to vote, we shall never be entitled to recall that right, and this country will probably eventually be controlled by people who are quite unfitted to govern.' [6]

In reality the Northern Rhodesian Government's proposals effectively disfranchised the African population for the foreseeable future. The vote was to be limited to British subjects of twenty-one years and over—and the indigenous African population were British Protected Persons by virtue of the Territory's Protectorate status. Hence, until such time as Africans took the necessary steps and became naturalized British subjects not a single one would be able to exercise the franchise. Furthermore, it was necessary for all intending voters to fill in an application form in English, and, apart from specific residential qualifications, to have an annual income of at least £200 or occupy a house or other building within an electoral area valued at no less than £250. Communal and tribal occupation of property was specifically excluded as a qualification under

[6] Hansard, 20 May 1925, col. 106.

the property clause.[7] For all practical purposes, therefore, the British Government agreed with the views of Mr. Ellis in so far as the years immediately ahead were concerned.

In the longer term, however, the settlers and the Imperial Government were at variance. The former considered the Black man inherently incapable of exercising the 'right of election': consequently Africans were to be maintained in a permanent state of trusteeship, the trustees being the Colonial Office in the first instance and the settlers whensoever Northern Rhodesia was granted independence. The British Government, on the contrary, maintained that men of all races were to be given equality of opportunity. But only after they had attained certain standards, and in the franchise these were related not only to a European standard of wealth but also, in the property qualification, to a European concept of living. Between the two extremes, the immediate future when the Africans were disfranchised and the distant future when the wards would be reaching maturity and participating in the franchise with Europeans, the British Government did not define its intentions. No plans were formulated whereby the standards of the wards were to be raised; consequently there was no time-table for the ending of British trusteeship and the attainment of independence. From the settlers' point of view, the supremely important factor was that without a specific bar against Africans participating in the franchise, there would be at some future time—and provided the Territory's economic development continued—a majority of Africans on the voters' roll, in view of the latters' overwhelming numerical superiority. And this would herald a Native state. Leopold Moore had already written in the *Livingstone Mail*, apropos of this, that it would be better to pay a White man three times as much as a Native rather than run the risk of evolving a Native as distinct from a White man's state.[8]

Thus within a very short time of the transfer of sovereignty, the settlers were forced to realize that if they wished to preserve White supremacy in Northern Rhodesia they had to force the British Government to agree to the granting of responsible

[7] *The Northern Rhodesian Legislative Council*, J. W. Davidson (London 1948), pp. 23–24.

[8] Quoted in *The Birth of a Dilemma*, P. Mason (London, 1958), p. 253.

government before the African emerged from his state of backwardness. Initially, however, circumstances combined to allay
settler fears and mute their political demands. The British
Government's intentions aroused suspicion and made the Unofficials watchful, but Officials of the Northern Rhodesian
Government were in broad agreement with settler views, and
the British Government itself had not propounded a policy
which was *immediately* disastrous. It would be many years before
there were Africans on the voters' roll. Meanwhile, the discovery of copper sulphide deposits and the development of the
Copperbelt promised a rapid economic transformation. Both
officials and settlers were more immediately concerned with the
problems arising from the attraction of large numbers of Africans to the urban locations. The key to the entire question was
considered to be the absence of tribal discipline, and consequently, the administrative policy pursued was meant to ensure that African workers stayed in employment only for a short
period, since this was felt to minimize both the breakdown of
tribal authority and preserve the cohesion of tribal life. In this
sense, the policy adopted by the Administration—and it was
supported wholeheartedly by the European settler community
—coincided with the feelings of the overwhelming majority of
the African migrant workers, who only came to work for limited
periods in order to achieve specific objectives.

To strengthen and support the tribal societies the Government introduced a system of 'indirect rule', following a recommendation to that effect by a conference of district commissioners and administrators in 1927. The Native Authority
Ordinance implementing it came before the Legislative Council
in 1929, and, as the Secretary for Native Affairs explained, it
introduced a more advanced form of Native administration
which gave to the chiefs the management of their own affairs
within the tribal areas. He hoped it would preserve and maintain all that was good in Native custom and tribal organization.[9] Under the terms of the Ordinance the Governor was
empowered to appoint chiefs, either alone or in conjunction
with headmen or elders, to be Native Authorities, which were
to have the power to make rules governing the maintenance of
law and order, the promoting of good government, and the

[9] Hansard, 18 March 1929, col. 235.

improvement of the welfare of those people resident in the area for which each was responsible. In addition, the Native Authorities were to collate and codify customary tribal law for the information of district officers, especially the laws governing marriage, divorce, the custody of children, and inheritance. A Native Courts Ordinance was introduced at the same time, establishing courts in the tribal areas, in which chiefs, either alone or with headmen and councillors, could hear and adjudicate on a range of civil and minor criminal cases according to customary tribal law.

At the time the introduction of indirect rule was considered a marked step forward in the system of African administration. No doubt it was in the sense that it initiated African political advancement. In reality, however, it was hardly an advance. Indirect rule was supposedly to strengthen the position of the chiefs and the traditional tribal administrative structures: the Secretary for Native Affairs stated that it would preserve all that was good in Native custom and tribal organization. But at the very time the new system was introduced, the development of the copper-mining industry was drawing thousands of African men and women from their village homes, thereby undermining the authority of the chiefs and destroying the tribal customs it was supposedly preserving. Moreover, the Government was active in encouraging these disruptive forces. It levied the poll tax, while in order to stimulate the flow of Native labour to the Copperbelt, an officially sponsored recruiting organization, the Native Labour Association, was formed.[10]

Missionary endeavour was having the same effect. As Dr. A. I. Richards remarked of the Bemba, 'whichever code they follow today, they are aware of a rival one, and conscious of their possible guilt, either as a Christian who breaks the rules of a pagan ritual and is never quite sure whether he will not be smitten by a fatal illness, or as a pagan, who is apt to fear the punishment of the White man or his God'.[11] In the Fort Jameson district, where numerous mission stations of many Christian creeds had been established, the White Fathers and the Universities Mission to Central Africa disallowed divorce, while

[10] *Modern Industry and the African*, J. Merle Davis (London, 1933), p. 160.
[11] *Bemba Marriage and Present Economic Circumstances*, Dr. A. I. Richards, Rhodes–Livingstone Papers No. 4 (1940), p. 27.

the Dutch Reformed Church accepted it: the U.M.C.A. insisted that all customary obligations had to be fulfilled before a
marriage between Christians could be solemnized, but the
White Fathers considered the payment or non-payment of
traditional marriage dues to be no concern of the Church. The
Dutch Reformed Church, on the other hand, had a rule for-
bidding the payment of any brideprice.[12]

This apart, the same inconsistencies and contradictions
underlay indirect rule as had underlain the British South
Africa Company's African policy. In the case of the Bemba, for
instance, while the Paramount and some of the lesser chiefs
were paid government subsidies, the wider administrative structure of the tribe was still not recognized, so that the hereditary
group of councillors known as the *Bakabilo* received no government subsidy despite the important role they played in tribal
affairs. Because of his declining power and influence, the Paramount Chief could no longer provide them with the traditional
payment of cooked food and beer: neither was his government
subsidy sufficient to pay them.[13] In the case of the Native Courts,
the chiefs were free to try only a limited range of cases according
to customary law. The remainder fell within the jurisdiction of
the district commissioners' courts, in addition to which all cases
could be taken there on appeal.

Why, then, did the Northern Rhodesian Government introduce indirect rule? First and foremost, there was still no real
appreciation of the underlying forces shaping the course of
events in the Territory. When the Native Authorities Ordinance
was debated only one doubting voice was raised, and that by
an Unofficial, who felt that the breakdown of the traditional
tribal societies had proceeded too far for indirect rule to be
successfully implemented. The Secretary of Native Affairs
assured him that this was not so. Moreover, the country was
still poised on the edge of economic expansion: though the
copper mines were being developed with great speed and opti-
mism, there was still no categorical assurance that their future
profitability was ensured, that the forces which had grossly

[12] *Marriage in a Changing Society*, Dr. J. A. Barnes, Rhodes–Livingstone Papers
No. 20 (1951), p. 102.
[13] *See* 'Tribal Government in Transition (The Bemba of North East Rhodesia)',
Supplement to *Journal of the Royal African Society*, October 1935.

accelerated the breakdown of the tribal societies were in any way a permanent feature of the Northern Rhodesian scene. In any case, the traditional tribal structures and in particular the chiefs, provided the only nuclei round which an administrative structure could be built. In the same way, customary law reflected the only pattern of social behaviour and sanction understood by the African tribes. Finally, the attempt to minimize the social dislocation characterizing the African urban communities by a system of constantly repatriating the African workers to the tribal villages was not only understandable; it was inevitable in view of the African's own desire to stay away from his village in employment for a minimum time.

Thus in the short term the contradictions inherent in the policy of indirect rule were unlikely to have important repercussions. But in the longer term, provided economic development continued on the same pattern, tribal institutions would become less and less effective as the basis for the administrative machinery in the rural areas. Moreover, tribal characteristics and values were at the root of the social disruption in the urban locations and were the cause of the friction between European employer and African employee. The Government's policy of indirect rule, of 'strengthening' tribal institutions, therefore militated against the bridging of the gap between the values of the African and those of the European, and was indeed likely to prolong the disruption it was meant to minimize.

But in 1930 an event occurred which shattered finally the settlers' confidence in the British Government's intentions. In June the Secretary of State for the Colonies in the then Labour Government, Lord Passfield, issued a memorandum on British Native policy in the African tropical dependencies.[14] While the greater part of its contents aroused the settlers to wrath, there was one sentence in particular which touched them on the raw. It ran: 'His Majesty's Government think it necessary definitely to record their considered opinion that the interests of African Natives must be paramount, and that if and when those interests and those of the immigrant races should conflict, the former should prevail.'

From the clamour which arose an impartial observer might have been forgiven had he gained the impression that a drastic

[14] *Memorandum on Native Policy in East Africa*, June 1930, Cmd. 3573.

departure from previous policy was actually being made. In the Union of South Africa the Minister of Lands, in the absence of the Prime Minister, issued a statement to the effect that since a radical change was being made in British Colonial policy, the South African Government should have been consulted. But it was not so. The doctrine of the paramountcy of African interests was a reiteration of a statement contained in a White Paper published in 1922, dealing with British policy in Kenya (Cmd. 1922), and indeed Lord Passfield's Memorandum was primarily concerned with East Africa. It contained little that was intrinsically new. What was the policy outlined? While emphatically stating that where there was a clash between the interests of indigenous and immigrant races those of the former were to prevail, it was also explicit that the other communities 'must severally be safeguarded'. The Colonial Office administrations in the tropical dependencies were to maintain order, administer justice, promote health and education, provide means of communication and transport, and generally promote the industrial and commercial development of the countries for which they were responsible. 'In all this range of work, persons of every race and every religion, coloured no less than white, have a right to equal treatment in accordance with their several needs.' But because of the duty involved in the trusteeship of backward peoples, the care and advancement of the African was a sacred trust which the British Government could not under any circumstances share. Though trusteeship placed the African section of the community in a separate category, it did not involve a separate system of administration but 'rather a specialized application and extension of the common administration of which the benefits are enjoyed by the whole population'.

The second part of the Memorandum detailed the actual application of this policy. The development of social and political consciousness in the indigenous peoples was to be based as far as was possible on tribal institutions, so that the African could be trained by methods and forms of organization having a traditional appeal. As his capacity increased, he was to have a larger share in the management of his tribal affairs and, ultimately, in the government at a national level. With regard to land, the first essential was to finally remove from the Native mind any feeling of insecurity, and land of an extent and character such as would meet a tribe's actual and future needs was to be made available and gazetted as Native reserves, which would then remain for its use and benefit for ever. Any individuals wishing to break away from the tribal pattern of life, however, were to have their equality of opportunity adequately safeguarded, for 'His Majesty's Government adhere to the principle of equality of opportunity in the disposal of Crown lands, irrespective of race, colour and religion'.

On taxation, the policy directives were equally firm. 'The levy of direct taxation on the Native should be definitely limited by his capacity to pay such imposts without hardship, and without upsetting his customary way of life. It is indeed a positive duty of the government to make sure that the Native has an effective choice in the way in which he meets his taxes, and every care should be taken to provide that taxation, whether central or local, does not in its result actually oblige the Native to labour for wages as the only practicable means of obtaining the money to pay his tax.' As to government expenditure: 'It is incumbent on governments to ensure that government expenditure on Native services in the annual budget should bear a proper relation to the revenue raised from the Natives and that the Natives should receive, directly and visibly, a fair return for the direct taxation he is called on to pay.'

Before examining the impact of Lord Passfield's declaration on European settler opinion in Northern Rhodesia, it is important to note not only discrepancies between previous practice and the policy he enunciated but the many contradictions implicit in the policy itself. The poll tax had been imposed in conditions where the great majority of Africans had no possible chance of earning the wherewithal to pay it without migrating to work in European employment. For years a substantial proportion of the total Territorial revenue had been contributed by direct African taxation: £101,448 out of £447,795 in 1924/5, and £124,386 out of £672,289 as late as 1929/30.[15] Indeed, in the very year the Memorandum was published the poll tax was increased by half a crown to compensate for the abolition of tax on wives other than the first, the tradition of polygamy having been severely curtailed by direct taxation. As to the benefits de-

[15] *Report on Native Taxation* (Government Printer Lusaka, 1938), p. 2.

rived by the African and European inhabitants of Northern Rhodesia from public revenue, despite the fact that from 1924 to as late as 1937 there was little difference in the receipts from African poll tax and European income tax, the Government capital grant for development and public works was so allocated that the amount of public money spent in the European area was four times the amount spent in the remainder of the country, although the latter was vastly larger, and seventy times the amount spent on facilities for African use.[16]

Presumably Lord Passfield was not unaware of these facts, and intended that his Memorandum should correct previous practice. Its inherent contradictions hardly ensured this. According to the Colonial Secretary, the commercial and economic development of the Colonial Dependencies was to be encouraged; but he made no mention of the British Government's intention of contributing to the cost. This presumably was to be left to immigrants, since the African was hardly able to take the initiative himself in such matters. Whatever bodies undertook such development, they would need African labour. And since, in the initial stages, Natives would be unwilling to work in paid employment in sufficient numbers, they would have to be forced from their villages by the imposition of a poll tax, as had occurred in Northern Rhodesia. The British Government was also to guarantee Native reserve areas to the exclusive use of African tribes in pursuance of their traditional mode of life; under these conditions, the indigenous Native population had no alternative but to migrate to work to meet taxation imposts.

The doctrine of African paramountcy epitomized these contradictions and demonstrated a serious unawareness both of the nature of the problems and of the history of Northern Rhodesia. There had been a continuous clash of interests between Black and White in Northern Rhodesia since a British administration had been established, clashes that had been consistently resolved in favour of the latter. Neither was this entirely a question of European greed or conviction of cultural superiority. The ramifications of European and African contact were too complex to be reduced to African interests or European interests. The suppression of slavery, it might be

[16] *These African Copper Miners*, R. J. B. Moore (Livingstone Press, 1948), p. 95.

thought, was entirely in the interests of the African. But would the Bemba have agreed, voluntarily? The Europeans had brought clothes, schools, hospitals; but would the Ngoni have welcomed them, knowing that they would also mean the end of their warrior state? The development of the Copperbelt would increase Northern Rhodesia's prosperity, provide money for African schools and services; it also accelerated the break-down of the African's own social-security arrangements within the tribe.

When the Legislative Council reassembled later in the year, Captain T. H. Murray, Member for the Southern Electoral Area, moved that the policy as adumbrated in the Memoran-dum on Native Policy in East Africa was not suitable to North-ern Rhodesia,[17] and in the debate which followed each of the Unofficials condemned it vehemently. Mr. Morris, representing the Northern Electoral Area, was particularly outspoken when dealing with the proposal that members of all races and creeds should have equal access to Crown land. 'I feel that here, Sir, we are dealing with something so fundamental that only the plainest speaking will suffice. The White man simply cannot contemplate the possibility of the Black man being allowed to buy a stand beside him in his townships or elsewhere, to build thereon a house and to rear therein a family. The original of this aversion may be race prejudice. It may be. The outcome is nevertheless a fact. It is not the fear of competing on even terms. It is the desire, the determination to maintain his stan-dard of living, health and cleanliness, to preserve his racial heritage, and hand it on unimpaired to his children. Unless the White man erects and maintains artificial barriers against the free intermingling of the races, there would creep in the spectre of miscegenation, leading inevitably to the complete absorption of the higher by the lower.'[18] Mr. Morris conceded that in time there might be 'compact Black provinces' from which 'per-chance there might at some distant future come representatives to a Federal Legislature, but not in numbers to dominate the Councils'.[19] The basis for settler policy in the vital field of African affairs was 'separate paths in matters social and racial, each

[17] Hansard, 18 November 1930, col. 28.
[18] Ibid.
[19] Hansard, 18 November 1930, cols, 37–42.

pursuing his own inherited traditions, each preserving his own race purity and race-pride'.

The publication of the Passfield Memorandum placed the then Governor of Northern Rhodesia, Sir James Maxwell, in a difficult position. He was caught between the Secretary of State for the Colonies, whose views were not only rejected by the settler population but were contradictory in themselves and in large measure inapplicable in the conditions pertaining in the Territory, and the settlers, whose demands, particularly with regard to racial segregation, were reasonable in the short term, in view of the differences between the standards, habits, and cultural patterns of Black and White, but unreasonable and contrary to the principles expounded by successive British Governments in the long term. When the Colonial Secretary tersely rejected the Unofficials' suggestion that he should meet a settler delegation, the public outcry became so loud that the Governor called a meeting in his office at Livingstone, then the capital of Northern Rhodesia, to give his interpretation of Lord Passfield's Memorandum.[20] After explaining why there was a large hospital for Natives at Ndola but none in the same town for Europeans, and denying that the Government offices in Livingstone were entirely run by Native clerks—two of the many accusations levelled at the Government as illustrations of the way in which Natives were favoured at the expense of the European community—Sir James pointed out that many of the directives in the Memorandum were already being implemented in Northern Rhodesia. Adequate land had been reserved for African use under the Crown Lands and Native Reserves Order-in-Council, 1928. Sixteen reserves had been delineated along the line of rail, where the African population feared further displacement at the hands of European farmers, following the publication of the Report of the Land Commission, appointed in 1924 to review the entire question. African political advance, based on tribal institutions in the Native areas, had already begun, following the enacting of the Native Authorities and Native Courts Ordinances.

Dealing with the question of the paramountcy of African

---

[20] An Address delivered by His Excellency the Governor at a meeting held in the Governor's office, Livingstone, on Monday, 23 October 1930—printed as an appendix to *Debates in the Legislative Council No. 12.*

interests, the Governor explained that 'where you have the interests of a group of Europeans conflicting with the interests
of a group of Natives it does not mean that the interests of that
group of Natives is to prevail simply because they are Natives,
but in my opinion it does mean that if you have some question
arising in which the interests of the Natives as a whole are at
variance with the interests either of the Europeans as a whole
or a group of Europeans, then the interests of the majority of the
population, that is the Natives, must prevail'. In his view, the
White Paper was essentially a statement of the Imperial
Government's duty to protect the Colonial underdog: that the
effective development of the Territory could not be based on the
protection of sectional interests. In conclusion, he stated: 'It is
the opinion I formed at the time, it is the opinion I still hold,
that there is nothing whatsoever in the White Paper which
means any change of policy on the part of the Government, and
there is nothing in it which in my opinion is detrimental to the
interests of the White settlers, or to other people of European
descent who have come to, and are working in the Territory.'

The Governor's interpretation of the concept of African paramountcy was hardly more logical than that expounded by
Lord Passfield: his conclusion that there was nothing in the
Memorandum which necessitated a change of policy on the
part of his Government palpably false. But what could the
Governor do? Lord Passfield might refuse to see a settler delegation; but Sir James Maxwell could not avoid facing them.
Moreover, by virtue of the settlers' unanimity and control over
the Territory's economic development, it was plain that even
had Lord Passfield's policy been a practical one capable of
implementation, it would have required a measure of force to
accomplish it. Simply to pass a measure through the Legislative
Council by virtue of the official majority was hardly synonymous with implementing it, particularly in view of the Unofficials' passionate convictions. In any case, the Officials too
were White men in Northern Rhodesia. Later in the same
legislative session, for instance, the Chief Secretary said in reply
to a demand by the Unofficials that Crown land be converted
from leasehold to freehold tenure: 'The policy of the Government is one of providing for the Natives sufficient land to enable
them to develop a full Native life in their own areas: sufficient

land to meet the inevitable expansion of the populations settled thereon and sufficient to enable the Government with a quiet conscience to release to European settlement other areas suitable for the purpose.' In his opinion, one of the dangers of freehold tenure was that European landowners would subdivide their land and lease it to Africans. 'We have to protect as far as we can the interests of the Native peoples in the reserved areas, and it is incumbent on us equally to protect the interests of the European.' [21]

Such views were expressed by other authorities at that time. The Royal Commission which had investigated the Closer Union of the Dependencies in East and Central Africa—whose report had stimulated Lord Passfield to issue his Memorandum —stated, almost in the same words, what the Chief Secretary told the Legislature: once there was adequate land reserved for Natives, it was then possible to encourage European immigration. The all-party delegation from the House of Commons which visited Northern Rhodesia shortly after the Memorandum was published stated bluntly that the policy of the paramountcy of African interests was unacceptable because 'the Natives of the Territory are wholly tribal, and adequate and suitable reserves, amounting in all to approximately 70,000,000 acres are provided for them'. Furthermore, 'no Native is compelled to work for the White man against his will. The law safeguards his welfare: it prescribes the conditions under which his services can be engaged and protects him against ill-treatment by his employer.' [22]

The flurry created by the Memorandum gradually subsided. Nevertheless, it left a permanent imprint on the politics of Northern Rhodesia. It had given the European settlers a tremendous fright: always suspicious, the publication of the Passfield Memorandum set the seal on their fears. From the very moment that Northern Rhodesia came under the jurisdiction of the British Government, leaders of the European community had cast around for a possible escape route from tutelage in the event of it becoming inconvenient. Since there could be no question of independence, this had usually taken the form of a political union with Southern Rhodesia, which in relation to

[21] Hansard, 25 November 1930, p. 105.
[22] 'Parliamentary Visit to Northern Rhodesia', *African Society*, Vol. 30, 1931, p. 9.

the vital question, African affairs, was virtually independent. Though the demand for such a union had been made with sufficient force to justify the setting up of a Royal Commission to review the closer association of the British dependencies in East and Central Africa, development on the Copperbelt had damped the ardour of those wanting a union with Southern Rhodesia. When two Unofficials advocated the amalgamation of the two Rhodesias in 1928, Mr. Leopold Moore, always a fervent opponent of Colonial Office rule, was stung to reply: 'The Hon. Member said it was preferable to be governed by a United Rhodesia than from Downing Street. . . . My experience is very much more limited than his, and I say that you can do even worse than Downing Street. I think if there was a chance of anything being worse than Downing Street it would be by submitting our affairs and direction to a United Rhodesia. Whatever money is available will be spent where the balance of voting power is, and that is not north of the Zambesi . . .' [23] When the first motion proposing Amalgamation was introduced into the Legislature in the following year, it was supported by only the mover and seconder. [24]

With the publication of the Passfield Memorandum, differences of opinion on the question of Amalgamation vanished. The urgent and over-riding need was to escape from the clutches of the Colonial Office, and the quickest and easiest route lay in amalgamating Northern and Southern Rhodesias under a constitution similar to the one enjoyed by the latter. Thus the Passfield Memorandum crystallized the political ambition of the European settler community. It also placed succeeding British Governments and Governors in Northern Rhodesia in a dilemma. The Passfield Memorandum was an attempt to define British policy more closely, to set out in greater detail the steps whereby Northern Rhodesia and its indigenous people were to progress from being wards of the British Government to ultimate self-government and independence. By virtue of its inherent contradictions, however, the policy could not be applied *in toto*. But since the Governor could not state this publicly, it appeared as though settler opposition alone was responsible for its rejection. This significantly influenced the attitudes of both

[23] Hansard, 23 April 1928, col. 127.
[24] Hansard, 21 November 1929, col. 166.

Officials and Unofficials in later years, the former being more loth than ever to offend settler susceptibilities, the latter believing that vigorous Unofficial opposition was sufficient to deflect the British Government from its purpose.

Another consequence of the contradictions in Lord Passfield's Memorandum was that it was subsequently divided into two components. The Governor naturally accented those parts with which the settlers were in agreement, such as the delineation of Native reserves, and the encouragement of commerce and industry. This was not controversial, and soon everyone forgot that it was part of Lord Passfield's Memorandum. But the phrase 'the paramountcy of African interests' was extracted by the settlers, who felt that it epitomized the British Government's intentions in the field of race relations, and who consequently used it to arouse enthusiasm for Amalgamation. Thus it became a permanent feature of the political vocabulary of Northern Rhodesia, until finally 'the paramountcy of African interests' and the Passfield Memorandum were synonymous.

The publication of the Passfield Memorandum, by clarifying and crystallizing settler political ambition, also brought the mutually opposed forces shaping the political destiny of the Territory into sharper relief. The settlers were determined to be rid of the Colonial Office so that they could control the pattern of race relations in Northern Rhodesia, based on Africans and Europeans living in permanently separated areas. But the nature of the economic development was not only undermining that pattern: the only place where Africans could resolve the clash between the communalism of tribal life and the individualism arising from their contact with the European's civilization was in the towns, in industrial employment. And every pressure, taxation, material desires, and the labour policy of the mining companies was drawing them there. As one of the men responsible for the handling of Native labour on a copper mine subsequently remarked: 'Throughout the big construction period, there continuously emerged from the African mass, Natives of outstanding ability, and it is due to this class of Native that it has been possible to build up the highly efficient labour force which we have today.' [25] The Natives of 'outstanding'

[25] 'The African Native and the Rhodesian Coppermines,' F. Spearpoint, Supplement to *Journal of the Royal African Society*, July 1937, p. 14.

ability did not become Black Europeans overnight. The tasks they performed were comparatively unskilled; their remuneration was linked with the low standards of tribal life. Nevertheless, they had crossed the first hurdle; within the working sphere, the clash between tribal attitudes and the demands of industrial efficiency had been resolved.

CHAPTER 6

POLICY CONTRADICTIONS EXPOSED—
THE FIRST AFRICAN STRIKE

I N retrospect, 1930 stands out as a significant year in the
political history of Northern Rhodesia. At the time, however, it appeared a turning-point of a very different kind.
From being in the midst of a boom, with four major copper
mines being developed, the country was suddenly in the grip
of an acute depression. On the world market the price of copper
tumbled from £72 to £27 a ton, thereby forcing the construction programme on the Copperbelt to be drastically curtailed.
By the end of 1931 only two mines, the Roan Antelope and
Nkana, together with the lead–zinc mine at Broken Hill, were
employing more than a clean-up and watchman force. Bwana
M'kubwa, Kansanshi, Nchanga, and Mufulira copper mines
were closed down. Displacement among Europeans was so
severe that in November 1932, 193 poor Whites were being fed
by the district commissioner at Ndola and 400 at Lusaka.[1]
Severe as would be the effects of such retrenchment in any
community, they were heightened in Northern Rhodesia by the
racial problem, by the White man's fear that his standards
might be undercut and lowered by the African. Consequently
the slump exacerbated racial bitterness. Africans long in the
service of the township authorities in Ndola complained of being unceremoniously sacked and their places filled with poor
Whites at double the rate of pay.[2] Each urban centre in the
country, and especially those on the Copperbelt, became centres
of drifting, displaced, and unemployed Africans. Since Africans
were not officially recognized as permanent members of the urban communities, large-scale unemployment simply meant that
those retrenched returned to their villages, to their homes. For
this reason, the depression was even welcomed by the Administration. The Secretary for Native Affairs, for instance, hoped

[1] J. Merle Davis, op. cit., p. 113.
[2] Ibid., p. 93.

that the increased numbers of Natives in the rural areas might
have a salutary effect on village and tribal life as a whole by
reducing the numbers of male absentees.[3]

This attitude overlooked the fact that working in paid employment had become part of the routine of living in most
African tribes. Money was necessary to satisfy the desires newly
stimulated in the African breast, and increasingly, to meet
tribal obligations. Retrenchment neither quenched desire nor
eliminated obligation. Even if it had, the original stimulus
forcing the African out of his village and into employment, poll
tax, still had to be paid. Only in those areas adjacent to the line
of rail, particularly in the Mazabuka district south of Lusaka,
could the African sell his agricultural produce and so earn
money to pay the poll tax without migrating to work. The areas
of comparatively dense African population, the plateau region
in the north, Barotseland, and the eastern districts round Fort
Jameson, were too distant from the only market in the territory,
the line of rail towns, for their traditional grain crops to stand
the cost of transportation and marketing. The Barotse had built
up a trade in cattle exports, but these had been stopped when
contagious cattle disease brought in from Angola had affected
the Barotse herds. Indeed, the Government officially recognized
that 'the Natives had to rely on the labour market as their main
source of wealth'.[4] But while the market for African labour had
shrunk enormously, the poll tax continued unchanged. For
many years there had been difficulties in collecting it, despite
the numbers of exemptions, as high as 78,000 in some years.
The depression naturally heightened these difficulties; in 1934
no fewer than 158,000 Africans defaulted on payment.[5] Ironically the Administration admitted: 'The default in tax payment
is not deliberate; it is the result of unqualified inability to meet
a situation which the people did not create and are unable to
control.'[6] The Native Authorities were said to be doing all they
could to help their people; but despite default on payment not
being deliberate, 6,080 Africans were committed to prison in

[3] *Annual Report for Native Affairs* (Government Printer Livingstone, 1932), p. 29.
[4] *Annual Report for Native Affairs* (Government Printer Lusaka, 1935), p. 5.
[5] In the years between 1920 and 1937 there were at least four occasions when
tax arrears exceeded the total liability on account of the tax. *Native Administration
in the British African Territories*, Lord Hailey (H.M.S.O., 1950), p. 80.
[6] *Annual Report for Native Affairs* (Government Printer Livingstone, 1932), p. 5.

1934 for failing to pay the poll tax.[7] Faced with the choice of payment or possible prison, many Africans continued to seek work in the urban areas, and particularly on the Copperbelt; to relieve the dangerous situation in the urban areas resulting from heightened racial tension and large numbers of un-employed Africans, the Government transported many Natives back to their rural homes, feeding them during the journey. Others, seeking to meet the demand for tax, walked to the Copperbelt. Significantly, the Africans' contribution to the Territory's revenue in 1931–32, when the depression was at its height, was, at £148,263, some £20,000 more than receipts from European income tax.

The slump had brought to the surface the fundamental contradictions inherent in the Government's African policy, as was pointed out at the time. 'It is strikingly inconsistent,' wrote Mr. Charles W. Coulter, a contributor to an independent in-vestigation into the conditions on the Copperbelt in 1932, 'to encourage tribal integrity on the one hand under the system of indirect rule (for without tribal integrity no chief can success-fully function), and on the other to encourage its disruption by the present chaotic economic system.'[8] As the same author pointed out: 'If the Native villages are to be regarded as reser-voirs of cheap labour which can be drawn off in any desirable quantity and poured back when no longer required, which can be used as an asylum for the unwanted or broken human wreckage, the consequences of the system ought to be frankly faced.'

Mr. Coulter, however, was unable to propound an answer to the dilemma. 'Stabilization [in the towns] will give us the opportunity on the industrial side of securing far greater effi-ciency, on the human side of making possible the growth of a stable society with all the advantages of family life, of a perma-nently raised standard of living, of education and outlook. But these gains must be bought by exposing the stabilized popula-tion to very great risks of unemployment, which it will become progressively more ill-fitted to face. If we are prepared, for its obvious advantages, to advocate stabilization and the complete severance of the urban worker from the land, we must also be

[7] *Annual Report for Native Affairs* (Government Printer Lusaka, 1935), p. 5.
[8] J. Merle Davis, op. cit., p. 104.

prepared to propound plans to deal with·unemployment when it next returns. But until it is possible to make such provision it is important that every bond of unity between town and country shall be maintained.' [9]

In the midst of an acute depression, reluctance to advocate a policy likely to expose the African working population to future hardships from unemployment was understandable, more especially when urban stabilization was complicated by the racial problem, by the settlers' refusal to contemplate the possibility of the African becoming a permanent member of the 'European' towns and settlements. And the depression inevitably sharpened European sensitivity, and the watch Unofficials kept on Government policy. The slump, for instance, also produced a sharp fall in the world price of maize, the principal cash crop grown in the Territory, in which a substantial export trade— relative to the overall size of the crop marketed—had been built up prior to 1930. With world demand contracting sharply, the small but relatively stable internal market assumed greater importance both to African and European producers. Since no organization for controlling the purchasing of the crop existed, traders began to buy maize from African growers, particularly in the Mazabuka area, at prices which would have eliminated the European maize farmer in the area. To remedy this, a system of control was mooted and the matter passed to an Agricultural Advisory Board which had been formed to advise on the marketing of Northern Rhodesian products. The Board recognized the importance of the home market, assessed its potential, and apportioned it between African and European producers in the proportion of 25 per cent. to the former and 75 per cent. to the latter. It recommended that a statutory board should be created which would purchase all maize supplies, and that whatever was offered in excess of internal demand should be marketed externally for such price as it could command. When these arrangements were implemented the result was that a large part of the African crop purchased was exported; consequently the price paid to Native growers was extremely low. The Agricultural Advisory Board foresaw this possibility and argued that a low price, by limiting African production, would save their lands from exhaustion, and thereby render the Native

[9] J. Merle Davis, op. cit., p. 178.

people a service.[10] When the Maize Control Ordinance (1935) implementing the Board's proposals came before the Legislative Council for debate no voice was raised in opposition. Indeed, one of the Unofficials, Mr. Charles Knight, after surveying the prospects for European and African agriculture, remarked: 'I think this maize control principle is complete co-operation.' [11]

The Unofficials reacted in a very different manner when the European and African Education Advisory Boards recommended that the departments of African and European education should be amalgamated, partly as an economy measure, and partly because, as the Governor, Sir Hubert Young, said, education in Northern Rhodesia could not be separated on a racial basis. The Unofficials opposed the move unanimously, and though a number of factors led the Governor to abandon the idea, it was significant that he decided to continue with the existing system 'in accordance with the desire expressed by the Honourable Elected Members'.[12]

The attitude of regarding the African as a rural dweller inevitably affected the manner in which the urban locations were administered. In the mine compounds the companies maintained a fairly strict discipline; medical and welfare services were well organized. At the Roan Antelope mine there was a 'welfare club house with games, writing facilities, newspapers, a gramophone, and a dry canteen', although the average daily attendance was reported to be poor.[13] But only at one of the mines, again the Roan Antelope, had an attempt been made to form an organization to bridge the gulf between White officials and African workers, and there a semi-official Native advisory council consisting of twenty-two outstanding tribal leaders, chosen from the location irrespective of tribal affiliations, had been formed. Its purpose was to keep the management informed of grievances among the African workers, on the one hand, and to inform Africans about changes in either legislation or company regulations, on the other. Conditions were very different in the locations of the non-mining townships. Generally, these had simply grown as the White settlements expanded;

[10] Quoted in *The Northern Rhodesian Legislative Council*, J. W. Davidson (London, 1948), p. 63.
[11] Hansard, 19 November 1935, col. 70.
[12] Hansard, 2 May 1936, cols. 5–6.
[13] J. Merle Davis, op. cit., p. 73.

when they were either large enough or menacing enough, a
'location manager was appointed to safeguard the interests of
the Natives in the interests of the Whites'.[14] In 1932 the Ndola
town location housed 4,400 Africans in 1,700 mud and wattle
huts, a plot of ground large enough for the erection of three
huts—they had to be separated by 12 feet—being rented for
half a crown a month, this sum including the cost of drinking-
water.

The depression seriously aggravated conditions in these locations. The Government and local authorities were forced to cut
expenditure and retrench personnel; at the same time large
numbers of unemployed Africans were channelled to them from
the more controlled mine compounds. To the alarm of the
authorities and the European community generally, African
crime began to increase rapidly. 'The list of crimes committed
in the mining area is becoming varied and makes by no means
pleasant reading. Pocket picking is common. Convictions have
been recorded in the courts for attempted arson, housebreaking
and theft, forging and altering food tickets and European orders on stores, receiving, possession of housebreaking tools, indecent curiosity, obscene writing, robbing with violence, and
indecent assault.' [15] The Government intensified its efforts to
repatriate the unemployed back to their villages. Nevertheless,
the trend towards greater urban stability was becoming more
marked. At the Roan Antelope mine in 1931, for instance,
single African employees stayed in employment for only 9·79
months; but the married men were resident for 20·25 months.
And of the labour force in employment at 31 December 1931,
45 per cent. were married men.[16] More significant were the comparable figures for the Broken Hill mine, which had then been
in operation for twenty-six years. Of the 748 African employees,
9·49 per cent. had been in continuous employment for over ten
years, and 27·54 per cent. for over five,[17] though the slump distorted these figures, since the mining companies naturally retained those employees who had been longest in employment or
who had acquired a greater degree of skill.

[14] J. Merle Davis op. cit., p. 78.
[15] *Annual Report of Native Affairs* (Government Printer Livingstone, 1934), p. 34.
[16] *Annual Report for Native Affairs* (Government Printer Livingstone, 1932), p. 27.
[17] J. Merle Davis, op. cit., p. 71.

The Merle Davis investigation discovered an even more in-
teresting manifestation of the same trend. In the Ndola town
location fifty-two of the more educationally and financially advanced Africans had formed a Native Welfare Organization
which met for discussions once a month. Similar organizations
also existed in Lusaka, Broken Hill, and in the Roan Antelope
mine compound. Furthermore, the leaders of three out of the
four organizations frankly admitted that they existed to safeguard the rights and interests of the Natives of Northern
Rhodesia.[18] Thus in the very centres considered by the Government and the European community generally to be the preserves of the White man, there was emerging an African element
stabilized within the urban context, which had formed associations based not on tribal loyalties but on discontent within the
urban framework. For the Native Welfare Organizations submitted memoranda to local district commissioners, and even on
occasion, to the Secretary for Native Affairs. As a matter of interest, the Commission's comments on the rural Native Authorities was in strict contrast. 'The orders and rules so far made . . .
show little initiative or originality. In practically all cases,
innovations have been suggested by the district officer.' [19]

The contradiction between Government policy and the forces
impinging on the African community was becoming apparent
in other directions too. Financed by Government loan funds, a
beginning was made in 1932 with the establishment of a trade
school at Lusaka. But as the annual report of the Department of
Native Education pointed out, 'There is little chance as yet for
the young artisan being able to set up in village work in the
province with success. The local Native standard of living is still
at too low a level to warrant a demand for his services as a
builder or carpenter, and the lack of money prevents his services being paid in cash. The Native idea of mutual service is
still a potent obstacle against an artisan working in a rural district.' Of course the African carpenter was not required to provide door- and window-frames in the tribal areas: life there was
keyed to shifting agriculture and easily erected mud huts built
in the knowledge that four, five, six years would see them abandoned. The only areas where African artisans could make use of

[18] J. Merle Davis, op. cit., p. 86.
[19] Ibid., p. 257.

their training was along the line of rail. And there, the European artisan forbade him to work for fear of losing his own employment.

In the sphere of academic education there were difficulties no less acute. Such educational facilities as did exist were concentrated in the rural areas. But where, for instance, were the schools to be sited? An area of fairly dense population might, within five or six years, become a tract of empty bush, a school devoid of pupils, as the villages moved on their cycle of cultivation. The alternatives were either to shift the schools with the villages or to have a central institution to which pupils could gravitate from the surrounding hinterland. The first necessarily meant schools of a primitive character, and while they could keep in close touch with the African population, the educational standards attainable were strictly limited. A central school could obviously override these difficulties, but faced in turn problems no less acute. For such schools to draw on suitable numbers, pupils either had to travel long distances or to board. The former was inconvenient; the latter too expensive for a community without the local means of earning money. In any case it meant a type of school beyond the resources of either the missions or the Government—and certainly of the local African people—as a glance at Government expenditure on African education quickly illustrates: £348 in 1924/5, £3,994 in 1925/6, and £8,493 in 1928/9. In the latter year even the total sum expended on African education was but £14,818.[20] In addition, African children in the rural areas were an integral part of tribal life. With cattle people such as the Tonga and Ngoni, they were the herders: in all tribes they were allotted specific tasks which inevitably interfered with schooling. Parents and elders were suspicious of the new institutions, partly because they were new; partly because they interrupted what were considered the proper—and sometimes vital—occupations for children; and lastly, because the schools were in the hands of missionaries, who interfered directly or indirectly with tribal customs, particularly those ceremonials in which chiefs and elders played a prominent part. Faced with such difficulties, it is not surprising that African education made little progress in the rural areas. Each year showed an increase in Government expenditure on

[20] *Annual Report of the Director of Native Education*, 1929, p. 7.

African education, increases in the number of schools and pupils. But real progress was desperately slow. By 1934 the total number of pupils had reached 71,000. But out of these 48,000 were below Standard 1, the first grade in primary education, while the average attendance was only 15,500.

The Government's declared policy was to encourage children to be sent back from the urban locations to the villages, or better still, for them never to be taken to the towns at all. In many respects this fitted in with tribal custom and African wishes, for in many tribes, including the Bemba, children once weaned were reared not by their parents but by their grandparents. And the elder generation of Africans rarely went to the urban centres. It is not surprising therefore to find that African educational facilities in the urban areas were almost nonexistent. By 1932 two small day-schools had been established by the mining companies, one at the Roan Antelope, the other at the Nkana mine, while a small Government-maintained school had been opened at Ndola. Three years later the latter was still the only institution undertaking serious educational work on the Copperbelt, and it had a capacity for only 238 pupils. Yet there were an estimated 4,000 children on the Copperbelt who were receiving no education at all. Paradoxically, it was officially admitted by the Director of Native Education that 'Native town dwellers, many of them divorced from their old tribal life, are becoming more and more clamant for attention.' [21] Meanwhile, the officially declared aim of the Department was 'to dispel illiteracy among the masses without bringing about a change so revolutionary as to dislocate tribal life'.[22]

But events were to make the Government aware of the urban African and the problems developing in the industrial areas. On 22 May 1935 all Africans employed at the Mufulira copper mine stopped work. Three days later, the Provincial Commissioner for the Western Province, in which the Copperbelt was situated, reported to the Governor that African miners at Nkana were likely to come out on strike. Consequently he ordered fifty extra European policemen to be sent to the Copperbelt towns, in addition to the ones already sent there from Ndola, the administrative centre of the province. On 27 May

[21] *Annual Report of the Director of Native Education*, 1935, p. 13.
[22] Ibid., 1934, p. 9.

troops were dispatched from Lusaka to reinforce the police. Two days later the Provincial Commissioner reported that African mine workers were rioting and that police had fired on them in self-defence. As a result, six Africans were killed and others wounded.

The Government appointed a Commission of Inquiry to investigate the cause of the disturbance.[23] The Commission found that the disturbance had developed, indirectly, from the manner in which a change in the rate of African poll tax applicable on the Copperbelt had been announced. Because of the extremely large number of African tax defaulters, the Government had appointed a committee to investigate African taxation generally. Its principal recommendations were that the poll tax should be graded according to the availability of work in a particular district, and that an African should pay according to the rate prevailing in the district in which he was working, not as had previously been the case, at the rate of the district in which he was registered. These recommendations were accepted, and subsequently changes were made so that Africans working on the Copperbelt and the line of rail paid a higher rate of tax and those in the rural districts a lower one, 15s. a head on the Copperbelt, 12s. 6d. in the Ndola, Broken Hill, and Livingstone districts, together with the remaining urban centres in the territory, and 7s. 6d. for the rest of the country. With the flat rate of tax previously in force, a majority of Africans had for some years been taxed at a rate equivalent to between one and a half and three months salary per annum.

Though the new rates were communicated confidentially to the Provincial Commissioners on 11 January 1935, the Native Tax Amendment Ordinance authorizing them was not signed until 20 May—though the new rates were made retrospective to 1 January. At Mufulira the district officer and the mine-compound manager discussed how best these changes could be announced. But their arrangements for informing the African public failed. African compound police raced through the location bawling out that the poll tax had been increased.

The effect was instantaneous. Crowds gathered at the mine-compound manager's office; the situation began to look omin-

[23] *Report of the Commission Appointed to Inquire into the Disturbances on the Copperbelt, Northern Rhodesia*, October 1935, Cmd. 5009.

ous. Work at the mine stopped. By great tact and patience, the district officer allowed the Africans to talk away their anger, listening at great length to their grievances. So well did he succeed in allaying their fears that by the following day everything in the township was quiet. African strikers from Mufulira subsequently contacted their fellow workers at Nkana, and as a result, work ceased there too on 25 May. Two days later work was resumed at Mufulira, while the arrival of troops in Nkana, where the atmosphere was more threatening, restored calm, and the night shift reported at full strength.

On the night of 25 May emissaries from Nkana also went to the Luanshya mine compound, and a rumour quickly spread that the strikes at Nkana and Mufulira had produced wage increases; that unless the men of Luanshya followed the same example, they would be looked on as old women. Work duly stopped. On 28 May, though the strike continued, the town was sufficiently quiet for the Provincial Commissioner to report that the troops would probably leave the Copperbelt for Lusaka on the next day. But on the following day police in the Luanshya mine compound attempted to disperse some Africans who were loitering near the compound offices. The Commission of Inquiry found that their action was ill-judged, because as a result, the group of Africans rioted and Europeans and Africans, both police and officials, were forced to seek shelter in the compound offices and eventually to fire on the African mob attacking them. With blood spilt, the disorders stopped. On the following day the troops were withdrawn.

This, the first African strike on the Copperbelt was another major milestone in the development of Northern Rhodesia. The Commission of Inquiry concluded that the impelling cause of the riot had been the sudden bawling out of the increase in taxation, without which the new rates would have been accepted. It seems clear, however, that the strike had other causes, for despite the heterogeneous nature of the population in the mining compounds, the enormous turnover in the labour force, and the lack of any kind of workers' organization, Native labour was withdrawn from three of the four mines on the Copperbelt completely and spontaneously. And in fact grievances about rates of pay, pay deductions, and rations had long been smouldering in the compounds: the bawling out of the taxation increase was not so much the cause as the spark setting off the conflagration. The strike in fact forcibly demonstrated the complete absence of any effective machinery in the locations whereby the authorities could ascertain genuine African grievances. The Commission pointed this out, indicating too that in their view the Administration was out of touch with the urban African. The only officially sponsored African organization which existed was the advisory council of tribal elders at the Roan Antelope mine, and this the Commission found, had proved inadequate, being of no assistance during the strike and having failed prior to it to bring a number of labour grievances to the notice of the mining companies.

As a result of the disturbance, the Government formed a Native Industrial Labour Advisory Board, consisting of representatives of employers of African labour and administrative officers, to advise it on African labour policy. The content of its advice can be judged from the annual reports of the Director of Native Education. In 1936, the year following the riot, he commented that there were few educational developments to record in the urban areas, since the educational problem was largely dependent on the policy to be adopted with regard to the stabilization of labour.[24] In 1937 he repeated that 'until the policy regarding the presence of school children in the industrial areas has been decided, the provision of education is at present limited to sub-standards and the first two standards [of primary education]. The Native Industrial Labour Advisory Board has recommended the removal of all children over the age of 10 from the industrial areas.'[25] In the following year he was saying: 'One of the greatest difficulties in the solution of the educational problem on the Copperbelt is how to reconcile the provision of really efficient schools with the policy of discouraging the growth of an urbanized population. The answer that suggests itself is the provision of equally good schools in the tribal areas, but apart from the expense involved, questions of distance between villages makes it almost impossible.'[26] Caught between physical difficulties in the rural areas and Government policy in the urban locations, African education made little progress. By

[24] *Annual Report of the Director of Native Education*, 1936, p. 7.
[25] Ibid., 1937, p. 15.
[26] Ibid., 1938, p. 16.

1938 there were 120,000 African children in schools of all kinds. But of these, 108,000 were in sub-standards A and B—while only ninety-nine boys and one girl were in Standard 6. Though the highest educational standard for which school facilities were available in the Territory, this was only equivalent to completing primary education. And this was a mere twenty years ago!

Nevertheless, the strike forced the Government and the mining authorities to cater for some of the urban Africans' needs. The system of tribal elders' advisory councils first introduced at the Roan Antelope was extended to all the mine compounds. With a measure of juridical power, the elders looked on themselves as direct representatives of their chiefs, and in this capacity dealt with such incidents, necessarily of a minor nature, as were referred to them. Those they could not handle, either because they were too serious or refused to yield to their advice, were passed on to the compound manager or the local district officer. But the elders' advisory councils functioned only in the mining compounds, and they did little to staunch the flood of litigation flowing into the offices of the district officers. With the Commission of Inquiry emphasizing the lack of contact between the Administration and the African community, the need to find some means of freeing the district officers from their court duties became urgent, and the idea was mooted that some form of Native court, similar to those operating in the rural areas, was needed in the towns. Serious objections, however, were raised against the proposal. The creation of urban courts would be tantamount to recognizing the permanence of the urban African communities; moreover, such courts would not be administering Native customary law, since the larger part of the litigation they would handle arose from incidents specific to the urban environment, or from a clash between two different traditions such as occurred in inter-tribal marriages. As a compromise, tribal councillors having a knowledge of customary law and experience of working in rural Native courts were appointed to assist district officers in the urban areas. Since customary law varied according to tribe and locality, the territory as a whole was divided into four 'customary law areas' in which the customs of the tribes were broadly similar. One Native Authority in each group then nominated a councillor to each of

the urban courts, so that each group of Native assessors contained men who between them had a knowledge of the customary law of all the tribes in the territory. Initially appointed for a
period of six years, the assessors were to return to their village
homes for six months after the first three in order to become
familiar again with the customs and laws they were administering.

The first assessors were appointed to three of the Copperbelt
towns in 1937. They proved to be of little help in easing the
district officers' work in the courts, and consequently consideration was again given to instituting properly constituted urban
Native courts, with the assessors undertaking the same kind of
functions as a chief and his councillors in the rural areas. This
idea was finally accepted, and the first Native court was inaugurated at Mufulira in 1938. By the end of 1940, similar
courts were functioning at Kitwe, Luanshya, Ndola, Chingola,
Lusaka, Broken Hill, and Livingstone. The area over which
they exercised jurisdiction was usually the bounds of a township
or municipality, together with an additional slice of adjoining
Crown land. All persons who were Natives, 'any member of the
aboriginal tribes or races of Africa, including any person having
the blood of such tribes or races, and living among and after the
manner of any such tribes or races', came within their competence, and though there were no hard-and-fast boundaries
between Native and Magistrates courts, in practice all petty
criminal and all civil cases involving Africans were heard before the former. But no Native court was allowed to try criminal
cases in which a person was charged with an offence in consequence of which death was alleged to have occurred, or which
was punishable under any law with death or imprisonment for
life. Neither could they try cases involving witchcraft, except on
the express approval of a district officer; nor those involving a
European as a witness. On all other counts they administered
Native customary law 'except in so far as it is repugnant to
natural justice or morality, or inconsistent with the provisions
of any law in force in the territory'.

About the same time as the Native urban courts were instituted, the Government introduced a system of African Urban
Advisory Councils in the main towns of the Copperbelt. Their
function was primarily to keep the officers of the Administration

in touch with African opinion, to advise them on matters of African welfare, and conversely, to make Government policy known to the African populace generally. Members of the Councils were partly elected by the tribal elders' councils and the 'boss boys'—Africans of long service on the mines who were responsible for a group of African labourers—and partly nominated by the district commissioners, who took the chair at all their meetings.

While the creation of this trinity, the tribal elders' councils in the mining compounds, the urban advisory councils, and the urban Native courts, implied a definite change on the part of the Government towards the urban African, nonetheless, there were certain ominous signs regarding their efficacy. The Commission of Inquiry into the Copperbelt riot had pointed out that the only tribal elders' council which then existed had proved of little value, either before or during that emergency. Neither was this surprising. Such authority as they had came either from hereditary title, age, or an unofficial delegation of chiefly power. The questions they considered were such as would be dealt with by a welfare officer in a modern industrial organization: smoothing out disputes between individuals, attempting to counsel and advise according to traditional tribal custom, and generally helping newcomers to the mine locations. In this sense they certainly fulfilled a useful function. But they did not have any real authority in the industrial field, since they were not empowered to negotiate with the mine management on behalf of their African employees. Indeed, it is doubtful whether many of them had either the ability or knowledge to undertake such responsibilities.

The urban advisory councils were hardly in a stronger position to render effective service to the Administration. Representatives from all sections of the African urban community sat on them; but again they had no power or influence in the vital spheres, the mine compounds. While there was joint consultation between a district officer and mine-compound manager on occasions such as when the poll-tax rates were revised, the day-to-day running of the compound was outside the jurisdiction of the district officers. They could be informed of discontent or grievances through those tribal elders or boss boys who sat on the urban advisory councils; but industrial matters were the

concern of the mining companies, and there was little of importance that did not fall within this category. The influence of
Government administrative officers was also declining in the
more important civil townships. When the European community was small and lacking in resources the controlling authority
was a Management Board, in which the Central Government
had a powerful say, through financial grants, through the district commissioner who was its chairman, and through the
Government's prerogative of nominating the remaining members of the Board, usually Government officers and leading citizens. As the settlement expanded, so this structure changed, the
local authority itself gradually taking over certain responsibilities from the Central Government. Moreover, elected representatives of the local community sat on the Board, and since
the qualification for the municipal franchise was ownership or
occupation of rateable property to a capital value of £250,
these were almost exclusively Europeans.[27] As a township developed local European citizens became increasingly influential
in local authority affairs. The end of this evolutionary process
was the granting of municipal status, by which time the local
authority was responsible for a wide range of administrative
matters, including the African compounds and locations within
its boundary. At this stage the district commissioner's authority
in relation to the African compounds and their inmates became
broadly similar to his influence in the mine locations. Long before the granting of municipal status, however, European rate-
payers exerted a considerable influence in local affairs, certainly
overwhelmingly greater than an advisory council of Africans.

Of the trinity, the Native urban courts were undoubtedly the
most important innovation. Yet even here Government plans
ran along a familiar channel. Any code of law regulating the
behaviour of Africans in the urban areas had of necessity to be
based on tribal customary law, and since tribal councillors and
elders were the authorities on such matters, it was inevitable
that they should form the nuclei round which the system of
urban courts was built. Nevertheless, as stabilization in the

[27] There was not, neither is there now, a legal bar to Africans voting. But the
great majority of African houses in the urban locations are not worth £250 even
today. Under the subsidized rental system, services are provided at cost: therefore
the property is exempt from rates. In 1958 no African had qualified for the municipal franchise.

urban areas increased, so divergence between the codes of law developed to regulate small, intricate family–village structures and the adaptations necessary to cater for the emergence of individualism and materialism would become more marked. Plainly the urban courts would have to move with this trend. And for this to occur the new laws would have to be collated, and magistrates and officials specially trained to frame and administer them. But the Government proposed that after three years in the urban areas, Native court assessors should return to their villages and refresh their memories about the tribal customary law they were administering in the urban areas. Moreover, the traditional elders and councillors constituted that section of African opinion most rigidly against change, most anxious to maintain the old ways in the face of the new, for they had a vested interest in seeing that customary law was administered, not only because it was from traditional custom that their authority sprang but also because it now gave them lucrative—in African terms—Government posts.

CHAPTER 7

OFFICIAL RESPONSIBILITY AND UNOFFICIAL CONTROL

THE African strike and riot profoundly shocked the European community in Northern Rhodesia. It reminded them of the extent to which they were outnumbered by Africans, even in the urban areas, of their vulnerability in the event of further disturbances. It also shattered the illusion that a policy of continuously repatriating Native labour back to the reserves protected their interests. Moreover, the manner in which the strike had been spread from one mine to the next indicated active African leadership during the emergency: if that leadership were consolidated, if an effective African workers' organization emerged, then the African mine workers might be able, at some time in the future, to dictate terms to the entire country, a frightening prospect from the settlers' point of view. Realization of these possibilities immediately produced demands from the Unofficials for a greater measure of political power—the Officials were accused of not being able to maintain law and order—while the Amalgamation of the two Rhodesias received renewed support. A general election was held in the Territory in the year of the strike, and all the Unofficials stood before the electorate supporting the demand for greater Unofficial power and for Amalgamation.

In January 1936 Northern Rhodesian Unofficials and representatives of the political parties in Southern Rhodesia met at the Victoria Falls to discuss the latter issue. Eventually they resolved in favour of 'the early amalgamation of Northern and Southern Rhodesia under a constitution conferring the right of complete self-government'.[1] In May of the same year a motion in similar terms was passed by the Southern Rhodesian Legislative Assembly. In his reply the Secretary of State for Dominion Affairs pointed out that the decision of 1931 'was definitely intended as settling the question for some time to

[1] *Rhodesia–Nyasaland Royal Commission Report*, 1939, Cmd. 5949, pp. 113–14.

come'; the British Government did not feel that during the subsequent five years the change in conditions had been such as to justify reconsideration of the question.[2] The rejection of Amalgamation, without any indication from the Imperial Government that it was willing to concede greater Unofficial responsibility, angered the settlers. One of the newly elected Unofficials, Colonel Stewart Gore-Browne, had already warned the Northern Rhodesian Government that he and his colleagues had 'decided, solemnly and seriously, after due consideration, that if the Constitution is not eventually altered in the sense we desire, that is by giving more power to the Unofficial element in the Territory, we shall collectively resign our present appointments'.[3] The Governor, Sir Hubert Young, was quick to point out that the decision on Amalgamation did not mean that there would be no constitutional changes for an indefinite time, and with his encouragement, the Unofficials suggested that the numbers of Officials and Unofficials in the Legislature should be equalized by adding a nominated member to represent African interests to the latter and reducing the numbers of Officials by one. The proposal was communicated to the Secretary of State, and subsequently accepted by the British Government.

The Secretary of State for Dominions and Colonies in the Imperial Government also offered to discuss the Amalgamation question with Rhodesian representatives when they were in London attending the Coronation of King George VI. Discussions duly took place, and were followed by a conference attended by the Governors of Northern and Southern Rhodesia and Nyasaland, the Prime Minister of Southern Rhodesia and Colonel Gore-Browne, which resulted in the appointment of a Royal Commission to inquire into the whole problem of the 'closer association or co-operation between Southern Rhodesia, Northern Rhodesia, and Nyasaland'. Amalgamation was not specifically mentioned; nevertheless, the decision to appoint a Royal Commission was, in the circumstances, a resounding victory for the settler representatives. The status of the Unofficials had in any case undergone a considerable change since the arrival of Sir Hubert Young as Governor in 1934. In his first address to the Legislative Council he had said: 'I regard Hon.

[2] *Rhodesia–Nyasaland Royal Commission Report*, op. cit., pp. 114–15.
[3] Hansard, 2 December 1935, cols, 197–8.

Elected Members as the permanent element in such a Council as this. They represent permanent local interests in a way that no official can do, least of all a Governor who has only a few short years to look forward to in which to learn what those interests are. I look . . . to Hon. Elected Members for advice upon all local matters affecting their own community, but also upon matters affecting that larger and less articulate community of Native Africans . . . Hon. Elected Members should in my opinion be consulted upon the application of a policy after the necessary legislation has been drafted, but wherever practicable, upon the policy before it is initiated.' [4] Such a view was very different from that of the first Governor of the Territory, Sir Herbert Stanley, who had regarded the Legislative Council more as an advisory body than a parliament. But since the Unofficials had continuously demonstrated their ability to thwart or to mould the policies pursued by the Northern Rhodesian Government, Sir Hubert Young was being no more than realistic.

Important changes were also occurring in the composition and the attitudes of the Unofficials. Colonel Gore-Browne in particular had made a mark in the Northern Rhodesian Legislature. Second to none in his desire to see the power of the Colonial Office in the Territory reduced, as his threat of collective Unofficial resignation bore witness, his entry into politics nevertheless marked the dawn of a new era. An old Harrovian and ex-Guards Officer, he first visited Northern Rhodesia in 1911 as a member of a boundary commission and had been sufficiently impressed with the land to return after the First World War to settle on a vast estate isolated in the heart of Bembaland. Perhaps it was the geographical position of his home which gave him an especial interest in African affairs: certainly he brought to the Legislative Council a knowledge of and interest in the African and his problems not previously conspicuous, either among Officials or Unofficials. It was he perhaps more than anyone who recognized the need for some kind of African representative bodies in the urban areas. In a speech to the Legislature in 1936, for instance, he described how he had addressed an African audience, consisting of 'educated Natives, clerks and capitaos', in Lusaka. Asked to speak on Amalgama-

[4] Hansard, 1 December 1934. col. 3.

tion, Gore-Browne refused, considering that such a discussion savoured of a political meeting, and he did not think it a good principle to encourage political meetings among Natives. Towards the end, however, an African asked him whether he did not think the Native peoples should be consulted on a question like Amalgamation. Gore-Browne agreed that they should, but asked in turn how Africans were to be consulted. The same African replied: 'Our chiefs will speak for us.' Immediately twenty others shouted out: 'No, they cannot talk for us, they do not know what we are thinking, they do not think anything about it.' [5]

While many of Gore-Browne's comments on Native affairs smacked of the traditional patriarchal attitude of the European settlers—he admitted that he preferred to treat the African with benevolent autocracy—he was strikingly different in other respects. For an Unofficial to address an African meeting was in itself a startling innovation: so was Gore-Browne's awareness of the need for some form of consultation with the African people on political issues. Later in the year he addressed the Legislature on the constitutional position. While contending that the Unofficials must be given additional responsibilities— he rejected the idea that the Officials had carried out the policy of Trusteeship in such a manner as to justify exclusive responsibility—he admitted that to continue to press for unadulterated Amalgamation was to demand the impossible. Closer association in Central Africa was conditioned by two factors: first, the British Government's responsibilities for the indigenous Natives, and second, what he described as the crux of the question, 'the fact that there are about 10,000 white people concentrated in a comparatively small area along the railway line, while behind and around them stretches a huge territory . . . inhabited by . . . a million and a half uncivilized Natives'. As an initial step towards solving the dilemma, Gore-Browne proposed that Northern Rhodesia should be carved into three separate blocks, Central Rhodesia, corresponding with the strip along the railway line, and North-East and North-West Rhodesias. The former would be a zone in which the White man's interests would be paramount, while in the latter those of the Natives would be decisive, although Gore-Browne hastened to add that

[5] Hansard, 4 May 1936, cols, 70–1.

Black labour in the White area would be well treated, and that Native paramountcy in the remainder of the country would not prohibit mining or other legitimate activities should the opportunity ever arise. Having thus split the territory, Gore-Browne proposed that Northern and Southern Rhodesia and Nyasaland be then linked together in a federation, North-East and North-West Rhodesia and Nyasaland being part of the federation but remaining under the aegis of the Colonial Office, while the White-dominated railway strip would be joined to Southern Rhodesia under a constitution similar to that enjoyed by the latter. Each area was to be allowed maximum independence, with the federal government responsible only for defence, communications, posts and telegraphs, customs, research, and civil aviation.

Gore-Browne recognized that a more flexible linkage than Amalgamation was necessary if the British Government was ever to agree to closer association between the three Central African territories; nevertheless, his proposals were Amalgamation under another name, since the whole purpose behind the settler community's demand for political union with Southern Rhodesia was to achieve responsibility for Native affairs in the European-settled zone. Since economic development was in the hands of European enterprise, this necessarily meant that the Native states would remain economic backwaters, their principal purpose, supplying the European settled areas with labour. His plan was to meet the Colonial Office's objections to full-blooded Amalgamation, while achieving the same ends from the European point of view. Gore-Browne's plan for achieving harmony between the races in the proposed state was unique—if a little blunted by the circumstances in which he set it. It was no more and no less than 'partnership'. Segregation and repression he rejected outright. 'The only solution to the problem . . . is to admit frankly that we regard the Native races as our partners, potential partners if you will, junior partners for as far ahead as it is possible to look, and to frame our Native policy accordingly.' [6] Certainly no one in Northern Rhodesia had talked previously of racial partnership, no matter at what distance in the future.

These suggestions by no means reflected the feelings of the

[6] Hansard, 29 October 1936, col. 249.

settler populace generally. But Gore-Browne's influence in the political field was to be immeasurably strengthened by virtue of the fact that fortuitously he supplied a missing element in the Legislative Council. Over the question of Native affairs there was a stalemate, Official responsibility being balanced by Unofficial control. Because of this, and because any Native policy emanating solely from the Official benches was suspected by the Unofficials, the stalemate could only be broken by associating the Unofficials more closely with African affairs. But hitherto the Unofficials had only been interested in African problems in so far as they affected the European community. Gore-Browne, on the other hand, was interested in African problems *per se*; he also had a special knowledge of African affairs. Consequently, he was appointed the first Nominated Member representing African interests. The settlers naturally welcomed his appointment not only because it associated one of them with Native affairs; it also heralded parity between Unofficials and Officials, and thereby demonstrated that the Territory was moving towards self-government and Unofficial power. That no one, Official or Unofficial, considered Gore-Browne's duties as involving any special responsibilities or obligations can be gauged from the fact that no machinery was devised to help Gore-Browne in his task of representing African interests—in a territory of 275,000 square miles, containing a multitude of different tribes thinly scattered over it. Neither was there to be any criterion whereby Gore-Browne's performance was to be judged. He was simply expected to meet as many Africans as he could, and to express in the Legislature what he considered to be their opinions. But Gore-Browne proved to be deeply conscientious, and while he never forgot that he was also a settler, he fearlessly expressed what he considered to be African opinion, whether this clashed with his own views or not. At the same time he was able to obtain Unofficial support for proposals which would certainly have met with considerable opposition had they come from the Official benches. This was particularly true with regard to the urban African community, for it was in this sphere that the Unofficials were most sensitive. Significantly, Gore-Browne took a leading part in establishing the African Urban Advisory Councils.

The 1935 strike convinced the European mine workers that

immediate steps had to be taken to safeguard their existing position. The development of the Copperbelt had, of course, altered the composition of the European community in Northern Rhodesia so that industrial workers and artisans became numerically the strongest class. During the construction boom a large number of the Europeans who flooded into the Copperbelt had no intention of settling permanently in the North. And the slump forced many more to leave the Territory. For those that remained, there was the constant fear that the mining companies might replace them with cheap African labour. By the time the strike occurred, however, the industry was recovering from the worst effects of the depression, and no European had been displaced by Africans. But the strike made the European mine workers realize that the danger emanated not only from their employers but from the Africans themselves. The only possible safeguard was to form their own trade union organization, as had the Europeans employed by the Rhodesian Railways, so as to be able to defend their standards from a position of strength. And in 1936 Mr. Charles Harris, a member of the South African Mine Workers' Union, visited the Copperbelt to help establish such an organization. This he did, and in the following year the Northern Rhodesian Mine Workers' Union was recognized by the mining companies in an agreement which, among other things, bound both parties not to call a strike or lock-out until conciliation had been tried and had failed. The numerical strength of the industrial workers was beginning to be reflected in the Legislature. Mrs. Catherine Olds was returned as Member for the Ndola Electoral Area in the 1935 general election, the first woman to sit in the Legislature and the wife of a copper miner. In 1938 the appointment of Colonel Gore-Browne to be Nominated Unofficial representing African interests left the Northern Electoral Area vacant, and a young engine-driver, an active trade unionist in the European Railway Workers' Union, Mr. Roy Welensky, was returned unopposed.

The mood of the Copperbelt at this time is well illustrated by an incident which occurred at Nkana in November 1937, when disturbances again broke out on the Copperbelt. On the first day of the month some Africans were digging a trench in the township at Kitwe. Two European youths were sitting near where they were working, when one of them suddenly re-marked that he thought the 'boys' were sitting down, picked up a clod of earth, peered round the corner, saw that one of them was sitting down, and threw the clod at him. He sub-sequently claimed that the African then swore at him and that in response he kicked and struck the African with his fists a few times. A struggle ensued in which he was bitten on the wrists. The African then ran away and reported the incident to the local police. The European youth was subsquently charged with assaulting a Native, appeared two days later before the local Acting Resident Magistrate, and was sentenced to four strokes with a cane, the sentence being carried out half an hour later. The only persons present were a medical officer of health and the European policeman who administered the punish-ment. The time was midday, 3 November. On the following day a mass meeting of Europeans at Nkana Club protested against what was described as the flogging of a European youth for assaulting a Native. Feelings ran high, and the local Member for the Legislative Council, communicated with the Governor, who happened to be in Kitwe at the time, and asked for an inter-view, which the Governor granted on the following day. That evening another meeting was held at the Nkana Club, and from 11.30 p.m. to 1.30 a.m. rowdy scenes of protest occurred. An official inquiry into the disturbance was ordered.[7]

This case appears to have been the culmination of a long series of incidents, each racial in character, each productive of bitterness among the local Europeans, who had conse-quently come firmly to believe that the local police and ad-ministrative officers favoured the African on all possible occa-sions. The official report put these into perspective by setting out what was considered to be justice and the role of the police in such matters. While the authorities had received numerous complaints from Europeans of African assaults, investigation usually proved that the European had struck first. The latter's attitude was indeed characterized by the kind of notes received at police stations from local European residents: 'This "boy" has refused to wash the dishes, please give him a good hiding.' Mr. Claxton, who played a prominent role in presenting

[7] *Report of an Inquiry into the Causes of a Disturbance at Nkana on the 4th and 5th November 1937*, E. E. Jenkins (Government Printer Lusaka, 1937).

evidence to the Commission of Inquiry and who was officially thanked for his help, expressed the feelings of the local European population when he said that 'the civil servants in this country seem to degrade a White man in front of the niggers'. Mr. Claxton considered the crux of the matter to be the prestige of the White man in the country. 'By what right,' he asked, 'has the magistrate to refer to the accused in this case and notify him that it is a Black man's country; he notified the boy that this is a Black man's country, and that he has to keep his hands off the niggers. I was always under the impression that this country belonged to the British Empire, not by right of conquest, but by right of acquisition, and the White man expects as much justice, no more, no less, than the nigger. But he will not have men administering justice in this country who are biased.'

The protests about the case had many varying facets. The youth had been caned without his parents being informed; Africans had witnessed the punishment; there had been no time for an appeal against the sentence. . . . The Commission of Inquiry found that all had been conducted within the framework of the law. No Africans had witnessed the punishment; neither was the youth, as the protests had intimated, an innocent. He had a previous conviction; his parents had proved unable to care for and discipline him, and he had been under probation and in the care of the police. The Governor promised to review the legislation covering the punishment of juveniles, and subsequently the incidents ceased. But a man who had been on the Copperbelt at the time said afterwards: 'I may say today, though things are quiet, that very little would be needed to fire the temper of the people into a disastrous destructive movement against the Natives.'

The report of the Royal Commission investigating Closer Association was naturally awaited with general eagerness. It was presented to Parliament in March 1939, a long and somewhat ambiguous document which expressed the view that the three territories faced fundamentally similar problems, and that they would therefore become 'more and more closely interdependent'. The acceptance of Amalgamation in principle was consequently recommended, although the Commission expressed the view that it should not be implemented immediately. Various reasons were given for this: the desirability of waiting until the White population of the three territories was larger, the need for giving the Northern Rhodesia and Nyasaland settlers more political experience, and the differences between the African policies followed in Northern Rhodesia and Nyasaland, on the one hand, and Southern Rhodesia, on the other. However, the Commissioners did not write very clearly about the causes or the consequences of this difference. Amalgamation was considered as the ultimate goal: as an interim measure the Commission recommended that Northern Rhodesia and Nyasaland should be amalgamated and an inter-territorial council established to co-ordinate certain matters of common interest between the three territories. Moreover, the Commission recommended that in Northern Rhodesia there should be an Unofficial majority in the Legislative Council and parity between Unofficials and Officials on the Executive Council.

The Royal Commission's report was debated in the Northern Rhodesian Legislature on 6 June 1939, when all the Unofficials, including Gore-Browne, deplored its ambiguity. The Commissioners' reasons for rejecting immediate Amalgamation were bitterly attacked, while the proposals for creating a measure of closer association were treated with disdain. Speaking on the proposal to amalgamate Northern Rhodesia and Nyasaland, Captain A. A. Smith (Nkana Electoral Area) declared: 'All that we should acquire by amalgamation [with Nyasaland] would be one and a half million Natives,' with the result 'that this divergence of Native policy [between Northern and Southern Rhodesia] will be carried further.' Suggestions were made for carrying out a referendum in the three territories on the issue. But the new member for the Northern Electoral Area, Mr. Welensky, warned the Council that if the Northern Rhodesian Native policy had to be adopted, then the referendum in Southern Rhodesia would be against Amalgamation. The leader of the Unofficials, Sir Leopold Moore (he had been knighted in 1937), condemned the Report with biting scorn. 'I simply dismiss the whole Commission as a waste of time and money by a lot of men who did not know what they were doing, never should have been sent out, were badly selected, and quite unfitted for their job.' [8]

To underline his feelings Moore resigned, though announcing

[8] Hansard, 6 June 1939, col. 496.

that if renominated he would stand for election again. Welensky in later years remarked that if Sir Leopold had warned the other Unofficials of his intentions, 'I think an organized attempt would have been made to get all the Unofficial members of the Legislature to resign,' [9] obviously thinking of the way in which the Unofficials had previously forced the hand of the British Government. The opportunity, however, passed. Sir Leopold Moore was returned unopposed at the ensuing by-election in Livingstone; but Gore-Browne had already been elected leader of the Unofficials.

[9] Hansard, 24 November 1949, col. 322.

CHAPTER 8

THE IMPACT OF THE
SECOND WORLD WAR—A SIGNIFICANT
CHANGE OF ATTITUDE

THE anger aroused by the Bledisloe Royal Commission
report was quickly overwhelmed by the repercussions of
another event, the beginning of the Second World War.
No longer was the Territory an African backwater, struggling
to recover from the effects of the depression: as the principal
copper producer in the Commonwealth, Northern Rhodesia
was vitally important to the successful prosecution of the war.
Maximum copper production was needed: unemployment and
underemployment within the line of rail area ceased, and consequently European mine workers and railwaymen were raised to
positions of unprecedented power and influence. The struggles
between Official and Unofficial in the Legislature were swept
aside. Mr. Welensky, as a leader of the European Railwaymen's
Union, was already a figurehead for the White workers in the
Territory: the advent of war raised him to national importance,
a fact which was quickly recognized officially by his appointment to the Manpower Committee, which, under the chairmanship of the Solicitor-General, was given the task of selecting
Europeans who could be released for service in the Armed
Forces. Unofficials were also appointed to the Executive Council, Welensky among them. The Unofficials thus achieved a
measure of political advancement inconceivable only a few
months earlier.

This swift change of circumstances brought other problems in
its train. In March 1940 the European daily paid mine workers
at Mufulira withdrew their labour without notice—except for
those engaged on safety and essential services. Four days later
they were joined by the Europeans at Nkana, strikers at both
mines taking action independent of the European Mine
Workers' Union and breaking their agreement with the mining

companies. Both made similar demands: that the basic rate of pay should be raised by 2*s.* per shift; a war bonus introduced to meet the increased cost of living; and the rates for overtime substantially improved. In one sense, the strike reflected the new power of the European mine workers. But the urgent need for copper had also brought close the possibility that Africans might have to be trained for work previously the exclusive preserve of the White man; consequently the strikers at both Nkana and Mufulira also demanded that the agreement between the European daily paid labour force and the companies should be amended by the introduction of a 'closed shop' clause. Officials of the European Union stressed that they were not against African advancement: 'the Union has always laid it down that there was no objection to any African being employed as a tradesman or in any other capacity, provided he was capable of doing a job of work as good or nearly as good as a European, and that he obtained the European rate of pay'.[1]

Neither was the Union totally opposed to a degree of labour dilution, the taking over of certain categories of work from the European by the African at rates differing from those paid to the European, although its leaders emphasized that whatever adjustments were agreed could only be of a temporary nature, for the duration of the war.

The strike was quickly settled in terms of the demand for increased remuneration. Moreover, after negotiations lasting until July 1940, a clause was inserted into the agreement between the European Union and each of the companies agreeing that 'during the war dilution of labour might be necessary, in which case it would be carried out after mutual consultation between the Union and the Company. After the war, working conditions on each of the individual mines will revert to the practice at present existing.' [2] The mining companies later stated that the agreement was made under pressure, the British Government insisting that the flow of copper should not be interrupted. In the following year the European Union again pressed for a closed shop, and, again following pressure from the British

[1] Evidence given to *Commission of Inquiry into Disturbances on the Copperbelt, Northern Rhodesia, July 1940* (Government Printer Lusaka), pp. 46–47.

[2] *Memorandum submitted by the Copper Mining Companies to the Board of Inquiry into the Advancement of Africans in the Copper Mining Industry* (Northern Rhodesia, August 1954), p. 2.

Government, it was agreed that all jobs scheduled in the agreement had to be paid at the rate laid down for European daily paid employees, and that everyone performing such work had to be a member of the European Union. Hence the new clause eliminated to all intents and purposes any possibility of African advancement, since all the skilled and practically all the semi-skilled jobs had to be paid at European rates and no facilities existed whereby an African could be trained to the standards of skill necessary to justify that rate of payment. Indeed, the Apprenticeship Ordinance, governing the conditions under which apprentices were indentured in the Territory, specifically excluded Africans.

After the strike of European mine workers at Nkana and Mufulira had been settled, rumours began to spread through the African compounds at the two mines that the Europeans had gained wage increases of up to £4 a day. In turn, rumours of an African strike began to circulate, and Government officials pressed the mining companies to announce an increase in the rate of African bonus payments. This was done. Nevertheless, on the day after the announcement a majority of African miners at one of the shafts at the Nkana mine failed to report for work. By the following day, the stoppage was complete and the strike had spread to the remainder of the mine at Nkana and to Mufulira. Police reinforcements and troops were dispatched to the Copperbelt when it became apparent that the temper of the strikers was deteriorating, for small incidents of violence began to occur, and Africans at the Nkana smelter were forcibly prevented from working by pickets.

Despite this, the mine authorities at Nkana decided to hold a normal pay parade at the compound office, and many Africans attended to claim pay earned before the strike began. A crowd of strikers, thinking that the men in the pay queue had either been working or were going to work, gathered outside the building and shouted insults and threats at them. A few stones were thrown. The police and military, present in case trouble developed, attempted to disperse the crowd by tear gas, but failed because of the absence of wind. The temper of the watching strikers worsened, and a fusillade of sticks, stones, and pieces of iron was hurled at the office. The strikers then began to move in on it, and to protect the property and the people sheltering therein, the troops opened fire. Thirteen Africans were killed, and four wounded so seriously that they subsequently died.

A Commission of Inquiry was appointed by the Northern Rhodesian Government, under the chairmanship of Sir John Forster, K.C., to inquire into the disturbance. The Commissioners found that its immediate cause had been the determination of the mine management at Nkana to hold a pay parade, while the African strike had stemmed directly from the previous stoppage of European mine workers.[3] In general, the state of affairs in the African compounds revealed by the Commission's report showed little change from that reported by the 1935 Commission of Inquiry. Of the two mines involved in the strike, only at Mufulira was there an effectively organized African tribal elders' council, and as had been the case at the Roan Antelope in 1935, the Commission found that it had proved inadequate to its tasks, failing to be of any assistance during the strike or to have successfully transmitted African grievances to the management prior to it. Yet grievances had been abounding in the African labour force. As a single instance, the wages being paid at the time of the strike were actually less than before the slump in 1930, 13s. 6d. and 22s. 6d. a ticket for an African surface and underground worker compared with 17s. 6d. and 30s. respectively.

But the Commission found a significant change in the attitude of the African mine workers. To some extent this was evident from the pattern of the strikes. At the Nchanga and Roan Antelope mines there had been no stoppage; at Nkana and Mufulira both European and African workers had struck, for the Commission discovered that the African mine workers were anxious to emulate their fellow European workers, to demonstrate that they had no less capacity in the industrial field. This was also the reason why the African strike had continued for so long; African workers were loth to return to work without gains commensurate with those of the Europeans. Consequently the Commission of Inquiry found African mine workers frustrated by the barriers erected against their further advancement by the industrial colour bar. Indeed, some Africans claimed not only that they were capable of performing satisfactorily work done

[3] *Report of the Commission Appointed to Inquire into the Disturbances in the Copperbelt, Northern Rhodesia, July 1940* (Government Printer Lusaka), pp. 50–51.

by Europeans; they went so far as to challenge the latter to a
production test, one shift being worked by Europeans the next
by Africans. Such a test would certainly have been impracti-
cable. Its real significance, however, lay not in its practicability,
but in indicating the extent and rapidity with which Africans
were being absorbed in the mining industry. Because of this
feeling of African frustration, the Commission included in its report a sentence of unprecedented importance in the history of
Northern Rhodesia: 'The mine managements should consider,
with representatives of the Government and the Northern
Rhodesian Mine Workers' Union, to what positions not now
open to him the African should be encouraged to advance.' [4]

Many of the recommendations of the Forster Commission
were accepted. In a statement agreed by the mining companies,
the Government announced that the minimum African wage
was to be increased by 2s. 6d. a ticket; that the African labour
force was to be divided into three grades, with the opportunity
of promotion open to all; and that a higher grade to accommo-
date Africans of special ability was to be formed. Cost-of-living
allowances were to be introduced, disciplinary reductions on
bonuses abolished, and overtime paid on the same basis as for
Europeans. The Commission's recommendation that adequate
married accommodation should be provided for African workers
was also accepted. 'But,' the statement continued, 'acceptance
does not commit the Government to a policy of establishing a
permanent industrialized Native population on the Copperbelt.' As for the suggestion that a conference should be called to
consider African advancement, the statement pointed out that
'the revised wages scales to which the companies have agreed
afford very considerable advancement on the present limits and
afford to Africans reasonable satisfaction during the next few
years of their aspirations towards higher remuneration.' Though
the Government hoped in due course to initiate discussions as
recommended by the Commission, many European mine
workers had joined the Armed Forces on promise of reinstate-
ment by the companies on their return from active service, and
in turn their places had been filled by other Europeans.
Though the Northern Rhodesian Mine Workers' Union had
agreed to a degree of labour dilution during the war period, 'it

[4] *Commission of Inquiry, Copperbelt Disturbances, 1940*, op. cit., p. 53.

would be impossible to maintain Africans in posts previously occupied by Europeans to the exclusion of others returning from the war. It may well be therefore,' the statement concluded, 'that these discussions will not lead to any early practical results.' [5]

The question of African advancement in the copper-mining industry epitomized the dilemma of both the Northern Rhodesian Government and the European community. No matter what the justification for reinstating European workers who had volunteered for war service when hostilities ended, it was not related to the question of African advancement. Neither was the Forster Commission's recommendation likely to lessen African frustration. For the duration of the war the question of African advancement would necessarily lie in abeyance. But with hostilities over, there would be returning European servicemen to be reabsorbed, the pent-up frustration of African workers to be dealt with, all in circumstances where a fall in the demand for copper was a possibility. To all intents and purposes, however, the Northern Rhodesian Government was already excluded from influencing the problem directly: African advancement was a question for the mine managements and the European Mine Workers' Union.

It was not only in the copper-mining industry that African problems were forcing themselves to the Government's attention. In 1937 the Director of Medical Services pointed out the unsatisfactory nature of much of the housing provided for Africans in the non-mining locations and suggested that local authorities should be made responsible for providing accommodation. The same point was emphasized by Major J. St. Orde Browne in an investigation into labour conditions in the Territory. Some of the African housing owned by the Livingstone municipal authorities he described as 'unsuitable in type, floors and walls being built with soft mortar which allows crevices forming a refuge for ticks, bugs and all sorts of pests. . . . Ventilation consists principally of the door, which must usually be kept open owing to the heat generated by the low iron roof. . . . Sanitation consists of the unsuitable bucket system, and water has to be fetched from distant taps.' [6]

[5] Reported in *East Africa and Rhodesia*, 27 February 1941, p. 412.
[6] *Labour Conditions in Northern Rhodesia*, Major J. St. Orde Browne (H.M.S.O., Colonial No. 150, 1938), p. 62.

The results of the first scientifically conducted social survey of an African urban community, undertaken by Dr. Godfrey Wilson, the Director of the newly formed Rhodes–Livingstone Institute, a research centre devoted to the study of social and anthropological problems in Central Africa, provided a fascinating picture of life therein, and illustrated how quickly the pattern of migratory labour was changing. Taking a 3 per cent. sample of the 6,640 men working in Broken Hill, Dr. Wilson estimated that 1 per cent. of the total were permanently urbanized in the sense that their permanent home was in an urban and not a rural environment. Furthermore, by defining a migrant worker as one who had spent from one- to two-thirds of his life in a town and from two- to one-third in a rural area since first leaving his village, Dr. Wilson estimated that only some 20 per cent. of the African male population were migrants. No less than 70 per cent. had spent more than two-thirds of their time since first leaving their villages in an urban area. Dr. Wilson's sample was admittedly small; nevertheless, it provided the first quantitative evidence of the existence of a permanent element in an African urban population, and more important, of the rapidity with which a majority of the African workers in Broken Hill were becoming urban rather than rural in domicile.

Dr. Wilson's survey showed that many of the features of the life in the urban compounds had changed little since the time when large-scale migrations had begun. Illegal beer brewing continued to be rife; the passion for acquiring European clothing had not abated. Indeed, the purchase of clothing constituted a kind of capital investment, and Dr. Wilson estimated that in Broken Hill, some 60 per cent. of Africans' total cash earnings were spent on the purchase of clothing. An additional sophistication was the perusal of illustrated brochures and the ordering of goods from United Kingdom mail-order companies, for to receive a parcel from overseas added considerably to a person's social prestige. Social relationships continued to be based on tribal custom, distorted by the needs of the urban environment and inter-tribal contact. As to the composition of the community studied by Dr. Wilson, there was an estimated 41 per cent. of young unmarried men in their teens and early twenties. Of the older men the majority were accompanied by their wives. Children were comparatively few, since they were sent back to the villages to be raised by grandparents. The housing and rations provided for the workers were both based on the assumption that they were all unmarried migrants; hence the preponderance of young men and the absence of children were also due to deliberately created circumstances.

Conditions were noticeably deteriorating in some of the African rural areas. In certain districts of the Northern Province the traditional *chitimene* cultivation technique was being modified by the absence of large numbers of males, so that instead of pollarding the branches the entire tree was felled. While this circumvented the problem of labour shortage, felling the trees necessitated a longer period for the woodland's regeneration. But the increasing population, allied in certain districts with the moving of the African population into arbitrarily defined reserve areas, forced the round of shifting cultivation to move at an ever-increasing speed. So serious were the problems of devastation and declining soil fertility that 780 square miles of land had to be bought by the Northern Rhodesian Government from the British South Africa Company in the Abercorn–Isoka district, while the Chartered Company itself gave an additional 1,481 square miles so that people from the worst affected areas could be resettled.

The same problems occurred even more acutely in the Ngoni reserves. Soil erosion had first been noticed there as early as 1933. Two years later an officer from the Department of Agriculture, posted to the area to investigate, reported that the problem could not be solved merely by action on the part of that department. Population densities of up to 135 to the square mile occurred, greatly in excess of the land's carrying capacity in relation to the system of cultivation practised. Another report was called for in 1938, which stated that the only solution was the acquisition of more land to provide for population overspill. Since the reserve areas were surrounded by the North Charterland Concession, the report recommended that the Concession should be purchased outright by the Government.

In the Mazabuka district of the Southern Province these problems were complicated, first, by the fact that the Tonga could sell their crops on the line of rail markets, and secondly, by the presence of European farmers growing the same crops in

adjacent areas. Land alienation for European settlement, particularly for soldier settlers after the First World War, had
caused African displacement and consequent overcrowding on
the boundary between Crown land and Native reserve. The
deterioration in soil fertility this had produced had been heightened by the use of ploughs and oxen in emulation of the European farmer and by a tremendous increase in the size of Tonga
cattle herds, which, because they were regarded as living bank
balances, were judged by quantity and not quality. Ironically,
the operation of the Maize Control Ordinance, introduced to
protect European maize farmers from the worst effects of the
depression, accentuated these problems. The provision of buying points and a guaranteed price for maize tempted the Tonga
into increasing the acreage of land they cultivated and into
moving into the densely populated districts adjacent to Crown
land, since these lay closest to the buying points. The low prices
paid to African cultivators quickly reduced the amount of
maize they offered to the Maize Control Board; but it failed to
induce any comparable movement away from the overcrowded
areas. And by 1939 the economic situation had so changed that
maize was being imported: the Northern Rhodesian Government was thus placed in a position where it had to encourage
African maize production, against African distrust in view of
their initial experiences of the Maize Control Board, and in the
knowledge that increased maize production could only aggravate an already serious situation. As the Director of Agriculture
remarked in his annual report for 1939, no progress could be
expected unless adequate funds for soil-conservation work were
made available. And the figure he mentioned as necessary—
£100,000—was staggering in terms of the Protectorate's
revenue and the money hitherto devoted to African projects.

Northern Rhodesia was in reality poised at a turning-point
in its history. Problems such as the rapid increase of soil erosion
in the Native reserves, the state of African housing and facilities
in the urban locations, and African frustration in the copper-
mining industry, could no longer be ignored. A new, positive
attitude was needed from the Northern Rhodesian Government
and the Unofficials if these African problems were to be solved.
As the Director of Agriculture had pointed out, the situation
in the Tonga reserves demanded a dynamic policy, a specific

programme designed not to bolster the traditional way of life but to revolutionize it.

In these circumstances the changes in British public opinion wrought by the Second World War were extremely significant. Addressing a Labour Party conference shortly after the outbreak of war, Mr. Clement Attlee, the party's leader, declared that 'the second principle of a peace settlement must be the recognition of the right of all nations, great or small, of whatever colour or creed, to have the right to live and to develop their own characteristic civilization. . . . The Briton must recognize that the African has as much right as he to a place in the world, and to a share in the bounty of Nature. There must be the abandonment of Imperialism . . .' [7] Such views were in a way directly descended from those expressed by Lord Passfield in his Memorandum on Native policy, though subsequent events had made it clear that Lord Passfield's ideas had had little support, even in London. But with the advent of the Second World War there was a general feeling that having called upon men of all races and creeds in the Colonies and Dependencies to assist in combating the onslaught of Nazism, with its racial ideology, a return to the pre-war attitudes with regard to the Colonies and the status of dependent people was impossible. Such feelings gained expression in the first Colonial Development and Welfare Act passed by the British Parliament in 1940, during the darkest days of the war, whereby the United Kingdom set aside funds for the express purpose of raising the standards of life in the Colonies, socially and economically. It was both an expression of faith in the future and an indication that an era in British Colonial history was at an end.

The influence of these combined internal and external pressures were soon to be seen in Northern Rhodesia. In 1943 the Governor took the unprecedented step of appointing a commission 'to inquire into and report on the administration of Native locations' (excluding the locations controlled by the mining companies). Even more startling were the commission's recommendations. In the introduction to the report, published in 1944,[8] the commissioners quoted Dr. Wilson's study of the

---

[7] Reported in *East Africa and Rhodesia*, 16 November 1939, p. 215.

[8] *Report of Commission Appointed to Inquire into the Administration and Finances of Native Locations in Urban Areas*, October 1944 (Government Printer Lusaka).

African community in Broken Hill, and stated unequivocally that the African and his family had to be treated as a permanent feature of life in the line of rail urban centres, and that in any long-term view, African stability in both the rural and urban areas was inevitable. Five years earlier, such expressions would have been considered nothing less than revolutionary, and while utterance did not imply acceptance, the mere fact that they were stated was profoundly significant.

The commissioners had found a state verging on chaos in the African locations. While a large part of the accommodation was owned by local authorities, there was no legislation compelling them to provide African housing. Though the Employment of Natives Ordinance placed an employer of African labour under obligation to house his employees, no mention was made of accommodating their families. The commission found that nearly all the housing they examined was of poor quality, while sanitation facilities were almost totally lacking. Of the 6,729 houses visited, only 689 had more than one room, this despite the fact that more than half the total male population living in them was married. Indeed, the commissioners felt that all the housing they had seen fell short of the minimum standards of decency and hygiene required for married couples. To remedy this state of affairs, the commission recommended that local authorities should be compelled to provide locations and build houses for all employed Africans, and that the housing should be of permanent materials with the minimum standard for married accommodation, two living-rooms, a kitchen, store, and veranda. Employers, the commissioners felt, should be made to assume full responsibility for housing both employees and their families. In order to plan and execute these proposals, the commission suggested that a new Government department should be created, to be solely responsible for the provision of African housing. With the information available to them, the commissioners estimated that the cost of meeting the demand for African urban housing would be no less than £1,000,000.

To ease the problem of overcrowding in the Ngoni areas, the Government opened negotiations with the North Charterland Exploration Company with a view to purchasing the latter's concession. The two parties failed to agree on a price, however, and the Company refused to refer the matter to arbitration. In

December 1940 the Government took power to acquire the concession compulsorily, though the actual sale, for £154,000, was
not completed until September 1941. Investigations revealed
that overcrowding in the reserves had been underestimated, the
new inquiries putting the surplus population in the Fort Jameson reserves at 90,000, with 22,000 in the Petauke reserves.
While the latter could be satisfactorily accommodated in the
newly acquired concession area, it was impossible, even with
this additional land, to achieve a correct population–land
balance with the Ngoni and Chewa tribes. The concession area
was consequently resettled to its maximum carrying capacity,
leaving some 56,000 people in excess of the land's carrying capacity in the Ngoni reserves.

In 1943 the Chief Secretary, Mr. G. Beresford Stooke, issued
a circular to all Provincial Commissioners regarding the problems likely to be raised by the return of the many Africans who
had volunteered for service with the Armed Forces. The
Northern Rhodesian Government took the view that full use
must be made of the demobilized soldiers to prosecute a campaign of Native development throughout the reserves. 'Are
Africans to be denied our culture?' the Chief Secretary asked.
'Are they to be condemned to live indefinitely under insanitary
and unhygienic conditions? Is it unreasonable to suggest that
within a measurable space of time it will be possible to bring
about conditions where, in every African village, Africans will
live in well-built cottages with adequate water supplies, a suffi-
ciency of good food, proper sanitation, and clean if simple
clothing? And that each village or area should have its skilled
craftsmen, and men and women trained to supply adequate
public services, health, educational, agricultural and so on?' [9]

The seal was finally set on this change in attitude when, in
1944, Mr. G. F. Clay was appointed by the Colonial Office as
Joint Development Adviser to the Northern Rhodesian and
Nyasaland Governments, and charged with laying the foundations for the post-war development of the two Protectorates. The
new attitude to Colonial development was made clear when Mr.
Clay stated in his interim report [10] that 'Social development and

[9] Reported in *East Africa and Rhodesia*, 9 September 1943, pp. 20–21.
[10] *Memorandum of Post War Planning in Northern Rhodesia*, G. F. Clay (Government
Printer Lusaka, 1945).

the basic services, under modern conceptions of the responsibilities of Colonial Powers, must be afforded to the indigenous population irrespective of the capacity of these populations to support such services'. He was forced to qualify this concept, however, in terms of the realities of Northern Rhodesia. 'It would appear,' he commented, 'that Northern Rhodesia, by virtue of its geographical position, its relatively small population scattered over a large area, and its comparatively poor soil, must avoid any tendency to extravagance in planning basic services, either in the organization or in the recurrent cost.' Nevertheless, he proceeded to suggest an outline plan that was certainly extravagant, at least by comparison with the ideas previously current. Primary development centres were to be built at five points in the Territory, each equipped to provide a wide range of social services and to train subordinate African staff, on whom would depend the dissemination of social advancement and improved welfare facilities. For Mr. Clay imagined these centres as focal points from which social uplift would pulsate out until standards in the entire length and breadth of the country were raised to those which the development centres would provide locally.

To support this concept by economic expansion was another question. Mr. Clay admitted that 'if a Native food production policy has no further objective than meeting the internal requirements of the territory, it would provide neither full employment for the rural community nor an economic and social standard comparable with that of the industrial worker'. Mr. Clay therefore suggested experimentation with new cash crops; the spreading of the area of economic production out from the line of rail by guaranteeing an average price to all producers; and the weaning of the European line of rail farmer from the prevalent system of maize monoculture to a more widely based mixed farming system, which would enable African producers to supply the more easily produced crops. Apart from the intrinsic difficulties in the latter, political and otherwise, Mr. Clay recognized that there had to be a revolution in African farming practice, a rapid change from extensive shifting cultivation to intensive stable farming. Moreover, 'the main stimulus for development must come from the local Native governments; but in most areas they are ill-fitted to take the lead in social or economic development'.

From the settlers' point of view, therefore, the Second World War produced contradictory results. On the one hand, it enabled the Unofficials to achieve an unprecedented measure of influence within the Government, and the Northern Rhodesian Mine Workers' Union to strengthen its grip on the copper-mining industry; on the other, the changed view of the responsibilities of Colonial powers ensured that once the war was over Northern Rhodesia would be subjected to external pressures, whether direct or indirect, to set in motion African advancement, social, economic, and political. Awareness of the latter induced a measure of disquiet among European political leaders and brought forward once again demands for Amalgamation. In 1941 Mr. Welensky formed the Northern Rhodesian Labour Party to fight the general election of that year, principally on the demand that Northern and Southern Rhodesia should be amalgamated. The party was strikingly successful, all its five candidates winning their seats. Its formation had been opposed by Colonel Gore-Browne, who argued that it was premature to introduce party politics to the territory. Welensky had replied that he was not introducing party politics, but merely wished to achieve Unofficial unanimity by having a dominant party in the Legislature.[11] Flushed with success, the new members of the Legislative Council made arrangements for another conference on Amalgamation with representatives from Southern Rhodesia. But their efforts proved abortive. As Gore-Browne said in the Legislature: 'We all know that the political issue of Amalgamation has to be deferred, and I am sure that we all see the justice of this and that none of us wish to embarrass the sorely tried Government at home by pressing this point at the moment.' [12] Moreover, as Welensky indicated in his reason for founding the Labour Party, there was no longer unanimity on the issue in Northern Rhodesia. The political advancement achieved by the Unofficials, together with wartime prosperity, combined to induce anew confidence that once the war was over Northern Rhodesia would quickly be granted self-government, and to offset the persistent criticism of Rhodesian affairs in the House of Commons. In the debate on the King's speech in November 1941 Mr. P. Noel-Baker (Labour) had stated that the most im-

[11] *The Rhodesian*, Don Taylor (London, 1955), pp. 58–59.
[12] Hansard, 30 March 1942, col. 17.

portant issue of political freedom raised at that moment was the proposed Amalgamation of the Rhodesias and Nyasaland. Mr. Arthur Creech Jones (Labour) asked if the civilization of Africa was to secure the White man in political and economic domination with the Black people menial and segregated, or if the policy was for a future Africa in which Black and White advanced and co-operated in freedom and citizenship. The question had to be answered before the war ended.

The division over Amalgamation came to a head in November 1943, when Welensky again moved in the Legislature that 'Northern and Southern Rhodesia be amalgamated under a constitution similar to that now enjoyed by Southern Rhodesia'.[13] Both Major McKee (Midland Electoral Area) and Mr. Geoffrey Pelletier (Ndola Electoral Area), who had entered the Legislature after defeating the Labour Party candidate in a by-election, abstained from voting, while Gore-Browne, as representative of African interests, voted with the Officials against it. The motion was consequently defeated.

Despite the resurrection of the Amalgamation demand, there was evidence of a marked change in the general attitude of the elected European members to African affairs. Gore-Browne, sensitive to the need for creating organizations to enable Africans to discuss their problems with the authorities, placed before the Legislative Council in September 1942 specific proposals for extending the system of urban advisory councils in the Copperbelt towns to all the urban areas, and for inaugurating Native Provincial Councils composed of members elected by the African Urban Advisory Councils and the Native Authorities. Of a purely advisory nature, Gore-Browne visualized them as assisting the Provincial Commissioners, and also helping the nominated member representing Native interests to discuss political issues with Africans.[14] Prior to the meeting, the other Un-officials had promised Gore-Browne their support, while the Officials were generally sympathetic. But during the debate Gore-Browne was asked from both sides of the House whether he was not expecting too rapid a change. Major McKee pointed out that many Europeans would ask where the proposal led, for while they had no inherent objection to Native progress, they

[13] Hansard, 25 November 1943, col. 152.
[14] Hansard 17 September 1942, cols. 148–68.

feared it might 'have effects detrimental to the contended rights of the European community'. Mr. Welensky declared, however, that the country had to expect direct African representation in the Legislature eventually: meanwhile, if African Provincial Councils would make the system of representation by Europeans more effective it was the duty of the Unofficials to support the proposal.[15] The motion was consequently passed without a division. When moving his Amalgamation motion, Welensky was also careful to use broader-based arguments, and instead of demanding it to protect European interests, as had been the case prior to the war, he argued that Amalgamation was necessary to secure the fullest social and economic development of the territory as a whole, for Africans, he suggested, would advance most rapidly in close contact with Europeans.[16]

But if Unofficial attitudes to African affairs were being modified, African political consciousness was also developing. The Forster Commission had discovered articulate African resentment against the industrial colour bar; likewise the Bledisloe Royal Commission had found that among the more educated urban African population opposition to Amalgamation was well developed. And when Welensky's motion of 1943 was debated in the African Regional Council (created subsequent to Gore-Browne's suggestion, and later converted to Provincial Councils) for the Western Province, Mr. Harry Nkumbula, a young schoolmaster and representative of the Kitwe Urban Advisory Council, declared: 'Now that this dreaded question has been discussed at the recent sitting of the Legislative Council it becomes necessary for the African to speak on the subject once more. The South African Native policy of economic and political discrimination and racial segregation is adopted as the official Native policy of the Southern Rhodesian Government. The Prime Minister of Southern Rhodesia has made it clear that his country is a White man's country and that the Black man shall always remain servant of the White man, if not a slave. On the other hand the Northern Rhodesian Government had from the time it took over from the South African Chartered Company given the African interests a very prominent place. Will the Prime Minister of Southern Rhodesia drop down his Native

[15] Hansard, 17 September 1942, col. 155.
[16] Hansard, 25 November 1943, cols. 152–63.

policy and follow suit with that of Northern Rhodesia and Nyasaland? If . . . the Dominions Office decided to hand over Northern Rhodesia and Nyasaland to Sir Godfrey Huggins, the Black peoples in the entire British East Africa will fast lose confidence in the British Imperial Government.' [17]

[17] *Regional Council: Western Province, Chairman's Report of the First Meeting* . . . 20 December 1943.

CHAPTER 9

THE POST-WAR YEARS—
THE STORM BEGINS

THOUGH the war years were notable for a marked change
in the attitudes of both Unofficials and Officials to African affairs, the overriding importance of devoting all
energies to the prosecution of the war prevented any commensurate translation into deeds. The cessation of hostilities was
thus akin to the lifting of a flood gate.

The pattern of events to come had been hinted at before the
war came to an end. In 1944 the then Secretary of State for the
Colonies, Colonel Oliver Stanley, showed sympathy with the
Unofficials' demand for increased representation. The Governor, Sir John Waddington, and Colonel Gore-Browne, as senior
Unofficial, were invited to London to discuss the constitution
and in October the announcement was made that the Unofficials were to be given a majority in the Legislature. The numbers of Officials (nine) and elected members (eight) were to remain unchanged; but the member nominated to represent
African interests was to be joined by two more Europeans
charged with the same duty, and there were also to be two additional Europeans nominated to represent other interests. The
new constitution came into effect in June 1945.

Another change introduced at the same time had a warmer
reception from the elected European members. The Colonial
Secretary announced the formation of a Central African Council
to promote joint planning in the two Rhodesias and Nyasaland.
Addressing the Legislative Council, the Governor explained that
'it will be the function of the Central African Council, working
through a permanent secretariat to be set up in Salisbury, to
promote the closest contact and co-operation between the three
governments and their administrative and technical services'.[1]
Welensky quickly indicated his reason for welcoming the
Council—it would leave the door ajar for Amalgamation.

[1] Hansard, 29 August 1945, col. 113.

In the United Kingdom general election of 1945 the Labour Party obtained a landslide victory: the party which throughout the war had been attacking the plan for political union between Northern and Southern Rhodesia, and indeed, the entire system of race relationships in the Rhodesias, had finally achieved power.

At the same time the split among the Unofficials over the Amalgamation issue had become absolute. When Welensky moved an Amalgamation motion in August 1945, for instance, Sir Stewart Gore-Browne, knighted in the previous year for public services in Northern Rhodesia, declared that: 'I am now convinced that there are two quite different ways of dealing with the problem of the African. One consists of treating him well, improving his standard of living and health, providing social security, but keeping him a servant. The other "ideology" is described, I think, as regarding him as a potential partner. I am convinced the African is right when he opposes Amalgamation with Southern Rhodesia because he fears it means he would be handed over to the first of the two alternatives, what we may call the South African ideology.' [2] Welensky's own attitude to African affairs was nevertheless changing rapidly. 'I stand back to no one in my desire to see the African progress,' he declared during the Amalgamation debate. 'If the only distinction between the African and ourselves is this question of education, and far more capable people than myself suggest it is, then it is a difference that will disappear.' [3] This did not mean that his fears were in any way lessened; indeed, he instanced his belief that education would progressively remove racial inequality, to demand that the Europeans be protected, since the African would otherwise take over 'post after post' as he advanced educationally.

With the elected European members apprehensive about the Labour Government's intentions, with support for Amalgamation increasing among the settler community and the Unofficials irrevocably split over the issue, a deterioration in the relations between the Officials and the Unofficials was inevitable. These were further aggravated when the constitution granting an Unofficial majority came into force. The Unofficials clearly

[2] Hansard, 29 August 1945, col. 113.
[3] Hansard, 28 August 1945, col. 62.

regarded it as conferring on them responsibility for controlling legislation and thereby Government policy, provided they were unanimous. Gore-Browne, who was elected chairman of the newly formed Unofficials' Association, declared in an issued statement: 'We, the Unofficials, with our power of veto will have the responsibility in the first instance for allowing anything to be done which is done in Council, apart from anything we may initiate ourselves.' [4] But events quickly proved this forecast optimistic. Despite the Unofficial majority, the attitude of the Officials continued unchanged. Indeed, this could scarcely have been otherwise: Officials dominated the policy-making body, the Executive Council; responsibility for every Government department rested with an Official. The old contradiction of Official responsibility and Unofficial control had been incorporated into the constitution. Tension could only have been reduced if the Unofficials and Officials could have agreed on a joint policy; but it was at precisely this juncture that the Unofficials were most suspicious, since the Officials were ultimately responsible to the Secretary of State for the Colonies. And he was now a member of the Labour Government.

But it was not only apprehension over the Colonial Office's African policies which were conditioning the Unofficials' relations with the Officials. The post-war years heralded a new economic era, in which development was no longer to be left to chance and individual enterprise. Five- and ten-year development plans were symbolic of the changed times, and millions of pounds from Colonial Development and Welfare Funds and internal sources were to be spent on improving education and welfare facilities, on developing new communications, and stimulating new economic projects. Aware of the dangers arising from the country's dependence on copper, the Unofficials were particularly anxious for the Government's post-war development plans to be published and implemented as quickly as possible. And because of the racial dilemma, they were equally anxious that European immigration should be encouraged on a large scale. But while the Officials might possess, individually and collectively, greater administrative experience than the Unofficials, of necessity they could not have the same sense of urgency. The system of which they were part did not allow it.

[4] Reported in *East Africa and Rhodesia*, 15 February 1945, p. 549.

Important decisions taken in Lusaka by the Governor and his Executive Council had to be referred back to the Colonial Secretary in London for approval; senior members of the administration were constantly being promoted from one post to another, many of them coming from another part of the Colonial Empire and having no experience whatsoever of Northern Rhodesian affairs. When the 1945 budget was debated, for instance, the Government was criticized by all the Unofficials for the delay in publishing its post-war development plans. Gore-Browne went so far as to state that if he had been sitting in the Legislature as leader of the Unofficial majority [5] he would have seriously considered asking the Unofficials to reject the budget as a protest against Government procrastination. Subsequently Welensky and another Unofficial, Mr. T. Page, resigned from the Executive Council, thereby terminating the wartime arrangement. Gore-Browne remained in the belief that he could best foster African interests by so doing.

The history of the British South Africa Company's mineral royalties epitomized Unofficial frustration in this sphere. The validity of the Company's claim to own the mineral rights of Northern Rhodesia in perpetuity was first raised by the settlers in the early 1920s, when the Territory was still under Company rule. But it was not until 1938 that the matter was brought before the Legislative Council, and then Captain A. Smith, the elected member for Nkana, moved that the matter should be referred to the Judicial Committee of the Privy Council, so that a decision on the legality of the Company's claim might be obtained. Though the motion was defeated by the official majority, the matter was considered by the British Government, who eventually issued a statement confirming that the Company's claims were valid and unchallengeable. From then, however, the matter was constantly raised by the European elected members in the Legislature. With the price of copper continually rising, the royalties paid by the mining companies to the British South Africa Company increased; so did the European community's awareness that very considerable sums of money were leaving the country as a direct result of the exploitation of its one major asset—a wasting asset moreover.

[5] The debate occurred before the constitution granting an Unofficial majority came into force.

Finally, in December 1945, through the advent of the Unofficial majority, a motion was presented and passed which
read: 'This Council does not accept as final the conclusions
reached by the Secretary of State in his despatch 374 of 31
December 1939, regarding the validity of the British South
Africa Company's claim to mineral royalties in respect of that
part of the Territory known as the Copperbelt.' Nothing came
of this, however, and one year later Welensky was asking in the
Legislative Council if he could be supplied with a copy of a
statement made by the Colonial Secretary to the effect that it
was the policy of the United Kingdom Government to re-
acquire mineral royalties which had been alienated. He had
heard it referred to on a B.B.C. news bulletin! After the lapse of
another year, Welensky asked the Attorney-General if the Executive could state whether the British Government had conveyed any information to them on the expropriation or purchase
of the mineral royalties claimed to be held by the British South
Africa Company. The Acting Attorney-General informed him
that there had been correspondence on the subject, but that no
decision had yet been reached.

If the mineral royalties issue highlighted Unofficial frustration, it also pinpointed the dilemma of the Labour Government. To recognize the consequences of an Unofficial majority,
and the need to streamline the administrative machinery by
granting the Unofficials greater responsibilities, would necessarily affect the Labour Government's ability to institute measures of African advancement. But the situation was changing
rapidly in the sphere of African affairs too. In December 1945,
for instance, Gore-Browne moved a motion in the Legislature
that there should be no further delay in the Government announcing its attitude to the report of the Commission of Inquiry
into African Housing—the report had been presented in the
previous year.[6] And in condemning the deplorable state of the
African urban locations, Gore-Browne was supported by the
other Unofficials. A Department of Local Government and
African Housing was formed in 1946 and £1,000,000 voted
from loan funds to finance housing construction. But little or no
progress was made in implementing the Commission of Inquiry's recommendations; indeed, because of the desperate

[6] Hansard, 18 December 1945, col. 396.

need and the shortage of building materials, a temporary housing programme was begun, the Government stipulating that the cost of each hut, together with services, was not to exceed £10. The first annual report of the new department recorded that no real progress appeared probable 'for some time to come'.

On another occasion, Gore-Browne raised the question of migrant labour, which he considered 'an obsolete, almost medieval method of providing labour'. While recognizing that labour stabilization was necessarily a long-term project, none the less it had to be faced. 'Our record in this country on the matter has not been particularly good,' the senior Unofficial continued. 'The late Secretary for Native Affairs maintained that there was no such thing as detribalized labour on the Copperbelt. All we had to do was send the workers back to their homes at frequent intervals.' [7]

Neither was Gore-Browne happy with the state of the Native Authorities. The Government had taken certain steps to reorganize their structure. Funds made available in the 1944 estimates had resulted in the raising of the salaries of Native Authority officials and the payment of monies to Native treasuries which brought their reserve funds to the equivalent of two years' annual recurrent expenditure on the basis of the new salary scales. Giving this information to the Legislative Council in 1945, the Governor remarked that 'with better pay, a hitherto unknown financial stability, and the gradual elimination of redundant Native Authorities, the structure of Native government may be regarded as undergoing steady change in the right direction, and it should not be long before improved performance . . . will become general'.[8] In addition, the Native Authorities Ordinance was modified so as to allow Native Authorities to make rules for raising rates in the areas for which they were responsible, and in his address to the Legislative Council in November 1946, the Governor stated that an increasing number of Native Authorities were submitting rules for the imposition of rates.[9] Gore-Browne expressed gratification at these moves. 'But I am not easy in my own mind . . .

[7] Hansard, 4 December 1946, col. 107.
[8] Hansard, 6 January 1945, col. 10.
[9] Hansard, 3 November 1946, col. 17.

about the general position of the Native Authorities. . . . I
know we have done away with a good many redundant chiefs,
but we have left a good many who have very little right under
modern conditions to remain chiefs.' [10] The Secretary for Native
Affairs reiterated the Government's wish that all Africans
should offer allegiance to the Native Authorities, especially
'when there is increasing political consciousness being mani-
fested among the more advanced section of the African community, who are beginning to voice a feeling of the inadequacy
of the present African administration. There is the danger that
if Native Authorities do not keep abreast of the times the more
advanced elements among the African population will tend to
become discontented and, still worse, will tend to form separate
political bodies instead of adopting the right course, which is to
co-operate and help to strengthen the Native administrations.
If this should happen I am convinced that a great disservice
will be done to the African population as a whole, and I am
sure that the Hon. the Senior Member [Colonel Sir Stewart
Gore-Browne] will exercise his very great influence among the
more advanced Africans in preventing this from happening.'

In 1946, at the suggestion of Gore-Browne, the Government
established the African Representative Council, an advisory
body modelled as to organization and procedure on the Legislative Council. Its members were drawn from and elected by
the African Provincial Councils, the Secretary for Native
Affairs presiding over its meetings. The Government undertook
to place before it all Bills likely to affect African affairs, and, as
far as this was possible, to take action on the Council's advice.
At the Representative Council's first meeting—it met once
annually for a few days only—a motion was moved asking that
Africans should be allowed to make valid wills, so that they
could leave their possessions to whosoever they wished. This
question of wills indeed epitomized the reason for the more advanced Africans' dissatisfaction with the Native Authorities. A
man who had lived for many years in the towns and who had
raised a family there, or a man who had built up a successful
business, might wish to pass on the fruits of his labour to his
immediate family. But this was not possible under customary
law in the matrilineal tribes. Indeed, a wealthy man's death was

[10] Hansard, 4 December 1946, col. 107.

a signal for all his legal heirs from the rural areas to descend on his home and remove his possessions. It was not impossible for a man's immediate family to be left destitute, and even if his relatives were willing to support them, they were hardly likely to be able to maintain them at the same standard of life. As the Rev. H. Kasokolo remarked, unless he could make a valid will 'my wife and children will be the subject of many threats by relatives that they will be forced to hand over everything'.[11] The Secretary of Native Affairs replied that while there was no objection to Africans making wills, they could only be recognized so long as they fulfilled tribal obligations.

Despite the fact that for more than ten years the more advanced Africans had been expressing dissatisfaction with the leadership of the tribal authorities, it was only towards the end of 1947 that the Provincial Administration reorganized the Native Authorities so as to allow Africans other than the hereditary leaders to participate in their work. In the case of the Bemba the superior Native Authority, that of the Paramount Chief, and the many inferior Native Authorities in the tribal areas were to be merged into one central Native Authority council on which all the existing Bemba chiefs, together with their traditional councillors, would sit, and act as agents for the Central Council in the areas for which they were responsible. The central council was also to be strengthened by the addition of official members, who would be executive officers paid according to merit, while leading Africans were to be invited to sit on it. 'Other Africans would be elected by the people so as to put the Council on a more democratic basis,' the Secretary for Native Affairs announced. In the urban areas, where there was maximum discontent with the traditional tribal leaders, the Secretary for Native Affairs offered no suggestions as to the next steps to be taken. Indeed, when announcing changes in the organization of the Native Authorities, the Secretary for Native Affairs admitted that the urban advisory councils were more effective in the Western Province than in towns like Broken Hill and Lusaka. But he merely expressed the hope that 'in the latter and other places where they [the Africans] are losing interest, steps will be taken to make them more effective bodies'.[12]

[11] *Proceedings of the African Representative Council,* 15 November 1946, col. 69.
[12] Hansard, 26 September 1947, col. 187.

In the circumstances it was hardly surprising that the hopes of the Secretary of Native Affairs regarding the formation of organizations independent of the Native Authorities were not being fulfilled. The Merle Davis commission had, after all, found that urban discontent had stimulated the formation of Native Welfare Societies as early as 1932. By the end of the Second World War numbers of these unofficial African bodies existed, especially on the Copperbelt. Moreover, they had become more active than the urban advisory councils and indeed often usurped the latter's functions of presenting African demands to the authorities. For many of the more politically conscious Africans in the urban areas were not only discontented with the Native Authorities: they were exasperated at the ineffectiveness of both the advisory councils and the unquestioning faith the tribal leaders and their representatives had in the Government. Chief Ikelenge, for instance, remarked in the African Representative Council in 1947: 'We know that Government has all the power, and we are the Government's children.'[13] A motion proposed by the same chief, asking for increased numbers of nominated European members to represent African interests in the Legislature, was rejected; so was another motion asking that the Europeans representing African interests be elected by the African Representative Council. As the Rev. H. Kasokolo explained: 'The Governor is like a father to this territory . . . he is the only one who can choose the right person to represent our interests.' [14] A proposal that Africans should be indirectly represented on municipal councils was likewise defeated.

The Government was admittedly in a difficult position. The racial discrimination practised in the urban areas and the industrial colour bar operative on the copper mines and the railway were heightening African political consciousness; but the Government was not in a position to interfere successfully in either sphere, since in the former the local authorities were dominated by the local European communities and in the latter European unions were strongly entrenched, while in the Legislature the Officials could not embark on a policy distasteful to the elected European members. However, the Officials gave no

[13] *African Representative Council No. 2*, July 1947, col. 70.
[14] Ibid., col. 160.

indication that they understood the fundamental reasons for African dissatisfaction; indeed, they appeared quite blind in their support for African tribal leaders. Ironically the Unofficials, under Gore-Browne's leadership, were often more realistic than was the Secretary for Native Affairs—although attacks on the Government in this sphere must be seen in relation to the Unofficials' dissatisfaction with their status in the Legislature generally. Thus after a serious strike of African railway workers employed by Rhodesia Railways in 1945, which began at Bulawayo and spread along almost the entire length of the railway in Northern Rhodesia, Welensky, himself a railwayman, declared in the Legislative Council: 'We are now witnessing a revolution among the African peoples. . . . We should face up to the position and guide it along proper lines. What I have in mind is the means of giving the African some method of presenting his views, his troubles to his employers . . . some machinery to give him the opportunity to negotiate. I do not think the African is yet fit for the trade union movement. I suggest the present system of using tribal leaders has served its purpose. The black man has got beyond that. What I have in mind is some form of central organization consisting of experienced trade unionists and elected representatives of the African workers.' [15]

In April of the following year, after wide publicity had been given to the view that the Government was to foster African trade unions, the Secretary for Native Affairs made a statement on the subject. 'It is the Government's policy to encourage the healthy growth of collective bargaining amongst the Africans on sound lines,' he declared. 'Ever since the Labour Department was formed [16] it has been the constant concern of its officers to consider how best this growth can be fostered. We came to the conclusion that what the Africans wanted at that time was to have representatives on a tribal basis. We did everything we could. I know that did not satisfy all Africans, and I do not suppose that anything would. Some of the Africans who felt that their tribal representative system was inadequate said that they wanted to form a separate organization, so with our help they

[15] Hansard, 24 November 1945, col. 60.
[16] In 1940 after the disturbance of the Copperbelt and as a result of the Forster Commission's recommendation that labour officers should be stationed on the Copperbelt.

formed a Bossboys' Association. We are doing everything we can to further the growth of collective bargaining,' the Secretary for Native Affairs concluded, 'and if trade unionism as we know it emerges naturally out of that we shall give it every encouragement.' [17]

Whether Officials or Unofficials were more or less advanced with regard to African affairs was in one sense immaterial, however, as events were to quickly prove. In 1946 another Northern Rhodesian delegation, consisting this time of the Governor, Sir John Waddington, Colonel Sir Stewart Gore-Browne, and Mr. Welensky, was invited to London, ostensibly for the latter to discuss with the Secretary of State for the Colonies the question of the British South Africa Company's mineral royalties in Northern Rhodesia. During the discussions the constitutional position was also examined, and agreement eventually reached on further changes. Two of the existing nominated Unofficials were to be replaced by elected European members. But the number of Unofficials representing African interests was to be increased from three to four: and two of these were to be Africans. Protest meetings were widely held in Northern Rhodesia once the news was announced: here were the fruits of a Labour Government in office. A majority of elected Europeans over Officials at last; but at the expense of two Africans sitting in the Legislative Council. However, Mr. Welensky remarked: 'I expressed the opinion that it was premature to give direct representation to Africans. But once the Secretary of State for the Colonies had made up his mind that this had to be done, once he had made up his mind to do this, I felt that the best thing was to accept it.' [18]

This decision exacerbated European feeling, and heightened the tension in the Legislature between the elected European members and the Officials. Other events were shortly to aggravate the situation. Although, contrary to the expectations of many, there had been no decline in the demand for copper following the ending of hostilities, the copper-mining industry had been racked by disputes between the European Mine Workers' Union and the companies. In August 1946 one of the elected European members suggested that the Governor should

[17] Hansard, 6 April 1946, col. 444.
[18] Hansard, 3 December 1946, col. 54.

appoint a commission to inquire into all the circumstances affecting the relations of employers and employees on the Copperbelt. The idea was welcomed initially by the European Union—at the time it was in dispute with the mine managements over two issues. When these were satisfactorily settled, however, the Union's attitude changed, for in the circumstances a commission of inquiry could hardly fail to examine the central question of African advancement. The Forster Commission had recommended a conference to examine the issue; but nothing had been done, and subsequently the problem had steadily become more serious and intractable.

When the companies' agreement with the European Union had been revised, early in 1946, the parties had agreed, after conciliation proceedings presided over by the Industrial Relations Adviser to the Northern Rhodesian Government, to delete the clause permitting labour dilution and replace it with the following: 'The company agrees that the work of the class or grade that is being performed, or job that is being filled, by an employee at the time of the signing of this agreement shall not be given to persons to whom the terms and conditions of this agreement do not apply.' [19] Since the agreement specifically referred to European employees in clause 1, the possibility of African advancement into job categories covered by the agreement was eliminated absolutely. The European Union did propose that the word European be deleted from the agreement, but the suggestion was rejected by the companies, who declared themselves unwilling to allow their African labour force to come under the control of the European Union.

Despite the unenthusiastic attitude of the Northern Rhodesian Government towards the development of African trade unions, it was officially announced in November 1946, presumably on a directive from London, that a Trade Union Adviser was to be appointed, one of whose duties would be to encourage the formation of African trade unions, an unwelcome development from the European Union's point of view. And in the following March Mr. W. N. Comrie, an experienced trade unionist from the United Kingdom, arrived in the Territory.

[19] *Report of the Board of Inquiry appointed to Inquire into the Advancement of Africans in the Copper Mining Industry in Northern Rhodesia* (Government Printer Lusaka, 1954), p. 7.

Shortly afterwards, the Bossboys' Committees on the copper mines were converted into Works Committees.

Furthermore, after an unsuccessful attempt had been made to reach an agreement on African advancement on the Copperbelt, the Governor in October 1947 appointed a commission to inquire into the advancement of Africans in industry. The commissioners were instructed to bear in mind 'the policy of the Government that Africans in Northern Rhodesia should be afforded the opportunities for employment in more responsible work as and when they are qualified to undertake such work', and to make recommendations as to what posts Africans should fill at once, what training facilities should be made available to facilitate their advancement, and about African wages.

When the Commission arrived in Northern Rhodesia the Northern Rhodesian Mine Workers' Union refused to co-operate with it, principally because of objections to the Commission's personnel and to the fact that no direct reference was made in its terms of reference to equal pay for equal work. When the Commission's report was published early in 1948 [20] it contained recommendations to the effect that Africans were capable of filling twenty-eight different categories of work in the mining industry immediately, eleven such jobs after a short period of training, nineteen jobs after a longer and more intensive period of instruction, and that 'the work or operations referred to should be transferred to Africans as early and as unprovocatively as possible'. With regard to the question of equal pay for equal work, the commissioners wrote: 'It would appear from the evidence placed before us that the African will not for some considerable time to come be able to take over all the duties of the European who had previously been performing the task. It is further clear that for some considerable time to come the African will require much more supervision than is at present required by the European. We have also in mind the policy of equal pay for equal work and responsibility, and on the assumption that the wage at present being paid to the European is equitable and that it requires three Africans to undertake completely the work of the European without any additional supervision, then the emoluments of the European should be

[20] *Report of the Commission Appointed to Inquire into the Advancement of Africans in Industry* (Government Printer Lusaka, 1948).

divided between the three Africans . . .' The Commissioners stated categorically however 'that no European at present carrying out the work or operations involved should be discharged to make way for an African. The African should only be promoted when the European ceases to be employed or is himself promoted.[21]

The report was received bitterly by the European Mine Workers' Union, and indeed all European trade unionists in Northern Rhodesia. When it was debated in the Legislature, Welensky declared that the Commission's proposal for subdividing European work 'must lead to the elimination of the European'.[22] As might have been expected, when the Commission's report was discussed at a meeting between the mining companies and the European Union the latter refused to agree to any amendment to the agreement, except on the condition of equal pay for equal work.

The publication of specific recommendations to the effect that a large number of job categories could be taken over immediately by African workers naturally sharpened African frustration and dissatisfaction, and partly because of this, the organization of African trade unions in the territory generally and the copper-mining industry in particular gathered speed. The executive of the European Union reacted by resolving to form African branches within the Union, and meetings were held to promote this proposal. But it came to nothing, and shortly afterwards the first African Mine Workers' Union was formed at Nkana with a membership of approximately 2,600. Subsequently, similar organizations were created at all the principal mines, and in 1949 they were amalgamated to form the Northern Rhodesian African Mine Workers' Union. It was recognized by the mining companies in August 1949.

The combined effect of all these developments was to bring about a marked deterioration in race relations. Gore-Browne pointed this out as early as April 1946 when he told the Legislative Council that African confidence in the European was deteriorating.[23] In the case of the settlers he believed this was

---

[21] *Report of the Commission Appointed to Inquire into the Advancement of Africans in Industry*, op. cit., p. 37.
[22] Hansard, 12 March 1948, col. 76.
[23] Hansard, 6 April 1946, col. 449.

because Africans felt that they had taken all the fertile land and left them with what was stony and unproductive. But African faith in both missionaries and administrators was also declining, and while Gore-Browne paid tribute to the work of the district officers, he charged the Administration generally with being out of touch with African affairs and urged that the times demanded a changed outlook. The principal cause of African dissatisfaction, Sir Stewart thought, was the colour bar. Its first manifestation was administrative in origin. 'I mean the restrictions on Black people which do not apply to White people. Some of these may appear very trifling, but, believe me, they are not trifling in the eyes of the African.' He then instanced African treatment in European shops—'referred to in almost any edition of any African paper'—and in post offices. 'Even in a small place like Pemba, where I suppose the number of Europeans who go to the post office in one day is strictly limited, an African has to go to a hole in the wall and stand in the road, in the rain if it is raining, and wait until any European who happens to turn up has been dealt with inside.' The same was true of railway stations and banks.

The Senior Unofficial then turned to the economic colour bar, its most important manifestation, and quoted letters to illustrate African feeling. One read: 'We Africans we do not want £60 a month for our work, and we realize that Europeans must be better paid, but we do feel that it is an injustice that a man who has worked four or five or perhaps ten or fifteen years underground should be receiving £4 or £5 a month whereas a European who comes fresh to the work from South Africa or England starts at £40 a month.' Another argued that 'once the colour bar is outlawed something approaching an economic revolution will set in. For the increased purchasing power of the Africans will precipitate production on a yet larger scale.' As for the social colour bar, Gore-Browne felt 'it is the sort of thing that must right itself as long as we keep our heads. If it so happens that it suits both the White man and the African to drink a cup of tea together, what can be the harm in that? It is only the absurd attitude that the supremacy of the White race is endangered by ordinary courtesy in these matters to Africans which is dangerous.'

In conclusion, Gore-Browne considered how the situation

could be remedied. In the post offices, the banks, and the railways, his recommendation was that African clerks should be trained to deal with African customers in a separate part of the building. On the plane of the economic colour bar, Gore-Browne merely recommended that a round-table conference of interested parties was necessary, as had been recommended by the Forster Commission. He was insistent, however, that the last thing he wished to see was European displacement. On the question of African trade unions, his comments were particularly forthright. 'I do urge that we should get on with it and not continue beating about the bush. We must accept that the African is calling out to be allowed to form trade unions at once.' Finally, Gore-Browne considered the solution based on miscegenation, which he declared 'commends itself to no single European and to no single African'. Indeed, he had been asked on many occasions by Africans to press for legislation which would make cohabitation between European men and African women an offence, as it was already for relations between European women and African men.

The Legislative Council had not listened to a greater bombshell. Furthermore, Gore-Browne had failed to inform the other Unofficials of his intentions, and, by speaking late in the day, allowed no time for any of them to reply. It was difficult to say which angered them most: the fact that the chairman of the Unofficial Members' Association had delivered such an unwarranted attack on the European, for that was how Gore-Browne's speech was interpreted, both by the elected members and the European electorate, or that he had done it without informing them, in a manner that precluded an immediate reply. The only speaker to follow Gore-Browne was the Acting Chief Secretary, who was obviously aware of the elected members' anger and embarrassed by what had just been said. He declared that 'I feel it would be wrong to let this opportunity go by without making an appeal in the name of the Government for the abandonment of this attitude of mind. This fear complex if not checked will lead to mistrust and mistrust will in its turn lead to dislike'.[24]

Not unnaturally a political storm broke over Gore-Browne's head. While he continued as chairman of the Unofficials'

[24] Hansard, 6 April 1946, col. 463.

Association, it became immediately clear that his day as a political leader was at an end as far as the European electorate was concerned. So incensed was the European community that the Governor finally agreed to convene a special session of the Legislative Council specifically to debate race relations, though in reality, it proved to be an attempt to refute Gore-Browne's charges.[25] The suggestion that race relations were deteriorating was unanimously rejected. Mr. Williams, an elected member, went so far as to suggest that 'there is no conscious or deliberate colour bar system in this country'.[26] The treatment of Africans in shops, banks, and post offices was generally explained away by the lack of facilities.

As a result of the storm his speech aroused, Gore-Browne resigned from the chairmanship of the Unofficials' Association, and Welensky was subsequently elected in his stead.

[25] Debated on 6–7 May 1946.
[26] Hansard, 6 May 1946, col. 41.

CHAPTER 10

MATTERS COME TO A HEAD— UNOFFICIALS DEMAND RESPONSIBLE GOVERNMENT

THAT African fears were strengthening and race relations deteriorating is amply evident from the changed tone of the debates in the African Representative Council during its meeting in 1948. Gone was the docility, the absence of poli- tical consciousness which had been so marked a feature of the debates in 1947. Instead there was a motion opposing the grant- ing of responsible government to Northern Rhodesia, a second demanding that there should be equal African and European Unofficial representation on both the Legislative and Executive Councils, and that African representation by nominated Euro- peans should be abolished. 'This country is ours and we don't want it taken away from us by other people,' declared Mr. Donald Siwale,[1] while Mr. Nelson Namulango, after affirming his belief in African paramountcy, insisted that 'we want Northern Rhodesia to remain a Native state'.[2]

Ironically, Gore-Browne was the cause of this sudden harden- ing in the views expressed by the delegates to the African Repre- sentative Council. On 12 January 1948 he had made another electrifying statement to the Legislative Council. 'The point at issue is simple enough,' he declared, 'but I am not sure whether members opposite, even now, realize quite what it is we want and what we mean to have. It is neither more nor less than re- sponsible government. We are one and all convinced that government by bureaucracy is no longer good enough for Northern Rhodesia.'[3] Gore-Browne did not disclose his plans for responsible government, but asked instead that they be con- veyed to the Secretary of State for the Colonies, Mr. Arthur

[1] *Proceedings of the African Representative Council*, July 1948, cols. 13–14.
[2] Ibid., col. 9.
[3] Hansard, 12 January 1948, col. 829.

Creech Jones, well known to the European communities in Central Africa as a persistent critic of Rhodesian affairs when the Labour Party had been in Opposition. Gore-Browne's speech ended with a threat. 'I cannot think that the Secretary of State will be so ill-advised as to force us to adopt the only alternative open to us . . . to use such powers as we already possess to paralyse . . . Government.'

The original spark firing Gore-Browne's outburst had occurred in 1947. In that year the Governor, Sir John Waddington, had announced his transfer. Mr. Welensky, in paying his tribute, reminded him that not once under the constitution granting an Unofficial majority had he found it necessary to use his veto. At the same time a new Chief Secretary, Mr. R. S. Stanley, was appointed, who, as Acting Governor, presided at the most important legislative session of the year, when the Government's budget proposals were introduced. In his speech from the Throne the Acting Governor complained of the unco-operative attitude of the Unofficials in preparing the financial estimates. It was a statement unlikely to endear the Acting Governor to the Unofficials under any circumstances; in the atmosphere of frustration and tension then current, it produced uproar. The Acting Governor had proposed that elected European members should join the Executive Council for the period necessary to prepare the Budget; Welensky, speaking on their behalf, had refused, and countered with the suggestion that the Standing Finance Committee should be expanded for the purpose. This, in turn, had been rejected by the Acting Governor.

'We are deeply concerned about the Government's attitude,' Welensky declared emphatically. 'If we are to have a fight, we might as well have it now in order to protect our interests. The last few days have demonstrated that the present constitution means nothing.' Gore-Browne then joined forces with Welensky. He told the Officials: 'We are invariably in the position that, whether we like it or not, when you want to consult us you do, and when you don't want to consult us, you don't . . .'

This altercation occurred on 18 November 1947. On 12 January 1948 Gore-Browne introduced his demand for responsible government. And the manner in which the Government handled it strained tempers still further. The Financial Secretary when he replied to Gore-Browne's statement in the House remarked that some Unofficials had made it clear that they regarded the proposals as no more than the prelude to amalgamation with Southern Rhodesia.[4] Gore-Browne immediately pointed out that his statement contained no such reference and asked the Financial Secretary to make this perfectly clear. 'The Government has taken very careful note of the statement of the Hon. the Senior Unofficial Member, and this will be transmitted to the Secretary of State for the Colonies,' the Financial Secretary concluded.

When details of the proposals were eventually announced, the new Governor might have been forgiven for thinking that the Unofficials had given him an unpleasant welcome to Northern Rhodesia. The proposed Legislative Council was to consist of ten elected European members; three Europeans nominated to represent African interests, two elected Africans, one African representing Barotseland, and four Officials—the Attorney-General, the Financial Secretary, the Director of Medical Services, and one other. On the Executive Council there were to be four Unofficial members and three Officials; an Unofficial was also to be president. The Governor was to be allowed to retain his veto over legislation, but clearly, with power overwhelmingly in the hands of the Unofficials, it was hardly possible for him to use it except in the very gravest circumstances. The proposals certainly contained sweeping changes. Nevertheless, Officials were still to remain part of the Government, and the elected European members accepted African representation, including two elected directly. Further, the numbers in the Legislature were so balanced that Amalgamation was still not possible, for Africans and Europeans representing African interests plus Officials equalled the numbers of elected Europeans. The main change, as Gore-Browne had said, was to make the Executive subject to the Legislature.

The proposals were rejected by African political leaders, however, whether within or without the Representative Council, for, like the Financial Secretary, they linked them with Amalgamation. One of the resolutions passed by the Kitwe African Society, a few days after Gore-Browne had made his speech, declared: 'Although the Unofficial members deny that their proposals will lead to amalgamation with Southern

[4] Hansard, 13 January 1948, col. 868.

Rhodesia, all Africans agree with Mr. Thornton [the Financial Secretary] that it is a way to Amalgamation.'[5] Gore-Browne later admitted that he had been ill-advised in making his demand without simultaneously publishing the actual proposals, though he also felt that the Government had handled it unfairly. Whether African leaders would in fact have accepted them had the Government's handling of the matter been more impartial is doubtful, however, for the more politically conscious Africans, members of such organizations as the Luanshya Welfare Society and the Kitwe African Society, constantly reiterated the view that the future political development of Northern Rhodesia must rest on the principle of the 'paramountcy of African interests'. And subsequent debates in the Provincial Councils and the African Representative Council made it clear that the tribal leaders took their stand on the same doctrine.

Previously, this unanimity between the rural and urban leaders had been masked, principally because the former had believed that the Northern Rhodesian Government and the Senior Member representing African interests supported this doctrine. In their view, slow evolution under the guidance of the Colonial Office and the officials of the Northern Rhodesian Government would at some time in the future lead to the establishment of an independent Native state. Such ideas were encouraged both by the support accorded them by the Northern Rhodesian Government and by virtue of their geographical isolation, for the Native Authority areas were in reality petty Native states. But in the urban areas the more advanced Africans had been forced to realize that power lay overwhelmingly in the hands of the local European population; that, over the years, the Northern Rhodesian Government had been powerless to eliminate racial discrimination and the industrial colour bar in the copper-mining industry, although prior to the demand for responsible government even the more militant Africans had hoped that in the long run the link with the British Government through the Colonial Office would set these matters right. Moreover, they were encouraged by Sir Stewart Gore-Browne's attacks on the colour bar and his consistent refusal to support Amalgamation.

[5] Hansard, 28 June 1948, col. 517 (Quoted by Sir S. Gore-Browne).

Gore-Browne's demand for responsible government shattered the confidence Africans had hitherto placed in him. It also made them realize that the link with the British Government, their 'safeguard' against the settlers, was not as strong and secure as they had imagined, and convinced them that their interests could only be represented satisfactorily by members of their own race. Both the principal racial groups were aligning themselves behind militant leaders, therefore, and inevitably this meant that Gore-Browne's days as a political leader—and indeed the days of liberal paternalism—were drawing to a close. African political leadership now passed to the more advanced detribalized Africans resident in the urban areas. In the African Representative Council meeting of 1948, for instance, a number of delegates expressed the view that many members were not capable of representing Africans' interests in the Legislative Council. Mr. Dauti Yamba, founder of both the Luanshya Welfare Society in 1942 and the Federation of African Societies four years later, was specifically mentioned in this connexion. 'If a person of that type were elected, he might be able to do much better work than any of our members here today,' one of the councillors declared.[6] The very fact that Africans were to sit in the Legislature in any case placed the English-speaking commoners at an advantage over the tribal and rural leaders, whose command of English was usually poor.

The repercussions of this development were profound. The debates in the Representative Council in 1947 showed that some of the delegates were prepared to support Government measures for the preservation of the soil and the development of the African rural areas, even if they were likely to be unpopular. Mr. Kakumbi forthrightly declared that the Africans in Northern Rhodesia were wasting the country's soil,[7] while another delegate likened the African to a child who had to take the pills recommended by the doctor, the pills being the new agricultural techniques recommended by the doctor, the Department of Agriculture. In view of the importance attached to the development of the African rural areas by the Government, and the scale of the changes implicit in the recommendations of

[6] *Proceedings of the African Representative Council*, 1948, col. 91.
[7] Ibid., 1947, col. 103.

the post-war development plan, this measure of African support was particularly important. In the Tonga chieftaincies in
the Mazabuka district, for instance, the Department of Agriculture had introduced schemes aimed at stabilizing the African
peasants on a particular piece of land and encouraging them to
adopt improved farming techniques. Their efforts had met with
little success, however, and by 1942 the Director of Agriculture
was writing that the time was ripe for firm and enlightened
action on the part of the Native Authorities. Without such
action, his department was powerless to do anything more than
exhort; and the experience of the previous six years had been
that exhortation in itself accomplished little.

To look for support from the Native Authorities was, considering the circumstances, optimistic. The long-term effect of
introducing stability and encouraging the progress of the more
advanced and enlightened Tonga agriculturists would be to reduce the numbers of cultivators, increase the area each cultivated, and force the less-efficient subsistence peasant cultivators
off the land. Such events are always productive of resistance and
protest in any agricultural community, particularly from those
forced off the land. But in the special circumstances of Northern
Rhodesia, protest was by no means confined to the latter. The
chiefs and traditional councillors who formed the Native
Authorities held power, apart from that reflected to them from
the Central Government, by virtue of their people's belief in the
supernatural qualities they were held to possess, especially with
regard to land and agricultural prosperity. Any measure tend-
ing to undermine this necessarily weakened a chief's real power.
And the emergence of a class of master farmers certainly would.
In view of this the Native Authorities could hardly be expected
to actively support the measures advocated by the Department
of Agriculture. Moreover, in failing to do so, they did no more
than adhere to the policy of the Provincial Administration,
which was based on supporting traditional tribal custom.

These contradictions were highlighted by an investigation
carried out by a team of agriculturalists and anthropologists.[8]
A number of 'master' farmers had in fact emerged in the area,
and, because they cultivated holdings larger than average they

[8] *Land Holding & Land Usage among the Plateau Tonga, of the Mazabuka District*,
Rhodes–Livingstone Papers, No. 14, 1948.

had been accused of exacerbating the problem of land shortage. The investigating team found, however, that the total land area farmed by such men was comparatively small and had done little to aggravate the problem. On the contrary, they pointed out that under existing conditions such farmers were merely transient phenomena in Tongoland. Their holdings had been built up partly because fortuitous family inheritances had provided them with contiguous patches of land, and partly because the more advanced techniques they used had enabled them to bring into use areas which could not be cultivated by the ordinary peasant. Such land remained communal, tribal land, for under Tonga custom the usufruct could be inherited. But when a master farmer died, his land, oxen, and implements would in turn be inherited according to tribal tradition, with the result that the holding, the stock, and the equipment would be distributed between numerous relatives and its economic balance destroyed.

Nevertheless, these contradictions had to be resolved in favour of the improved farmer if the Tonga area was not to be completely devastated, and by 1946 the Director of Agriculture was talking of action on 'the revolutionary scale required by the situation'.[9] The problem was enormously complicated even if no other factors had to be considered. But in reality there were many others. The more advanced Africans who were ready to support measures for the conservation of the soil were also more politically conscious, and for this reason the Government found their views on other questions embarrassing. Hence their firm support for the tribal leaders, and their tardiness in granting advanced Africans a limited participation in the work of the Native Authorities. Moreover, the research team discovered that the overwhelming majority of the Tonga firmly believed that the sole cause of their troubles arose from one fact, the alienation of Tonga tribal land for European settlement. It was beyond dispute, of course, that land alienation had exacerbated overcrowding. But even if this land were handed back *in toto* to the tribe, it was only a question of time before it too would be devastated by erosion gullies unless the Tonga way of life was radically changed. However, while the European remained in possession of the land, the Tonga refused to co-

[9] *Annual Report*, Department of Agriculture, 1946, para. 34.

operate in any measures sponsored by the Government, suspecting that they were merely the prelude of a drive to improve the land preparatory to it being occupied by settlers.

The problems of the remaining African reserved areas were no less acute, for the latter did not have the advantage of proximity to markets. When the post-war development programme was eventually published in 1947 it was considerably more pessimistic than had been the Development Adviser, Mr. Clay. While the third aim of the Ten Year Development Plan was 'to assist the African population to develop itself under its Native Authorities with all possible speed',[10] the report stated that 'agricultural work should be concentrated on regions which are in the greatest need of assistance or which afford the best opportunity for development by virtue of their position, population, and soils. The ultimate aim is to produce conditions which will enable thriving concentrations of population to be established. Large inhospitable regions will have to be neglected at first in the hope that conditions in the more favourable regions will be made so attractive that there will be voluntary movement into them from the remainder.'[11] The concept of general territorial development implicit in Mr. Clay's recommendations was thus abandoned, and when the Development Plan was reviewed in 1948 this became even more apparent. Recognizing that the Native areas away from the line of rail possessed only one economic asset, the sale of the labour of their man-power, and that the cause of the high percentage of male absentees from the villages was economic, the review stated that the first objective must be to achieve an agricultural revolution in limited areas by getting the maximum number of villages in the shortest possible time to abandon cultivation by traditional implements on a subsistence level. This was to be achieved by creating peasant farming schemes, which, as they became established, would become the centre of marketing facilities, co-operatives, rural industries, and housing schemes. Indeed, all rural development, the report recommended, should be confined, in so far as was practicable, to such areas.

The consequences of this modified concept were far reaching.

[10] *Ten Year Development Plan for Northern Rhodesia* (Government Printer Lusaka, 1947), p. 8.
[11] Ibid., p. 28.

In the first place, because the remote regions were to be left outside the schemes for development, the population therein would
remain dependent for economic opportunity on migrant labour.
In the short term therefore the drift into the towns from such
areas would necessarily continue. In those areas where economic development was planned there had to be a socio-
agrarian revolution on the same pattern as was needed in the
Tonga areas, involving precisely the same conflicts. And while
there was no European settlement immediately adjacent to
most of these areas, nevertheless the impact of the technical
revolution would be all the greater, because there had been no
previous opportunity for the tribes to become familiarized
either with an exchange economy or the methods needed to establish peasant farms. Moreover, the strictly agricultural problems proved more intractable than had been thought. The review of the Development Plan in 1948 noted, for instance, that
should peasant farming schemes prove popular, the railway
belt would in due course provide all the maize and pulses
needed to supply the line of rail market. Hence the more distant
areas would lose their market for maize, and consequently it
was essential to find them alternative crops. In the event, this
proved impossible, and apart from certain areas of the Eastern
Province adjacent to Petauke, the peasant farming schemes
foundered because the farmers were able neither to compete
with those crops grown along the line of rail nor to find alternative ones for which there was a market.

   In strict contrast, European-financed economic development
along the line of rail proceeded at an ever-increasing pace in the
post-war years. Copper production remained at a high level;
new secondary industries were started, while European immigrants attracted to the land, particularly by the current high
prices for flue-cured tobacco, brought European agricultural
activity to record levels. Thus the lack of balance between the
highly industrialized mining area, the prosperous railway belt,
and the rest of the country—which the Development Plan described as giving a 'general impression of being practically stag-
nant' [12]—was being accentuated. But so long as the African-
reserved areas continued economically dependent on agriculture,
the combination of poor soils, adverse climatic conditions,

[12] *Ten Year Development Plan for Northern Rhodesia*, op. cit., p. 54.

tsetse fly, and distance from markets, apart from any other factors, mitigated against any substantial improvement. The crux of the matter was that the Territory's entire economy was dominated by that small fraction of its total surface area which lay along the line of rail and the Copperbelt. Unless this could be broadened, and that implied the injection of European capital, initiative, and skills into the African areas, they would be perpetually condemned to remaining rural slums.

But the land divisions in the Territory arose directly from the racial dilemma. In 1947, following intensive investigations, the Government introduced legislation whereby all land in the Territory not previously set aside as Native reserves, or alienated on freehold title, was to be divided into either Crown land or Native Trust land.[13] 'Crown land,' the Secretary for Native Affairs explained in the Legislature, 'will be potentially or actually available for non-Native settlement on an economic basis and for mining development, neither of which it is desired to restrict. It will include land certified as a result of ecological survey to be suitable for European settlement and all land known to contain potential mineral resources. Natives and non-Natives may acquire land in Crown land areas under the same conditions. That right is preserved by article 42 of the Northern Rhodesia Order-in-Council, 1924.' With regard to Native Trust land, the Secretary for Native Affairs continued: 'What we seek to establish beyond any possible doubt is that there is sufficient land for the aboriginal inhabitants of this Territory and for their increase, and that in Native Trust land there should be no alienation of land, whether to Africans or non-Africans, unless Your Excellency is satisfied, after consultation with the Native Authorities, that such alienation will be for the general benefit, including the aboriginal inhabitants.'

Thus, apart from Barotseland, in which African land rights are secured by treaties, the Territory is divided into 54,240 square miles of Native reserve, created by Orders-in-Council and guaranteed by the British Government for the exclusive use of the Natives of Northern Rhodesia in perpetuity; 5,324 square miles alienated in freehold and individual title before the British Government assumed direct responsibility for the administration of the Territory; 16,610 square miles of Crown land; and

[13] Hansard, 11 February 1947, col. 808.

170,810 square miles of Native Trust land. In the Crown land areas equality of opportunity existed only in theory. African settlement therein was confined almost exclusively to the urban areas, where the overwhelming majority of Africans lived in tied cottages. And while it was legally possible, no Africans had ever leased Crown land. Indeed, it was regarded by the settlers as exclusively European, its existence a safeguard for their way of life. Likewise the African looked on the Native Reserves and Native Trust land as exclusively African, for they provided him with his only security. A land policy which *prima facie* aimed at setting racial fears at rest ensured, therefore, that the greater part of the African-reserved areas would remain rural slums, given over to subsistence agriculture, and inhabited by the young, the very old, the sick, and women; that the drift of Africans into the urban areas would continue; and that there would be no solution to the problems of the urban African locations.

If the land divisions arose directly from the Territory's racial dilemma, likewise their maintenance constituted its principal political problem, for this economic unbalance had inevitable political repercussions. The flood of Africans into the urban areas, for instance, stimulated the settlers to demand that the area available for European settlement should be extended, and this aroused African apprehension, already sharpened by the increased rate of European immigration in the post-war years. The demand for responsible government united the traditional leaders and the more advanced Africans into a unanimous determination to defend African security at all costs. Thus the only Africans who were prepared to support agricultural reforms became as suspicious of the Government's measures as were the traditional leaders. In these circumstances, problems which were immensely difficult became to all intents and purposes insoluble.

Neither was there any likelihood that racial tension would abate. The Unofficials were resolved to put an end to their frustration by wresting from the British Government recognition of the power and authority which they considered had been conferred on them by the creation of the Unofficial majority. Apart from the demand for responsible government, the mineral royalties issue had also come to a head. In January 1948 Welensky had raised the question again, warning the Officials that if he did not receive a reply from the British Government by March he would move a vote of no confidence.[14] No reply was received and on 22 March Welensky duly moved a motion asking the Colonial Secretary to reconsider his decision and to take steps 'to ensure that these mineral rights are vested in the people of Northern Rhodesia'.[15] Welensky pointed out that with the price of copper standing at £132 per ton, the British South Africa Company's mineral royalties amounted to £1,250,000 annually, and that fully half the total value of the country's mineral production, some £15,000,000, left the country, mostly as dividends. 'I do not suggest that people who have invested their money are not entitled to a return,' Welensky declared. 'But the people who own this country, who have made this country, are entitled to at least a fairly reasonable proportion of the money.' He then delivered another ultimatum. 'In the event of the United Kingdom Government not acceding to our request, I think the time has come . . . when we should tax the royalties . . . and I shall suggest a fifty per cent. royalty tax.'

A Northern Rhodesian delegation was subsequently invited to London for discussions by the Secretary of State for the Colonies.

[14] Hansard, 7 January 1948, col. 690.
[15] Hansard, 22 March 1948, col. 366.

CHAPTER 11

FEDERATION IS SUGGESTED—BUT THE STALEMATE REMAINS

O N 24 March 1948, while the furore over the Government's handling of the responsible government proposals was at its height, Gore-Browne addressed the Legislative Council again, and expanded his ideas on the constitutional development of Northern Rhodesia.[1] The first step to be taken, he considered, should be the amalgamation of Northern Rhodesia and Nyasaland under a constitution similar to the one he had postulated for Northern Rhodesia. The advantage of this, he held, was two-fold. First, it would make a greater amount of human material available, both European and African, from which to fashion the Government—he thought the large number of advanced Africans in Nyasaland a particular advantage in this respect; and second, since the economies of the two countries were complementary, Nyasaland could help solve Northern Rhodesia's food shortage at the same time as Northern Rhodesia could supply Nyasaland with manufactured goods from her developing secondary industries. Whether such a union would have been acceptable to Africans, Gore-Browne could not say; but he quoted a Nyasaland chief with whom he had talked as being in favour of it. If such a union took place, and only then, Gore-Browne maintained, it would be possible to federate the two northern Territories with Southern Rhodesia, 'and so bring into being that Central African state which seems to my mind to be essential for the welfare, and if the worst comes to the worst, possibly even for the very existence of the three territories'.

There was an obvious continuity of thought between these proposals and those postulated for responsible government: in both Gore-Browne based his suggestions on an immediate emancipation from the dominating power of the Colonial Office with the guaranteeing of existing African rights, more

[1] Hansard, 24 March 1948, col. 440.

especially those pertaining to land. Only then did he consider it would be possible to link the two Rhodesias and Nyasaland, and then only through a federation, a union which allowed the individual states to continue to exercise a large degree of responsibility for their own affairs, beside permitting the Colonial Office to retain a definite interest and influence in the two northern Protectorates.

The suggestion was thrown out somewhat casually. Nevertheless, at the opening of the very next session of the Legislative Council, some ten weeks later, Mr. Welensky was saying to the Governor, in reference to the Northern Rhodesian delegation's visit to London to discuss the responsible government proposals: 'We do want an opportunity of discussing the Federation issue with the Secretary of State for the Colonies.' [2] The federal idea was by no means new: Gore-Browne had been first in the field with concrete proposals for such a scheme in 1936. Ten years later, Colonel Oliver Stanley, Secretary of State for the Colonies during the latter period of the war, had told Welensky that there was no possibility of either major political party in Britain agreeing to Amalgamation, and that he thought a form of federation might be more acceptable.[3] The impracticability of Amalgamation had indeed become increasingly obvious, and the re-introduction of the proposal for a federation came when an alternative was desperately needed.

The Colonial Secretary was thus faced with a bewilderingly complex set of demands from Northern Rhodesia. On the question of the British South Africa Company's mineral royalties and the federation of the two Rhodesias and Nyasaland, Mr. Creech Jones declared that His Majesty's Government were not in a position to commit themselves. But he agreed to modify the composition of the Executive Council so that four Unofficial members of the Legislative Council, including one of the Europeans nominated to represent African interests, could sit on it. Under the new arrangements, the views of the Unofficial members were to carry the same weight in the Executive Council as they did in the Legislative Council, subject to the Governor's reserved powers. This was immediately interpreted by the Un-

[2] Hansard, 8 June 1948, col. 23.
[3] Mentioned by Mr. Welensky in the Northern Rhodesian Legislative Council, Hansard, 24 November 1949, col. 329.

officials to mean that provided they were unanimous, their views on the Executive Council would prevail. It was further announced that one or two of the Unofficials would be given responsibility for a group or groups of Government departments when the 1948 constitution came into force, and that the meetings of the Legislature would be presided over by a Speaker, and not by the Governor as had previously been the case.

But events in Africa were moving whether His Majesty's Government were prepared to commit themselves or not. In May 1948 Field Marshal Smuts and the United Party had been swept from power in South Africa by the Nationalist Party led by Dr. Malan. For the European communities in the Rhodesias, this was an event touching them closely. The new party was pledged gradually to cut South Africa's ties with Britain, ties very strongly felt in the Rhodesias. Moreover, English-speaking Rhodesians were well aware of the number of Afrikaans-speaking South Africans north of the Limpopo, whose sympathies might be attracted by the new Nationalist Government. The need for creating a large Central African state with strong links with Britain and powerful enough to resist the influence of South Africa began to be felt all the more keenly.

A political crisis developed in Southern Rhodesia shortly afterwards. In June 1948 the Deputy Leader of the Opposition in the Southern Rhodesian Assembly proposed that an all-party delegation should be sent to London to press for the granting of Dominion status to the Colony. For Southern Rhodesians were not only perturbed by events to the south; many saw in the trends developing in Northern Rhodesia an equally dangerous threat to their security. The Prime Minister, Sir Godfrey Huggins, managed to side-step this demand, but shortly afterwards a general election was precipitated when his Government was defeated over a matter concerning the Central African Council, an institution highly regarded by the Colonial Secretary, Mr. Creech Jones, but equally unpopular with European politicians in the Rhodesias, especially in Southern Rhodesia. Though Sir Godfrey Huggins's party won in the subsequent election, a victory widely accredited to the success of the Nationalist Party in South Africa, for the leader of the Opposition, Mr. J. H. Smit, was suspected of viewing sympathetically a union between

Southern Rhodesia and South Africa, it was clear that the Government would soon be forced to take a decision on the Colony's future constitutional development. But if union with South Africa gained no favour with English-speaking Europeans, it was equally clear that the development wholeheartedly supported for many years by Sir Godfrey Huggins, amalgamation with Northern Rhodesia, was equally unacceptable to the British Government.

It was at this juncture that the two Rhodesian leaders met in London, Welensky having attended the British Africa Conference convened by the Colonial Secretary, while Sir Godfrey was attending the Commonwealth Prime Ministers' Conference. Discussions with Mr. Creech Jones had convinced Welensky that the British Government would never support Amalgamation, and consequently he set out to persuade the Southern Rhodesian Prime Minister that the only way to achieve the closer association of the two Rhodesias was through Federation. In this he was successful; indeed, Sir Godfrey announced before leaving London that he was prepared to call a conference of Northern Rhodesian Unofficials and representatives of the political parties in Southern Rhodesia to discuss the matter.[4]

The Federation conference convened by Sir Godfrey Huggins took place at the Victoria Falls in February 1949 under the chairmanship of Sir Miles Thomas, chairman of British Overseas Airways Corporation, and at that time, of the Southern Rhodesian Development Co-ordinating Commission. Sir Godfrey Huggins led the Southern Rhodesian delegation, which consisted of several Cabinet Ministers and M.P.s, including members of the Opposition, and Welensky the Northern Rhodesian delegation of elected European members of the Legislative Council. Leading members of the European community in Nyasaland also attended. No Africans were invited to the conference, though the African Voice Association of Southern Rhodesia sent a European observer and Colonel Sir Stewart Gore-Browne attended in the same capacity as a representative of the Northern Rhodesian African community.

This arrangement was in itself sufficient to arouse the suspicions of Africans in Northern Rhodesia; the Southern Rhodesian Prime Minister's opening address confirmed their worst

4 See *The Rhodesian*, Don Taylor, pp. 103–7.

fears. For some time to come, he declared, Africans must be ruled by a benevolent aristocracy in the real sense of those words. For obvious reasons, conditions in Central Africa did not permit the introduction of a full democratic system, for Natives were not yet ready to participate in elections, although he agreed that Africans could be nominated to an upper house. However, existing African land rights in the two Protectorates would be guaranteed by the Federal Government.[5] The conference then went into private session. From the European delegates' point of view, the conference was a striking success. It agreed that a federation consisting of Northern Rhodesia, Southern Rhodesia, and Nyasaland was both workable and desirable; in two days of intensive discussion the basis for a constitution was drafted. In almost every other respect, however, it was disastrous. The fact that it was being held was widely publicized; but after Sir Godfrey's opening speech, its deliberations were shrouded in silence. If the intention had been to antagonize African opinion in the two northern Protectorates it could scarcely have been achieved more successfully. It has been said that much of the subsequent bitterness in Central Africa could have been avoided if this first Federation conference had been handled more competently, and particularly if Africans had been associated with it.[6] The underlying circumstances hardly allowed of any great variation from what actually took place. The fundamental aim of the assembled delegates was to create a new state sufficiently endowed in men and material resources to achieve and maintain independence, so that in the racial field European interests could be protected. From the Northern Rhodesian and Nyasaland delegations' point of view, this could be achieved only through the active support of Southern Rhodesia, for that Colony possessed the European population and the resources in indigenous administrative and technical personnel without which the two Protectorates could not hope to maintain independence and at the same time protect European interests. But Southern Rhodesia insisted that Federation should not result in any closer contact with the British Government and the Colonial Office; indeed, Federation was seen, basically, as a safeguard against Afrikaner nationalism from the

[5] Reported in *East Africa and Rhodesia*, 24 February 1949, p. 765.
[6] See for instance *The Rhodesian*, D. Taylor, p. 109.

south and Black nationalism from the north, which Southern Rhodesians felt was being actively encouraged by the British Government. It was hardly surprising therefore that the views of the Southern Rhodesian delegates, and in particular those of the Prime Minister, should have dominated the arrangements for the conference and the composition of the draft constitution.

The European elected members returned to Northern Rhodesia well satisfied. On 29 March 1949 Welensky asked the Chief Secretary in the Legislature for the loan of two Government officers, the Financial Secretary and the Attorney General, to assist him on the committee which was to be established by the Prime Minister of Southern Rhodesia to prepare a constitution for the proposed Federation. On the following day the Chief Secretary announced that the Government would be very glad to give the assistance requested, but pointed out that the officers would be acting in their personal and professional capacity, which would in no way prejudice the position of the Government regarding the proposals. The initiative with regard to Federation clearly lay with the Central African leaders, for the Colonial Secretary had immediately announced that he regarded the Victoria Falls conference as unofficial, and that he was not prepared to comment on the issue until such time as he received definite proposals from Central Africa. Welensky and Sir Godfrey Huggins had originally planned to prepare a draft constitution quickly and to submit it to another delegate conference in Central Africa for approval. This proved more difficult than they had supposed, and finally the Southern Rhodesian Prime Minister had to send his Minister of Justice and Attorney General to London to discuss the constitutional difficulties encountered.

The proposals announced at the Victoria Falls conference thus provided the only material from which the constitution of the proposed Federation could be judged. From the African point of view, this was disastrous. When Sir Stewart Gore-Browne, accompanied by the two African members of the Legislative Council, toured the Territory explaining to Africans what Federation entailed, he found, not unexpectedly, adamant opposition. As he himself admitted, the proposals enunciated at the Victoria Falls conference were Amalgamation scarcely disguised. African reaction to his responsible government proposals hardly suggests that his original suggestion for linking Northern Rhodesia with Southern Rhodesia would have received a warmer reception. Indeed, the swift growth of African fears had brought about the event feared by the Secretary for Native Affairs. In 1948 the Federation of African Societies had been renamed the Northern Rhodesian African National Congress, an avowedly political organization led by the detribalized Africans resident in the urban areas. And it soon became apparent that Congress was actively organizing African opposition to the Federation proposals.

But further progress over Federation was unlikely, for Northern Rhodesia was trapped in a political stalemate. The British Labour Party had repeatedly stressed their determination that under no circumstances would they grant increased political power to the settler communities in Central Africa without a commensurate increase in the power of the African communities. Active support for the creation of the Federation could hardly be expected therefore from the British Government of the day. But neither was the Colonial Secretary in a position to reject Federation categorically. Already the pressure exerted by the Unofficials had forced him to modify the views he had so frequently expressed while in Opposition. The decision to allow four Unofficials to sit on the Executive Council; the agreement that their combined views should carry the same weight as in the Legislative Council; the appointment of two elected Europeans to be Ministers responsible for groups of Government departments; all were moves in the direction of increased Unofficial power, and increased political influence for the European community, for which there had been no comparable and balancing advance for Africans. Indeed, the new Member for Agriculture and Natural Resources controlled Government departments which most closely affected African life, which touched that most sensitive chord in African fears, land.

This stalemate can be seen reflected in the manner the question of African paramountcy was handled. With the more politically conscious African leaders declaring their support for this 'principle' in the post-war years, the Unofficials were naturally anxious to force the Government to agree to abandon it. In 1945 the Northern Rhodesian Government accepted a motion

moved by Major McKee, an elected member, 'that the interests of Africans and Europeans in the Territory are interlocked,
and . . . that a policy of subordinating the interests of either
section of the community to those of the other would be fatal to
the development of Northern Rhodesia'.[7] The then Secretary of
State for the Colonies announced his concurrence with the sentiments expressed in the motion. But in December 1945 Welensky again asked the Chief Secretary whether the British Government had modified its views on the paramountcy of African interests as defined in a supplement to a Gazette dated 17 June
1930.[8] The Chief Secretary did not mention the text of Major
McKee's motion in his reply, but reiterated that the operative
document was the report of the Joint Select Committee of Parliament of 1931, and that the policy of His Majesty's Government in this respect was unchanged.

The question then lay dormant for several years, until the
demand for responsible government brought it into prominence
again. In March 1948 Welensky asked for an unequivocal 'yes'
or 'no' to the question: 'Did the doctrine of African paramountcy . . . still apply to Northern Rhodesia?' On this occasion the Chief Secretary did refer to Major McKee's motion
and pointed out that the Northern Rhodesian Government had
accepted it.[9] Welensky retorted that it meant nothing. 'I am
somewhat surprised at my Hon. Friend saying it means nothing,' the Chief Secretary replied. 'It is a very clear statement . . .
and the idea of partnership . . . is in fact enshrined in these
statements.' But a few days later, in response to another question from Welensky, the Chief Secretary told the Legislature:
'The interpretation of this Government of the assurance received from the Secretary of State is that under any system of
partnership the interests of one section of the community
could not be subordinate to those of any other section.[10] This
was no more meaningful than the original doctrine of African
paramountcy in the circumstances of Northern Rhodesia;
nevertheless, it was an advance from the point of view of the
European community. Moreover, in view of African declara-

[7] Hansard, 4 July 1945, col. 459.
[8] Hansard, 11 December 1945, col. 154.
[9] Hansard, 12 March 1948, col. 124.
[10] Hansard, 23 March 1948, col. 419.

tions subsequent to the demand for responsible government, the Colonial Secretary consented to the calling of a special meeting of the African Representative Council in August 1948 at which the Secretary for Native Affairs stated that 'the main point is that the development of Northern Rhodesia is based on a genuine partnership between Europeans and Africans. There can be no question of Government adopting a policy of subordinating the interests of either community to those of the other. The . . . interests of Northern Rhodesia can be served only by a policy of whole-hearted co-operation between the different sections of the community'.[11] In attempting to redefine the official attitude to race relations in Northern Rhodesia and in granting the Unofficials increased political power, Mr. Creech Jones was bowing before an irresistible pressure. But in view of his own suspicions, these steps were taken reluctantly, a retreat at the last possible moment. Moreover, many back-bench members of his own party in the House of Commons still reiterated their belief in the paramountcy of African interests, and any concession to the settlers was seen as a betrayal of the African cause. Those expressing such views had not the advantage of the Colonial Secretary's close view of the balance of power in Northern Rhodesia; and he could scarcely inform them of the reality without overtly admitting to the Africans in Northern Rhodesia that there was little which the British Government could do to protect their interests. Even if he had, the only probable outcome would have been the loss of his own reputation and position in the Labour Party.

Yet a further recognition of the power of the Unofficials in Northern Rhodesia was inevitable. When the amended Legislature met in Lusaka in November 1948 the Governor announced in his opening address that Mr. G. B. Beckett, the Member for the South-Western Electoral Area, had consented to become the Member for Agriculture and Natural Resources, with control over the departments of agriculture, veterinary services, forestry, game and tsetse control, and water development and irrigation. 'It is my belief,' the Governor concluded, 'that these changes will be of benefit for this Territory by assisting the smooth working of the administrative procedure, and by

[11] Quoted by the Governor, Sir Gilbert Rennie, in his Address to the Legislative Council, 22 June 1949.

enabling Unofficial members to assume greater and more intimate responsibilities.' [12] Events hardly confirmed the Governor's view. A few days later Welensky announced his intention of tabling a motion asking for permission to introduce a royalties tax on Northern Rhodesian mineral production. 'I fully appreciate what this means,' he declared. 'It means that we shall carry it because my colleagues are with me. We shall carry it in spite of the declaration of the Secretary of State for the Colonies in 1939.' Once the motion was passed, Welensky proposed asking the Governor for permission to introduce a Bill which would affect the country's finances. 'That permission, I take it, will be refused to me in view of the Secretary of State's declaration of 1939. But I want to warn the Government . . . if that permission is refused, there will be trouble in this country.' [13]

Welensky was patently right: the Unofficials were determined. Moreover, they had chosen the ground for testing whether the British Government would finally acknowledge the consequences of an Unofficial majority with great skill, for it was the one great issue on which all the Unofficials were united. In keeping with his earlier promise, Welensky moved on 24 March 1949 that the time was opportune for the introduction of legislation providing for the imposition of a special tax on royalties recovered from minerals in the Territory. The motion was seconded by one of the new African members in the Legislature, the Rev. Kasokolo, who supported Welensky's contention that land and mineral rights had been vested in the chiefs, and that under no circumstances should they have signed away such tribal assets. All the Unofficials spoke and voted in favour of the motion, with the exception of Mr. N. Nalumango, the second African member. The Officials, on the Governor's advice, refrained from voting. The motion was thus carried, and as the Financial Secretary remarked: 'In view of the importance of the motion, and its implications, the Secretary of State will have to be consulted.' Welensky had made it abundantly clear, however, that 'either we, the Unofficials, have some say and play our part in the Government of this country, or we have not. If we have not, let us . . . get away from this suggestion that we

[12] Hansard, 10 November 1948, col. 4.
[13] Hansard, 25 November 1948, col. 263.

are part of the Government, and let us play our proper role, that of the opposition.' [14]

Friction was again mounting between Unofficials and Officials, this time over the interpretation of the phrase that the unanimous views of the Unofficials would carry the same weight on the Executive Council as in the Legislature. While it had not overtly reached the same proportions as in 1948, Welensky, as leader of the Unofficials, had refused to nominate a second elected member to ministerial status until the matter had been clarified. The crux of the entire situation was the mineral royalties issue. And a decision, in view of Unofficial unanimity and determination, could no longer be postponed.

It was at this juncture that Mr. Creech Jones announced his intention of visiting Northern Rhodesia, the first Colonial Secretary to do so. He arrived in the Territory in April 1949 and after a series of meetings with the Governor and the Unofficials an official statement was issued which stated that 'the conclusion reached in the London discussions last July . . . should be understood to mean that, without prejudice to the constitutional position of the Executive Council, the Governor will accept the advice of the Unofficial members of the Executive Council when the four Unofficials are unanimous, except in cases where he would feel it necessary to use his reserved powers'.[15] Commenting on the results of his meetings with the Colonial Secretary, Welensky exclaimed triumphantly: 'They were very satisfactory. Interpretation of the phrase is now quite clear: we have it in writing.'

Progress was also made with regard to the mineral royalties issue. After a preliminary meeting between Welensky and the President of the British South Africa Company, Sir Dougal Malcolm, who was also visiting Central Africa at the same time as the Colonial Secretary, the latter invited both to begin negotiations under his chairmanship in London. Preliminary agreement was eventually reached in August 1949 after a series of meetings between a Northern Rhodesian delegation and representatives of the Chartered Company, whereby the Company agreed to surrender the mineral royalties free of charge to the Northern Rhodesian Government on 1 October 1986, and

[14] Hansard, 24 March 1949, col 192.
[15] Reported in the *Bulawayo Chronicle*, 18 April 1949.

in the meantime to pay a 20 per cent. tax on the net income from royalties. It was a personal triumph for Welensky, and set the final seal on the reality of the Unofficial majority.

But over the third issue, the supremely vital one of Federation, matters turned out very differently. During the course of his tour, the Secretary of State received more than a dozen addresses from African bodies, all of them opposing Federation, and though he refused to comment on them publicly, the mere absence of comment confirmed European belief that Creech Jones supported their sentiments. And as a local newspaper commented, 'should Federation fail, there will inevitably be a gradual change in political trends in Northern Rhodesia, and Europeans are likely to look further south than Southern Rhodesia for encouragement and support in what would be no more than a battle for survival'.[16]

Despite the care which Creech Jones took not to offend European susceptibilities, he inadvertently drove European suspicion and distrust into open anger, into an outburst of anti-Colonial Office sentiments unparalleled since the publication of the Passfield Memorandum. During a brief visit to Southern Rhodesia, the Secretary of State made a reference in Salisbury to the fact that by virtue of the British Government's guarantees to Africans, 'permanent White settlement in Northern Rhodesia needed to be controlled'. In view of the tenseness of feeling in Northern Rhodesia it was an unfortunate statement, for with so much of Northern Rhodesia reserved in one form or another for African use there was obviously a limit placed on European settlement. Moreover, it was doubly hurtful by being made in Southern and not Northern Rhodesia.

Welensky read the Colonial Secretary's statement in a local newspaper immediately prior to leaving for a political meeting in Livingstone, and in a Press interview at Lusaka airport on his return he delivered his answer. 'The Colonial Secretary's statement is completely unacceptable,' he declared, 'and if the British Government wants to implement it they will have to bring their troops to this country to carry it out. The European community will not under any circumstances recognize the paramountcy of African interests. If Mr. Creech Jones persists in this policy I shall not hesitate to appeal to the people of

[16] *Bulawayo Chronicle*, 22 April, 1949.

South Africa and Southern Rhodesia for support in counter action. I shall also contact the elected members of Kenya to make sure that we take concerted action in the interests of the Europeans in Central and East Africa.' [17]

The Colonial Secretary was extremely angry at what he considered an unjustified outburst, and during the remainder of his tour did his best to rectify the damage. In a broadcast to Africans made just before he left for London he declared that 'now there are many Europeans in this country, they give you work, increase the country's wealth and contribute by taxation to services and development which you as well as they want. I know that in some places there may appear to be a conflict of interests between some Europeans and Africans, but this we are trying to prevent and smooth away.' [18] And at a Press conference Mr. Creech Jones again reiterated that 'it is clear that for the economic well-being and social development of the Territory, the European must have a permanent place'.

Nevertheless, his visit resulted in a further deterioration in race relations, which in the circumstances was hardly surprising. The two major racial groups looked to a future based on diametrically opposed premises; an end to the prevailing uncertainty was desperately needed. But Creech Jones, trapped between the support accorded the African cause by his own party and the power of the European community in Northern Rhodesia, could only attempt a precarious balance between the two racial points of view, unable to discourage African demands for 'paramountcy' on the one side, or those of the European for political power on the other. Thus when Mr. Skinnard, a Labour M.P., asked the Colonial Secretary in the House of Commons on 13 May 1949, after his return from Northern Rhodesia, for an assurance that nothing would be done about a federation of the territories in Central Africa which would result in increased political power for the European minorities, Mr. Creech Jones replied that the present and future interests of Northern Rhodesia could only be served by a policy of wholehearted co-operation between the different sections of the community. Yet in *The African Weekly*, a newspaper published in Lusaka for Africans, there had appeared on 27 April 1949 the

[17] *Bulawayo Chronicle*, 2 May 1948.
[18] Ibid, 22 April 1948.

statement that if there was any conflict of interests between Europeans and Africans, then African interests would be paramount. According to the newspaper, this assurance had been given by the Secretary of State for the Colonies, Mr. A. Creech Jones, to a delegation of the Northern Rhodesian African Congress in an interview in Lusaka on 14 April 1949.[19]

In view of this contradiction, Welensky asked the Chief Secretary whether the Minister had been correctly quoted. The Chief Secretary replied that while no full verbatim record had been taken, some notes made at the time were available. From them, the Minister's statement appeared to be diametrically opposed to what had been published in the *African Weekly*. The relevant passage read: 'Previously the view was that if there was conflict of interests, and such conflict could not be resolved, then the interests of the indigenous people would be paramount. This was in any case a purely hypothetical situation and the previous definition no longer had any force at all. His Majesty's Government would in accordance with their position as trustee see that the interests of Africans were adequately safeguarded. As stated in the Official declaration in 1948, the two communities must work together for the good of the Territory.'

Mr. Welensky then asked as a Supplementary Question: 'Could I ask if my Hon. Friend would state categorically in simple language that paramountcy is dead and that the policy followed in this country is a policy of partnership of all peoples in the interests of all its peoples?' To which the Chief Secretary replied: 'If by paramountcy the Hon. Member means a policy of subordinating the interests of one section of the community to those of the other, then I can say that paramountcy is dead. If paramountcy means that the interests of one section cannot be subordinated to those of the other, then paramountcy is very much alive.'

[19] Quoted by Mr. Welensky, Hansard, 24 June 1949, col. 70.

CHAPTER 12

RECOGNITION OF REALITY

THE first step in resolving this impasse was for the European leaders in Central Africa to modify their original approach to the Federation issue, for them to place the Colonial Secretary in a position where he had to make a decision on it. For this reason, Welensky's motion 'that in the opinion of this House the time is opportune for His Majesty's Government to take the lead in creating a Central African federation consisting of Southern Rhodesia, Northern Rhodesia and Nyasaland',[1] moved in the Northern Rhodesian Legislature in November 1949, was of exceptional significance. It indicated Welensky's appreciation that nothing could be achieved from Central Africa, and of greater importance, that a Federal constitution based on the ideas expressed at the Victoria Falls conference had not the slightest chance of acceptance by a British Government. Welensky indeed admitted that the Victoria Falls conference had hardened African opinion against Federation. But his argument that this was largely unjustified because nothing definite had been decided was naïve. And while Welensky could justifiably point out that certain African leaders in Northern Rhodesia were deliberately distorting facts in order to arouse the suspicions of the more unsophisticated members of the African community, in reality distortion was hardly necessary in view of Sir Godfrey Huggins's opening speech.

In support of Federation, Welensky used many of the arguments propounded in his post-war speeches in favour of Amalgamation. But on this occasion, he deliberately slanted them to show that Britain, too, stood to gain from the creation of a powerful Central African state with strong British ties. He pointed out that it was impossible to ignore the trend of events in South Africa, where Nationalist ministers were continuously referring to the desirability of creating a republic, possibly outside the Commonwealth. In a future war, Welensky declared,

[1] Hansard, 24 November 1949, col. 322.

South Africa might remain neutral: hence it could no longer be considered strategically safe. There was the question, too, of defence. Britain was no longer the power she had been in 1938: her capacity to defend Central Africa was doubtful, and each of the existing states were incapable of defending themselves. Indeed, not until there was the underlying economic strength, and this could only be obtained through Federation, would the three Territories be able to undertake their own defence. That each state would gain economically from the creation of the Federation—and this was particularly true of Northern Rhodesia, which was absolutely dependent on copper—Welensky did not doubt. None of the three territories possessed markets sufficiently large for secondary industries to be successfully established. And as far as the Protectorates were concerned, how, Mr. Welensky asked, was it possible to guide and inspire economic progress when the strings of government were controlled from 6,000 miles away?

Such arguments were not, and indeed had never been, in serious dispute. The essence of the Federation controversy, as in the case of Amalgamation, was African affairs, and in dealing with this Welensky admitted that the indigenous population disliked change, that the only form of government acceptable to them was one consisting of Colonial Office officials. 'Well, Sir, need I say to the House that that attitude is resented by the settler community of this country? Year after year we have voted vast sums of money for the purpose of providing facilities of all kinds for the Africans. That money was not provided by His Majesty's Government. It was provided by the enterprise, the driving power, and the initiative of the Europeans of this country, and to suggest we are unfit to take part in the government of this country is resented by the Europeans.[2] I do understand and sympathize with the African's dislike of changes,' Mr. Welensky continued, 'but if anyone allows the African to believe that the only choice left to him will be between remaining what he is today or becoming part of a Federal state then someone is being dishonest. The position in this country, our mineral wealth, our strategic position, will not permit of this country remaining a backwater. We have to develop it, and if we do not develop it, I have a feeling that other nations may not be pre-

[2] Hansard, 24 November 1949, col. 346.

pared to see us retain these vast open spaces and this vast mineral wealth without developing it, and I say in the interests of the European section and in the interest of the Africans that this part of the world should be developed.'

The tone of Welensky's speech was very different from that made by Sir Godfrey Huggins at the opening of the Victoria Falls conference, though it was hardly likely to soothe African suspicions. Moreover, the motion was seconded by Mr. van Eeden, a Northern Rhodesian born son of a Dutch Reformed Church missionary, who had entered the Legislature as Member for the Midland Area in the 1948 general election. And he told the Legislature bluntly that 'the main reason why we need a Federal state in Central Africa is because this will enable us to loosen the grip of the Colonial Office on the territory'.

After recounting African opposition to the projected Federation, Colonel Sir Stewart Gore-Browne announced that he and his three colleagues, the second European nominated to represent African interests and the two African members, would vote against the motion. 'Apart from our duty to represent African opinion as it actually is, we feel that in view of the universal African opposition to Federation, we cannot honestly say that the time is opportune for His Majesty's Government to take the lead in creating a Federal state; and further, we must in all honesty make it clear that we ourselves are opposed to the proposals made at the Victoria Falls, in so far as they were made public there, on the grounds that to us they appear to be Amalgamation under another name,' Sir Stewart declared.

On 28 November the Acting Chief Secretary, Mr. Thornton, replied to the debate. Welensky's motion had finally forced the Northern Rhodesian Government's dilemma to the surface, for the Officials could hardly vote for the motion, thereby informing the Colonial Secretary, who was opposed to Federation, that, in their opinion, the time was opportune for him to take a lead in creating it. But if they voted against it, the inevitable consequence would be another bout of friction with the elected members. They consequently took the middle course and abstained. The motion was therefore passed by the votes of the elected members against those representing African interests. With prior knowledge that this would happen, the Acting Chief Secretary carefully explained: 'I wish to make it clear to Africans especially that the passing of this motion would in no way indicate or imply that His Majesty's Government will agree to take the action suggested. . . . On the other hand we do not propose to vote against the motion, as we do not wish to prevent the motion from going forward; we do wish the motion to go forward as an expression of views of the majority of the Unofficial members of the Council. Moreover a vote against . . . would be regarded by many as a vote against Federation, and this Government . . . has an open mind on the question of Federation.' [3]

Though the decision now lay absolutely with the Colonial Secretary, his personal dilemma had in the meantime become more acute, and, consequently, though a decision had to be made, and indeed was desperately needed, the months slipped by with no sign of a lead from London. Meanwhile, race relations in Northern Rhodesia continued to deteriorate, and the political leadership of the African community was increasingly monopolized by the more militant leaders of the National Congress. At this juncture, however, fortune intervened in the guise of another general election in the United Kingdom, for at the polls, as part of a general swing away from the Labour Party, Mr. Creech Jones lost his seat. The Labour Party was still returned to power, though with a greatly reduced majority, and Mr. Attlee, the Prime Minister, appointed Mr. James Griffiths to succeed Mr. Creech Jones as Colonial Secretary. Welensky had an early opportunity of meeting Mr. Griffiths when he went to London as a member of a Northern Rhodesian delegation to discuss possible changes in the Territory's constitution, it having previously been agreed that the constitutional arrangements introduced in 1948 would be reviewed after an interval of thirty months. Welensky suggested that more Unofficials should be given executive responsibilities, in his view not a very sweeping change, especially as he only asked that the numbers of Unofficial ministers should be increased from two to four. Mr. Griffiths took an entirely different view, considering Welensky's proposal a marked forward stride in the political progress of the European. Before giving any answer, he wished to examine what possible prospects there were for African progress. There the matter rested—except that Welensky

[3] Hansard, 28 November 1949, col. 404.

warned the Colonial Secretary of the possible consequences if he waited until the last moment before announcing any changes.

Welensky also took the opportunity of once again outlining the advantages of creating a Federation in British Central Africa. 'Everyone knows the arguments, I have used them so often here'—Mr. Welensky was reporting to the Legislature on his visit to London—'but I only endeavoured to persuade the Secretary of State to agree to one thing, and that was to the proposal to hold a conference, which I personally would prefer to see held here in Africa, to try and bring this matter to finality.' [4] The two Secretaries of State—Welensky also saw Mr. Patrick Gordon-Walker, Secretary of State for Commonwealth Relations—neither rejected, nor agreed to, his proposal, but reiterated Britain's obligation to the African people north of the Zambesi. 'I fully understand it,' Welensky remarked, 'but I do want to say this in regard to the future. Northern Rhodesia is fast getting to the stage when we want to know in which direction we develop.' During the course of the next three weeks, Welensky continued, he would be meeting Sir Godfrey Huggins to consider the next steps to be taken in the Federation campaign.

It proved to be another fateful meeting, for from it emerged the proposal for a London conference to re-examine Closer Association. Sir Godfrey Huggins apparently considered that the principal reason why all attempts to discuss Amalgamation or Federation had been so unfruitful was that they had been held at too high a level, between a Secretary of State and Southern Rhodesian Ministers, and consequently he cabled Mr. Attlee, the British Prime Minister, who was also acting for the Secretary of State for Commonwealth Relations at the time, suggesting that a conference of officials of the Colonial Office, the Commonwealth Relations Office, and the Southern Rhodesian, Northern Rhodesian, and Nyasaland Governments should be convened.[5] The telegram was sent in August 1950. On 8 November James Griffiths announced in the House of Commons that His Majesty's Government had decided that there should be a fresh examination of the problem of Closer Association. And as Sir Godfrey had suggested, the study was to be undertaken by officials who were to meet for this purpose

[4] Hansard, 2 June 1950, col. 41.
[5] *The Rhodesian*, op. cit., p. 128.

early in 1951. Mr. Griffiths reiterated, however, that none of the participating Governments would be bound by the results of the conference, which was of an exploratory nature, to ascertain whether closer political association between the three Central African states was either desirable or practicable.

Superficially, the decision was surprising. Mr. Creech Jones immediately voiced his opposition to it, since he considered that the conference itself would give some kind of recognition to the principle of Federation. And indeed, an agreed scheme implementing Federation could not fail to enhance the political power of the European communities in Central Africa. Why, then, did the Labour Government consent to the conference being held? In the first place, a decision on the Federation issue could not have been withheld for very much longer. Vacillation had already produced a marked deterioration in race relations in Northern Rhodesia. And in view of the pressure being exerted by the settler communities, outright rejection without official examination would certainly have had serious consequences, particularly in Northern Rhodesia. In this sense, the idea of a conference of officials was astute, for officials could not be accused of unnecessary bias in favour of the European, particularly as the Southern Rhodesian delegation would be heavily outnumbered by representatives from the Northern Rhodesian and Nyasaland Governments and the Colonial and Commonwealth Relations Offices. Moreover, in the wider African context the Nationalist Government was forging implacably ahead with its plans for maintaining permanent White supremacy south of the Limpopo, while in the Gold Coast, the constitution had been changed so that internal self-government under an African Prime Minister was shortly to be inaugurated. Thus if a new central state shunning racial nationalism was to be created, steps had to be taken urgently. This was realized by some of the senior members of the Labour Government. Mr. Gordon-Walker, Secretary of State for Commonwealth Relations, said for instance during a tour of Southern Rhodesia prior to the convening of the officials' conference, that the Labour Government had far less prejudice on Closer Association than most people imagined, and that it would indeed be happy if the officials produced a unanimous report.[6]

[6] *The Rhodesian,* op. cit., p. 132.

In the event, they did. Closer Association the officials considered was necessary; and the need for action urgent. In their report [7] the economic interdependence of the three Territories was pointed out, as was the need for integrated economic policies, both internally and externally. While each Territory was relatively prosperous, as individual economic units all were vulnerable, since Southern Rhodesia was dependent on the sale of flue-cured tobacco, and Northern Rhodesia even more on copper. Rail, trunk road, and air communications needed to be planned on a broader basis; the unification of certain public services, almost impossible to achieve while the three remained separate states, would secure greater efficiency. Moreover, Closer Association would enable the maximum use to be made of the capital resources of the entire region, in finance, raw materials, power, labour, and technical skill. The general quickening of economic expansion which would follow would bring advantages to all the inhabitants of the area, and in particular a more rapid advance in the provision of social services for Africans. But apart from these considerations, the officials felt that a crucial stage had been reached in Central Africa. 'European political development is already well advanced; and there is a growing political consciousness among Africans. The latter is in part due to the improvement and expansion of the social and economic services; but there can be no doubt that thinking Africans as well as Europeans in all the Territories are becoming increasingly anxious about the course of Native policy south of the Limpopo.' There, in the opinion of the officials, was the prime reason for urgency in implementing closer political association between Northern Rhodesia, Southern Rhodesia, and Nyasaland.

But what of that great stumbling block, the divergence of Native policies north and south of the Zambesi? In 1950 a comparative survey of the Native policies followed in each Territory had been compiled by the three Secretaries for Native Affairs sitting under the chairmanship of the Chief Secretary of the Central African Council, and this document was used at the conference to assess the aims and objectives of each. In Southern Rhodesia the Land Apportionment Act of 1931, with its

[7] *Central African Territories: Report on Conference on Closer Association* (H.M.S.O., March 1951), Cmd. 8233.

subsequent amendments, defined exclusive African and European areas. In the North, while this racial separation was not embodied in law, except that Native reserves were set apart for the exclusive use of Africans in Northern Rhodesia, there was in reality a considerable degree of geographical racial separation. Under the Colonial Office, it was held that in order to fit the African to take his place in the community as a full partner with citizens of a more ancient civilization, he must be induced to play a full part in the politics and administration of the whole territory. In Southern Rhodesia, on the other hand, the first necessity was considered to be the raising of the African's standard of health, material well-being, and education. This difference of emphasis was reflected in the African's greater political progress in the two Protectorates. Native Authorities had wider responsibilities in local administration. In Northern Rhodesia there was the African Representative Council; in Nyasaland the equivalent African Protectorate Council. But in Northern Rhodesia, Africans were British Protected Persons, and as such, were not allowed to vote unless they became naturalized British subjects; in Nyasaland there were no direct elections. Africans in Southern Rhodesia, on the contrary, shared a common voters' roll with Europeans, although only a handful were registered thereon. But the differences in policies north and south of the Zambesi were not entirely confined to the sphere of political advancement. In the Northern territories, particularly in Northern Rhodesia, African trade unions were officially fostered and recognized. In Southern Rhodesia they could not be officially registered, although they were given a limited *de facto* recognition. But in both Northern and Southern Rhodesia certain wage agreements made between European trade unions and employers' organizations had created an effective industrial colour bar in certain spheres of employment by laying down European wage standards. In Southern Rhodesia such agreements could and did receive statutory recognition under the Industrial Conciliation Act.

The officials came to the conclusion, however, that the most striking feature of the survey was the degree of similarity between the policies and practices in the three territories rather than the differences. There were no differences, for instance, between the policies pursued in the important spheres of education, health, agriculture, animal health, and forestry, in the way they affected Africans. And the Southern Rhodesian Government spent considerably larger sums on these services than did the two northern Governments. Even in those spheres where there were important differences, the officials considered that they were largely a question of method and timing. The ultimate goal of all three Governments, they felt, was broadly the same: the economic, social, and political advancement of Africans in partnership with Europeans. Thus in the officials' view differences in Native policy could no longer be regarded as a valid argument against Closer Association. On the contrary, they felt that positive advantages were to be gained by it from the point of view of Native policy, although they were far from explicit as to what these were. Because of this, and the political and economic reasons compelling urgent action, they not only recommended Closer Association but advanced a detailed plan for achieving it.

They rejected two possibilities which had been suggested: Amalgamation, and a Central African League, the latter proposal postulating that each Territory retained its existing constitution, powers, and status, but entered a 'League' to which all three would, by agreement, hand over certain functions and powers to be exercised by it on their behalf. The former was rejected because of African opposition; the latter because it would not only be too complex and cumbersome to work, but would be quite unacceptable to the Europeans of Southern Rhodesia. The solution recommended by the officials was a federal system. 'We believe this would enable the territories to be knit together effectively for common action in those spheres where it would be most beneficial for all of them, while leaving unimpaired the authority of the individual territories where this seemed most appropriate and recognizing the responsibility of His Majesty's Government in the United Kingdom towards the African people.' The division of functions between the Federal and Territorial Governments was strictly defined, roughly on the principle that those functions and services affecting external relations and transcending territorial boundaries would belong to the former, and those impinging closely on the daily life of the African people to the latter. In particular, all aspects of African Administration, and social and technical services, were to be reserved to the Territorial Governments. 'Under our proposals, the political development of Africans, both in national politics and in local government would go forward as at present in the three Territories.'

The Federal legislature, the officials recommended, should be a single chamber of thirty-five members, of whom seventeen would represent Southern Rhodesia, eleven Northern Rhodesia, and seven Nyasaland. Three members from each Territory would represent African interests, two from each of the Northern territories being Africans. To ensure that African interests would be adequately safeguarded in the legislature, there was to be an African Affairs Board and a Minister of African Interests. The latter would be chairman of the former, and would be appointed by the Governor-General from among the members representing African interests in the Federal legislature. He would also be a member of the Federal Cabinet. The other members of the African Affairs Board would be the three Secretaries for Native Affairs, one elected or unofficial member, and one African drawn from each territory. All legislation would be scrutinized by the Board before publication, and if any Bill was considered detrimental to African interests it had to be reserved by the Governor-General, after passing through the Legislature, for the signification of His Majesty's pleasure. It would then have to be referred to the Secretary of State for the Colonies.

The reception accorded the Officials' Report was, considering the circumstances and the nature of the proposals, much as was to be expected. Mr. Griffiths announced that they were a constructive approach to the problem of Closer Association, but that the British Government could not take any decision until they had been fully discussed in the three Central African Territories. Welensky and Sir Godfrey Huggins in turn were as enthusiastic as the Colonial Secretary was non-committal. Meanwhile officers of the Provincial Administration in Northern Rhodesia were given instructions to explain—but not to recommend—the proposals to the African population. Their reception can be gauged from the reports of the various Provincial Commissioners. In the Western Province district commissioners met 'a great deal of unintelligent and at times vituperative criticism'.[8] One elderly man at Fort Rosebery declared

[8] *Annual Report of Department of African Affairs, 1951*, p. 4.

with vigour that he was strongly opposed to all things which affected the everyday life of the African community coming under the control of the Territorial Government in Lusaka, let alone a Federal Government. 'Let these things remain in the hands of the Boma, [the district commissioner's office] as they always have been' was his attitude! In the Northern Province 'it became obvious at an early stage that the whole question had been prejudged by the African intelligentsia, who had firmly made up their minds to say "No" to any proposals designed to change the status quo. Even after lengthy explanations had been given, it is doubtful if more than a very small percentage of the African population had at the outset much idea about the proposals contained in the report. There is no doubt that local leaders of African opinion are being briefed as to what they should say from Congress headquarters'.[9] The Provincial Commissioner for the Southern Province wrote that the publication of the Officials' Report had created the feeling among all Africans that they 'must sink or swim together'.

The Colonial Secretary, when he presented the Officials' Report to the House of Commons, announced that both he and the Secretary for Commonwealth Relations would visit Central Africa after there had been sufficient time and opportunity for the proposals to be discussed. This visit was made in August and September of 1951, when Mr. Griffiths toured the Protectorates extensively, testing African opinion and explaining to them the gist of the Federation proposals. The Ministers' visit ended with another conference at that favoured site, the Victoria Falls, which was attended by representatives of the four Governments concerned and delegations from the African Representative Council in Northern Rhodesia and the African Protectorate Council of Nyasaland, although at one point it looked as though no Africans from Nyasaland would attend. In order to allay the apprehensions felt by the African communities in the two northern territories, the conference agreed that in the event of some form of Closer Association being implemented, certain rights would be enshrined in the constitution, namely that the Protectorate status of Northern Rhodesia and Nyasaland would be accepted and preserved, thus excluding any possibility of the amalgamation of the three territories unless a

[9] *Annual Report of Department of African Affairs ,1951*, p. 23.

majority of the inhabitants desired it, and that land and land settlement questions in Northern Rhodesia and Nyasaland would remain, subject to the ultimate authority of His Majesty's Government in the United Kingdom, the responsibility of the Territorial Governments, in accordance with the existing Orders-in-Council. It was agreed, too, that the political advancement of the Africans in the Protectorates, both in local government and the Territorial Governments, should remain, again subject to the ultimate authority of the United Kingdom Government, the responsibility of the Administrations in each territory.

But most important of all, the representatives of the four governments endorsed the principle of Federation, adding as a corollary that in the conditions of Central Africa it could only be based on a policy of economic and political partnership between Europeans and Africans. But at the end of the conference it was announced that before further progress could be made, additional discussions were necessary. The conference was therefore adjourned until the following year. Apart from the need for further discussions, the issue had to be postponed because Mr. Attlee, the British Prime Minister, had announced while the conference was still in progress that there was to be another general election in the United Kingdom. Much as the announcement had irritated the Rhodesian leaders, for it was assumed that the Colonial Secretary had had some prior knowledge of the decision, and that consequently the conference was from the beginning condemned to being abortive, a general election held out the possibility that the slender majority of the Labour Party might be turned into a Conservative victory. And Welensky and Sir Godfrey Huggins had always believed that their cause would receive a more sympathetic hearing from a Conservative Government.

In the event, their hopes were justified. The general election did return the Conservatives to power, and Mr. Winston Churchill once again became the British Prime Minister.

CHAPTER 13

A NEW STATE IS BORN—AFRICANS DEMAND PARTNERSHIP

THE man chosen by Mr. Winston Churchill to fill the office of Colonial Secretary was Mr. Oliver Lyttelton, and his attitude, and that of the new Government, towards the projected Central African Federation was quickly made clear. On 21 November 1951 Mr. Lyttelton announced in the House of Commons that His Majesty's Government were in full agreement with the conclusions reached at the second Victoria Falls conference and that a Federal scheme on the general lines recommended in the Officials' Report was favoured. The assurances then given about African guarantees were specifically endorsed, and the Colonial Secretary promised to initiate further consultations and discussions as had been promised by Mr. James Griffiths. To this end there was to be a further conference on Federation to be held in London in the following July.

Africans in Northern Rhodesia reacted bitterly to the Colonial Secretary's statement. It had already become apparent that the African community generally repudiated the official statement issued after the Victoria Falls conference convened by Mr. Griffiths, that Africans would be prepared to accept Federation on the lines recommended in the Officials' Report, after partnership had been defined and put into operation. The Governor therefore called a special session of the African Representative Council in December 1951 and asked the delegates to state whether they agreed or rejected the statement. He also invited them to join with Officials and Unofficials in the task of defining partnership. The Council dealt with the latter request first. Mr. Walubita, a delegate from the Southern Province, immediately moved that the Council did not wish to partake in any such discussions, and asked instead that the Government define partnership and submit the definition to the African advisory councils for comment.[1] There was always a

[1] *Proceedings of the African Representative Council*, December 1951, No. 8, col. 11.

tendency for the delegates to adopt the attitude that they were merely mouthpieces for the people they represented, and thus for them to avoid commenting on a controversial subject until they had consulted their 'constituents'. But on this occasion the tendency was strengthened by a unanimous feeling that the delegates from the Council to the Victoria Falls conference, by agreeing to the statement that Africans would agree to Federation after partnership had been defined and put into practice, had betrayed the views of the African people and enabled Mr. Oliver Lyttelton to proceed with plans for a further conference on Federation. Consequently the Council refused to participate in defining partnership—fearful lest this in turn might lead to a further advance towards Federation. And after a long and acrimonious debate, the delegates changed the statement that Africans 'would consider' to 'might consider' Federation, after partnership had been defined and put into practice.

Whether Africans were prepared to co-operate or not, the British Government was plainly intent on pressing forward with all possible speed. In the House of Commons the Colonial Secretary announced that he had invited Sir Godfrey Huggins and the Governors of Nyasaland and Northern Rhodesia to visit London in January 1952 for preparatory talks in connexion with the full Federation conference which was to be held in July. Mr. James Griffiths, principal Opposition spokesman on Colonial affairs, sharply expressed his disapproval: it was a mistake he felt, to hold yet another meeting with no Africans present, and moreover, broke a definite promise he had given at the second Victoria Falls conference. A renewed outburst of protest followed the January conference: for while the British Government reiterated once again that Amalgamation was not a political possibility in Central Africa, the conference had agreed to advance the date of the Federation conference from July to April. In the opinion of many members of the Opposition in the House of Commons, matters concerned with Federation were being indecently hurried.

Neither was this opinion unique to the Labour Party. Many influential sections of the Press were hostile to the Government's plain intention of reaching a decision on Federation with all possible speed. The Africa Bureau was formed specifically to expound the African's case against Federation and to provide in

London and elsewhere in the United Kingdom a public plat-
form for African spokesmen from Central Africa. It received
support from members of all political parties and other influential personalities with no political affiliations. The Federation issue was rapidly becoming of front-page importance, a
controversial Colonial subject in which, for the first time for
many years, a wide section of the British public felt themselves
involved.

In Northern Rhodesia meantime, the tempo of African opposition was quickening. The political leadership of the African
community had passed almost entirely into the hands of members of the African National Congress. When the first term of
the first two African members of the Legislature came to an end
in 1951, the Rev. Kasokolo and Mr. N. Namulango, both of
whom had always been moderate in their expressed opinions,
were displaced by two active members of the National Congress, Mr. Dauti Yamba and Mr. Pascale Sokota. Even in Congress the same trend was evident, for the first president, Mr.
Godwin Lewanika, was subsequently ousted by Mr. Harry
Nkumbula, who many years earlier had strongly opposed
Amalgamation (see Chapter 8, p. 114). Under Mr. Nkumbula's leadership, the National Congress quickly became a widespread organization, with organizing secretaries in each province and branches in even the remotest corner of the Territory.
Congress propaganda was directed particularly at chiefs and
Native Authorities, especially over land questions, a topic on
which both chiefs and commoners were particularly suscep-
tible. And a measure of their success was the sudden increase in
active opposition to Government-inspired measures, such as
contour ridging and general conservation work, which became
so strong in certain districts that Government officers had to be
withdrawn.

Symptomatic of the current mood was the following statement issued by Congress early in 1952. 'Realizing that the Tory
Government is about to attempt to force through Federation
against the unanimous wishes of the African people, in the absence of normal constitutional power to prevent such a move,
Congress adopts in principle mass protest action, and resolves to
begin a campaign to organize the people for such action.
Further, Congress appoints a Supreme Action Council of nine,

including five seats to be filled by the Trade Union Congress (African), to plan such action, this Council to be empowered to issue orders for action in the name of Congress up to and including the serious step of calling for a national stoppage of work. The Council shall have the power to call for mass action at any moment during the time of the Federation crisis that they think tactically wise.' As soon as the resolution was passed, Congress ordered all African men in the urban areas to send their women and children back to their villages, while Mr. Nkumbula was reported as saying that European lives would be made intolerable if Federation was imposed against the wishes of Africans.[2]

Against this background of strife, controversy, and publicity, the delegates to the Federation conference assembled at Lancaster House, London, in April under the joint chairmanship of the Marquess of Salisbury, Secretary of State for Commonwealth Relations, and Mr. Oliver Lyttelton, Secretary of State for the Colonies. Though Official and Unofficial representatives from the three Central African territories were present, there were no African delegates from the two Protectorates. They had been invited; indeed, delegates from both the African Representative Council in Northern Rhodesia and the African Protectorate Council in Nyasaland were actually in London at the time, and both had had informal discussions at the Colonial Office before the conference opened. But they refused the official invitation to attend as delegates, despite the Colonial Secretary's assurance that the Conference was not taking a decision on Federation, but merely drafting a constitution which would be promulgated for discussion. But almost every African in Northern Rhodesia was suspicious of the Government's intentions; hardly one was not opposed to Federation; hardly one who knew anything of politics but was convinced that by participating in the Victoria Falls conference Africans had enabled the British Government to proceed with Federation. It was not surprising that they should have refused to co-operate. Instead, the African delegates held meetings and conferences of their own in a widespread campaign of protest against what they described as the imposition of Federation.

While the conference was being held, Mr. James Griffiths

[2] Reported in *East Africa and Rhodesia*, 6 March 1952, pp. 787–8.

initiated a debate on the subject in the House of Commons, in which he again accused the Government of having decided on Federation in advance and of bulldozing it through regardless of opposition. And indeed the matter was already almost settled, for though Mr. Oliver Lyttelton announced during the debate that the draft constitution would not be binding, except in the sense that once agreed no party would be expected to withdraw from it unilaterally without discussion, the communiqué issued at the end of the conference stated that agreement had been reached on a draft constitutional scheme. The conference also recommended that three Commissions should be appointed as soon as possible by the Governments of the United Kingdom, Southern Rhodesia, Northern Rhodesia, and Nyasaland, to make detailed examinations of the financial consequences of Federation, the establishment of a Federal Civil Service, and the constitution and jurisdiction of a Federal Supreme Court. These Commissions were appointed in June 1952, and their reports were presented to Parliament by the Secretaries of State for the Colonies and Commonwealth Relations on 29 October. To allow adequate time for them to be studied, the British Government announced that the final conference on Federation would be convened in London on 1 January 1953.

By this time, support for and opposition to the proposals had crystallized into two groups, neither of which was swayed by the arguments advanced by the other. In the United Kingdom those against Federation felt that it was morally wrong for the British Government to create the new state in view of the expressed opposition of African leaders in the two Northern Protectorates and the special relationship in which the British Government stood to the indigenous population of Northern Rhodesia and Nyasaland. But the British Government and European leaders favouring Federation countered this by declaring that the overwhelming majority of the African population had no idea of what the proposals actually meant, and that African leaders, particularly in the National Congress movements in Northern Rhodesia and Nyasaland, were deliberately distorting the proposals so as to ensure that the African public rejected them. It was generally agreed, however, that Federation would bring economic benefits to the three individual states; and Mr. James Griffiths, on behalf of the Labour Government of the day, had endorsed the principle of Federation. Thus the central issue in the controversy was whether the opposition of the African communities in the two northern Protectorates was really justified.

The essence of the African case against Federation was that it would result in political power passing into the hands of the local European communities in general and that of Southern Rhodesia in particular; that this would inevitably lead to a deterioration in their status; a halting and even reversal of the measures of African advancement inaugurated by the Colonial Office; the loss of African reserved land, since the British Government would not be in a position to maintain its guarantees; and the creation in Central Africa of a state of affairs similar to that in the Union of South Africa. Over the question of land, Africans pointed out that in Northern Rhodesia some 225,050 square miles out of the total land surface of 287,640 square miles were reserved for African use; in Southern Rhodesia 50,701 square miles were reserved for African use, and 75,910 for European occupation. But only some 54,240 square miles of land in Northern Rhodesia were reserved specifically for African use in the form of Native Reserves, however; the remainder was Native Trust land. And the British Government was not in a position to grant Africans the absolute security they desired even if it agreed to convert all the Native Trust land into Native Reserves. In answer to a question in the African Representative Council, the Secretary for Native Affairs stated that 'there are companies who own the mineral rights in Native Reserves and Native Trust land. The rights of such persons, where in existence before the creation of either Native Trust land or Native Reserves, are preserved by article 8 (1) of the Northern Rhodesia (Crown Land and Native Reserves) Order-in-Council, 1928, or by article 6 (1) of the Northern Rhodesia (Native Trust Land) Order-in-Council, 1947.' While there were arrangements whereby compensation was to be paid for land alienated for mining developments, Native Authorities had no say whatsoever in any decision as to when or where such developments would occur, though the Secretary for Native Affairs promised that they would be consulted. In any case, no government could undertake to reserve absolutely and in perpetuity such a vast land area; provisions had to be made for game and forest reserves, and sites for hydro-electric schemes.

Of the other issues raised by African leaders in Northern Rhodesia for opposing Federation, the principal ones related to the racial discrimination practised in Southern Rhodesia; the industrial colour bar and in particular the Industrial Conciliation Act; the fact that no African trade unions had been formed, and indeed could not be formed; that there were no Africans in the Southern Rhodesian Legislature; that separate Black and White areas were defined by law; that Africans needed a multiplicity of passes in the urban areas; that the chiefs in Southern Rhodesia had no status, since the system of direct rule followed there had stripped them of power, dignity, and their traditional place in African society. The Industrial Conciliation Act of Southern Rhodesia certainly constituted an effective barrier to African advancement within industry in the urban centres, which were considered European. But was there any practical difference between the legal barrier erected in Southern Rhodesia and the *de facto* barrier constituted by the agreement between the copper-mining companies and the Northern Rhodesian Mine Workers' Union? Indeed, the copper mines in Northern Rhodesia constituted the largest single enterprise in the two countries. Consequently it could be argued that the industrial colour bar on the Copperbelt was far more onerous than the provisions of the Industrial Conciliation Act in Southern Rhodesia, for there was a greater development of secondary industry in the Colony and wide variations between the opportunities open to Africans as between one firm and another. Certainly no African trade unions had been formed in Southern Rhodesia; but it was extremely unlikely that any would have developed in Northern Rhodesia if the copper-mining industry had not existed, for it at once provided a more pressing need and enabled the African Mine Workers' Union to be more easily organized than would have been the case if its members had been spread across a multiplicity of industries situated in widely spaced urban centres. For with the exception of the African Railway Workers' Union, the other African unions in Northern Rhodesia were industrial organizations in hardly more than name. And in Southern Rhodesia, where the largest single unified industry was the railways, an African

industrial organization did exist and had been granted *de facto*
if not *de jure* recognition. In any case, while the Northern
Rhodesian African Mine Workers' Union had achieved improved conditions for its members, the vital problem of African
advancement remained.

As to racial discrimination in public places in Southern
Rhodesia, it could scarcely have been more serious or prevalent
than in the Northern territory. In every principal post office
Africans had either to enter by separate doors or were compelled to wait at the African counter, to be served as and when
the European counter clerk thought fit. In the smaller post
offices, consisting usually of one room, no Africans were allowed
to enter, but were compelled to wait outside to be served
through a hatch in the wall. In the banks there were either
separate entrances or completely separate facilities. No Africans
were allowed to enter the European-owned cinemas and restaurants in the 'European' part of the town; the European-
owned stores, which were often the only ones with a large
range of products on sale, were also barred to them. Service was
again through a grilled hatch in the wall. Should there be
Europeans in a store, then an African had to wait until they
were served, even though many of them had been sent by
European housewives! These matters had been graphically
outlined by Gore-Browne in his race-relations speech in 1946.
But matters had not changed perceptibly in the years following.

The residential areas in the urban centres of Northern
Rhodesia were also strictly segregated, the only Africans who
were allowed to live in a European residential zone being
domestic and personal servants who lived in little cottages tucked
behind the bungalows owned or occupied by Europeans. This
division into Black and White areas was not entrenched in law as
was the case in Southern Rhodesia under the Land Apportionment Act. However, the mining townships were under the direct
control of the mining companies, and in the other important
urban centres the local authority was controlled by the European residents in the town. In any case, there was no such thing
as a permanent African urban dweller in Northern Rhodesia,
since an African's period of residence was by law limited to
such time as he was in employment. As to Africans having to
carry passes in Southern Rhodesia, every African in the line of

rail urban areas in Northern Rhodesia had to carry a document indicating that he was in employment and had paid his poll tax; a resident in a municipal location had to carry a pass indicating this; and no African could enter the European portion of an urban area after dark without specific authorization. Any African not complying with these rules was liable to arrest.

With regard to the status and dignity of the chiefs, it was true that the Northern Rhodesian Administration considered them leaders of their people. But they were also Government servants, no less responsible for carrying out Government policy, in so far as it affected a particular Native Authority, than were the district commissioners. And while the Government was always at pains to appoint a chief from among the traditional tribal heirs to the chiefdom, likewise it had little compunction in dismissing one should he by any chance fail to carry out his responsibilities efficiently or oppose Government policy. Indeed, many of the chiefs were artificial creations, born of administrative convenience. And as administrative convenience changed, as when the Native Authorities were reorganized for example, many of them were discarded. In any case, the Northern Rhodesian Government's support for the traditional tribal authorities had often been condemned by many of the Africans who opposed Federation on the grounds that the status of the chiefs had been reduced in Southern Rhodesia.

What of the argument that the creation of the Federation would give the European minorities permanent political power in Central Africa? Under the Federal constitution, as prepared by the London conference in January 1953,[3] the legislative powers of the Federation, designated the Federation of Rhodesia and Nyasaland, were vested in a Federal Legislature, which consisted of a Governor-General, as the authority empowered to assent to Bills, and a Federal Assembly. The latter was to consist of a Speaker, to be chosen by the Assembly from within or without the House, and thirty-five members, made up of twenty-six elected members, six specially elected African members, and three European members charged with special responsibilities for African interests. Of the elected members, fourteen seats were allocated to Southern Rhodesia, eight to Northern Rhodesia, and four to Nyasaland. While the Federal

[3] *The Federal Scheme* (H.M.S.O., February 1953), Cmd. 8754.

Assembly was empowered to pass legislation defining voting qualifications for Federal elections, subject to the Bill being passed by an affirmative vote of two-thirds of the total membership of the Assembly, excluding the Speaker, and reservation for the signification of Her Majesty's pleasure, the first general election was based on the franchise laws governing election to the Territorial legislatures. Nyasaland was excluded from these provisions until such date as the Nyasaland Legislative Council passed a resolution making them effective, since there were no direct elections in the Protectorate. For the first Federal general election therefore, the elected members from both Southern and Northern Rhodesia were bound to be European, since the high franchise qualifications in those Territories excluded all but a handful of Africans. Moreover, no Africans in Northern Rhodesia, even if fulfilling the means and educational qualifications, could vote unless they first became British subjects by naturalization. When the regulations governing elections in Nyasaland were published the franchise qualifications were broadly the same as in the two Rhodesias; but they applied only to non-Africans.

African representation in the Federal Assembly was to be effected by two Africans and one European representing African interests from each Territory. Those Africans from the two Protectorates were to be elected by bodies 'representative of Africans', in reality the African Representative Council in Northern Rhodesia and the African Protectorate Council in Nyasaland, while the two Europeans representing African interests were to be nominated by the respective Governors. In the case of Southern Rhodesia, Africans and the European representing African interests were to be elected by voters registered on the common roll. Each voter thus had three votes: for the elected constituency member; for one of the African members, two special constituencies, Mashonaland and Matabeleland, being created for the purpose; and for the European representing African interests. Because of the composition of the common roll, the two African members and the European representing African interests would all be elected by European voters. Thus of the thirty-five members in the Federal Assembly, the twenty-six elected members would be Europeans, while the two Africans and the European representing African interests from Southern Rhodesia would be elected by Europeans.

But the Federal Assembly was constitutionally limited to legislating for a specific range of subjects. These included defence, external affairs, economic and financial matters; services such as railways, posts and telegraphs, and civil aviation; agriculture in Southern Rhodesia, exclusive of forestry, irrigation, and African agriculture; primary and secondary education for non-Africans; and higher education for all races. Hence the Federal Assembly was primarily responsible for economic matters and subjects specifically non-African. All matters directly affecting African affairs were left within the jurisdiction of the Territorial Legislatures.

Moreover, to protect African interests within the sphere for which the Federal Legislature was responsible, a standing committee of the Federal Assembly was created, known as the African Affairs Board, which consisted of the three Europeans representing African interests and one African member from each territory selected by a majority vote of all those directly concerned with representing African interests. A chairman and deputy chairman were to be selected by the Governor-General from among the members of the Board. Under the constitution, the African Affairs Board was empowered to make representations to the Federal Prime Minister, or through him to the Executive Council, on any matter within the competence of the Federal Government which the Board considered desirable in African interests. In particular, it was to draw attention to any Bill introduced into the Federal Assembly which, in the Board's opinion, differentiated against Africans by making them subject or liable to any disadvantageous conditions to which Europeans were not subjected. Any Bill passed by the Federal Assembly which the Board considered differentiated against Africans had to be reserved for the signification of Her Majesty's pleasure and referred to 'a Secretary of State, together with the Bill'.

Finally, constitutional amendments were required to be passed by an affirmative vote of two-thirds of the total membership of the Federal Assembly, excluding the Speaker, and then to be reserved by the Governor-General for the signification of Her Majesty's pleasure. Furthermore, Her Majesty's assent to a constitutional Bill was required to be signified by Order-in-Council if one of the Territorial Legislatures objected to a Bill, or if requested by the African Affairs Board on the grounds that it was a differentiating measure. The power to amend the constitution by Federal law included the power to establish and constitute a second chamber of the Federal Legislature and to prescribe its functions. No Bill amending the constitution by changing the Legislative Lists wherein the spheres of responsibility of the Federal and Territorial Legislatures were defined could be introduced into the Federal Assembly until after ten years of the Federal constitution coming into force, unless a draft of the Bill was laid before each Territorial Legislature and each passed a resolution stating that it did not object to the Bill being introduced into the Federal Assembly. Finally, a constitutional review conference was to be held within seven and not more than nine years of the constitution coming into force, to be attended by delegates chosen by the Governments of the Federation, each of the constituent territories, and the United Kingdom.

There was no denying therefore that the Federal Assembly could and probably would be dominated by the bloc of European elected members; moreover, their combined votes constituted more than the requisite two-thirds majority required to amend the constitution. Balancing this, however, was the fact that the Federal Assembly could only legislate for matters primarily of non-African interest, and that even then there were safeguards against discriminatory measures. Moreover, the British Government and the three Central African Governments agreed that Amalgamation was not a constitutional possibility; that the Protectorate status of Northern Rhodesia and Nyasaland was to continue: and that the pledges given by the British Government, especially in respect of African land rights in the two Protectorates, would not be infringed by Federation.

The Federal constitution, in other words, was an almost perfect mirror reflection of the existing constitutional position in Northern Rhodesia. The Federal Assembly had been given responsibility for a range of subjects which either directly concerned Europeans or were of an economic nature; in Northern Rhodesia elected European members had been given responsibility for groups of Government departments on broadly the same basis. Elected members dominated the Federal Assembly, as did the Unofficials the Northern Rhodesian Legislature. Why then were African leaders in Northern Rhodesia so adamantly opposed to the creation of the Federation? Because the British Government's plain intention of pressing forward with Federation finally shattered an African illusion: their belief that the British Government and the Officials of the Northern Rhodesian Government could protect African interests and ensure that Northern Rhodesia became a Native state on the same pattern as the Gold Coast in West Africa. It came as the culmination to a series of disillusioning events: the demand for responsible government, the indecision of the Labour Government in the face of increasing European pressure for emancipation from the Colonial Office, and finally the Officials' Report recommending that Northern Rhodesia should be joined politically with Southern Rhodesia. True, the official policy of the Federation was to be racial partnership: it was enshrined in the preamble to the constitution. But where in the Rhodesias did Africans see any sign of it? In these circumstances they were not unnaturally bewildered, angry, and disillusioned.

The fundamental fact was that the centre of gravity of power had shifted from London to Central Africa. Despite the experiences of the last two Secretaries of State when the Labour Government was in office, this was not appreciated by the Labour Party generally. Mr. Creech Jones, who took a leading part in the anti-Federation campaign outside the House of Commons, even argued that 'it is important to remember that the Africans in Nyasaland and Northern Rhodesia are not conquered subjects: their lands have not yielded to our arms . . . no political scheme can be enforced affecting their territories without their consent. The two northern territories are in fact Protectorates, and British control is only by invitation and treaty. Their status cannot be evaded. The treaties with the African chiefs include the concession to the British South Africa Company, which in 1900 stipulated it to be a treaty or alliance between the Barotse nation and the Government of Queen Victoria.' [4]

That Northern Rhodesia and Nyasaland were British Protectorates was incontrovertible. But to argue that British control over them had been established by invitation only; that no force of arms had been used; and that because of this, no change in the political status of either territory could be made without

---

[4] *African Challenge, the Fallacy of Federation*, A. Creech Jones (Africa Bureau, 1952).

the consent of their respective African populations, was, considering their early history, scarcely justified. The only treaty between the British South Africa Company and a Native potentate in Northern Rhodesia which had been recognized by the British Government was that signed with Lewanika, Paramount Chief of the Barotse. But had Mr. Creech Jones forgotten so quickly the background to this concession revealed in the mineral royalties debates in the Northern Rhodesian Legislature? In the first place it was doubtful whether, under tribal customary law, the chief of a tribe could sign away mineral and land rights without the consent of his people, since these assets were vested in him as trustee for the tribe as a whole. The Rev. Kasokolo, one of the African members, had spoken in the Legislature in support of this view. But Lewanika signed away not merely his own people's heritage; he had signed away those of every other tribe in Northern Rhodesia. Did Mr. Creech Jones seriously argue that British trusteeship over Ngoniland had been at the request of Mpezeni? As to obtaining the consent of the African people to any change in the political status of the territory, was there any citable precedent for this? As Mr. Welensky pointed out, were the African people consulted in 1924, when the responsibility for administering the territory was transferred from the British South Africa Company to the British Government? Indeed, the very fact that the British South Africa Company, a commercial company controlled ultimately by shareholders, had been responsible for the administration of the Territory scarcely suggests any great concern for the welfare of the African people.

In Nyasaland the Jumbe treaty was cited in support of the argument that no political change could be effected without the consent of the African people. Mr. Henry Hopkinson, Minister of State for the Colonies, took the treaty with him when he toured Northern Rhodesia and Nyasaland in August and September 1952. It read:

'The Marquess of Salisbury, Her Britannic Majesty's Principal Secretary of State for Foreign Affairs, is commanded by Her Majesty, the Queen of the United Kingdom, of Great Britain, and Ireland, the Empress of India, etc., etc., etc., to state that the Letters addressed to Her Majesty by the Chief Jumbe on the 3rd day of Shewal. . . . have arrived safely. Her Majesty

and Her Government have learnt from them with much satisfaction the friendly relations which exist between Jumbe and
Mr. Johnston, the Representative of Her Majesty's Government
in Nyasaland. Mr. Johnston has also reported in the same sense.
It is the wish of the Queen and Her Government that this state
of things continue, and that the Chiefs of Nyasaland may always
be guided in peace and prosperity by the advice which they
may receive from Her Majesty's Government.' [5]

The letter was dated the Foreign Office, 15 August 1892. It
could scarcely be construed as a treaty: certainly not a document binding the British Government to accept the advice of
the Nyasaland chiefs as to their future, political or otherwise.
Indeed, the last sentence gave quite the opposite impression.

Emotional sympathy with the African, the under-privileged
of Central Africa, was understandable. But the crucial issue
was not whether the British Government, by agreeing to
Federation, was abandoning its responsibilities and handing the
Africans in Northern Rhodesia and Nyasaland over to the re-
pressive policies of the European minorities; it was whether, by
agreeing to Federation, the British Government was utilizing
its remaining power and influence in Central Africa to strike
the best bargain it could in view of its African responsibilities.
In Southern Rhodesia political power was exclusively in the
hands of the European settler community; and Sir Godfrey
Huggins, the Prime Minister, had already said that unless
Federation was implemented quickly, the Colony would have
no choice but to seek independence. In the event of Federation
failing and Southern Rhodesia having to stand alone, the resulting loss of confidence among Europeans in Southern Rhodesia
might force them to look to the Union of South Africa for support. This could scarcely augur good from the point of view of
the Africans in Southern Rhodesia. In the event of Federation
failing, the European population in Northern Rhodesia would
have pressed for self-government as quickly as possible, which
would have led to increased friction between the Unofficials and
the Officials and to the Unofficials wresting more power from
the British Government, as they had on numerous other occasions in the past. The problem in Nyasaland, as far as the
British Government was concerned, was primarily economic.

[5] *The Rhodesian*, op. cit., p. 158.

186   RACE AND POLITICS

Scenically beautiful, Nyasaland was geographically isolated and economically poor. It possessed no mineral deposits on the scale of Northern Rhodesia, while its cash crops were developed only on a small extent. Any prospect for substantial economic expansion in Nyasaland, it could reasonably be argued, would only come from the Protectorate being linked with the two Rhodesias. And while its communications with them were poor (the main road from Southern Rhodesia passed through Portuguese East Africa), nevertheless they were the strongest bonds Nyasaland had with any of its neighbours. At the same time Europeans in Southern Rhodesia were apprehensive about Nyasaland. A large percentage of the migrant workers on which the Colony's economy depended came from Nyasaland. If the Protectorate was allowed to develop under the Colonial Office it would eventually become a Native state, a development unwelcome to Southern Rhodesia for both political and economic reasons.

By agreeing to establish the new state with all possible speed, the Conservative Government ended the prevailing mood of political uncertainty. In the field of race relations, they persuaded the European leaders to accept that the principle of 'racial partnership' should be written into the preamble to the constitution, and that Africans should be directly represented in the Federal Assembly, a startling innovation for Southern Rhodesia, where no Africans sat in the Legislature and where, since there were a greater number of Southern Rhodesian subjects on the Federal Legislative List, the responsibilities of the Federal Government were more extensive than in the two Protectorates. Moreover, by persuading the European leaders to agree that the Federal constitution should not be reviewed until at least seven years after its inception, the British Government was able to maintain its position in the Protectorates and in Central Africa generally for a longer period than might otherwise have been the case. And while the concept of partnership was not defined, its moral influence was not to be underestimated, for it provided an alternative ideal to apartheid, with its associations of racial separation and repression.

As the Federation campaign mounted—for there were Europeans in Southern Rhodesia frightened by partnership— so there was a corresponding realization among African political leaders in Northern Rhodesia that the only way to protect their interests was through sharing political power with the European settlers. When Mr. Griffiths toured the Territory in 1951 he was presented with a seven-point memorandum by the Kitwe branch of the Northern Rhodesian African National Congress. It demanded the institution of universal adult suffrage; reinstitution of the policy of African paramountcy; increased African representation in the legislature; removal of all forms of colour bar and segregation; assistance in higher education to enable Africans to take degrees; African members of the Legislative Council to be given portfolios; and the continuance of Colonial Office rule until such time as Africans were in a position to demand self-government on their own terms.[6] By the time Federation was implemented, these points formed the basis for African political leaders' demands. Mr. L. N'gandu, speaking in the African Representative Council, was to put the position succinctly: 'I think, Sir, and I contend that a fair award would have been this: Federation for the European and equal representation for the African.' [7]

That the decision on whether Federation would be created or not depended on the European voters in Southern Rhodesia was the final African disillusionment—the final Federation conference agreed that there should be a referendum among the voters registered on the Southern Rhodesian common voters' roll. With the referendum establishing the reality of Federation, the final vote in the referendum was 25,580 in favour of Federation and 14,929 against, African aggressiveness in Northern Rhodesia reached its climax. On 22 May 1953 Mr. Dixon Konkola, the President of the African Railway Workers' Union and an active member of the Northern Rhodesian African National Congress, led a group of Africans into what was the European section of the Broken Hill post office and demanded to be served. It proved to be the first of a series of direct attacks launched by Congress on racial discrimination in public places. Attempts were made to boycott certain European-owned butchers' shops in the towns along the line of rail, on the dual grounds of the bad quality of the meat sold to Africans and the

[6] Reported in *East Africa and Rhodesia*, 20 September 1951, p. 42.
[7] *Proceedings of the African Representative Council*, Nos. 11, 12–15, December 1953, and 11–13, January 1954, col. 149.

practice of serving them through hatches in the wall. The truth of both complaints was incontrovertible. A variety of cheap meat known locally as 'boys' meat was sold for African consumption, though meat was often scarcely a correct description, the parcels usually consisting of bones, old pieces of meat, and refuse not normally saleable. Furthermore, they were pre-wrapped so that Africans could not see what they were buying; and anyone demanding that the packets should be opened received very short shrift from the European butchers. It was in any case difficult to argue or protest when the butcher was on one side of a wire grille and the customer on the other. Such boycotts frequently took a militant form, with Congress pickets seizing any purchases made by Africans and destroying them by trampling on them in the street. Occasionally violence was used. This aspect of the boycotts was used in many quarters to condemn them, and the Government took measures to protect any purchaser who wished to use the shops, which were interpreted by Congress as deliberate attempts to break the boycott.

The outcome, however, was to focus public attention on such acts of discrimination, and steps began to be taken to modify them. Partnership in the context of Black–White relationships had become the currency of the Federation (which officially came into existence on 23 October 1953), and while the evidence of every urban centre showed that, at best, partnership was a future possibility, once the word was used, it was impossible for Europeans to defend such practices without defeating one of the arguments they themselves had used to justify Federation.

Within a comparatively short time of the Federation being created, tension relaxed in Northern Rhodesia. This was true of the rural areas in particular. In the Northern Rhodesian African Representative Council meeting of July 1953, Mr. D. Siwale, a tribal councillor from the Abercorn district of the Northern Province, had stated that 'one wonders how this Federal Government is going to work, because it is going to be imposed against the wishes of the people of this country. I am afraid it is going to be a police state, because it is going to be forced by the police, for the Africans will not comply with Federal laws.' [8] But there was no influx of settlers from South-

[8] *Proceedings of the African Representative Council*, No. 10 July 1953, col. 106.

ern Rhodesia: district officers and district commissioners continued with their round of duty in exactly the same way. With the principal fears of the rural dwellers proving thus unfounded, the united front displayed by African leaders during the anti-Federation campaign began to break, as the differences between Congress leaders and the traditional tribal authorities began once again to assume importance. Moreover, the division was actively encouraged by the Government, in that pressure was brought on the chiefs and tribal leaders to ban Congress activities in their districts. Passions quickly subsided in the towns, too, for similar reasons, and although this did not imply a change of heart in the African public generally regarding Federation, Congress bluff had been called. An illiterate and generally apathetic public had been roused to expect certain dire consequences: their failure to materialize consequently deflated interest.

The old sources of suspicion and discontent continued, however, and these Congress worked on assiduously, using them wherever possible to stir strife and maintain tension. In the rural areas this was most easily done in such areas as the Tonga and Ngoni chieftaincies, where problems associated with overcrowding and land alienation had caused long-standing suspicion of Government and settler motives. And though the chiefs were aware that Congress was a potential usurper of their authority, suspicion of Government intentions kept them uneasily balanced between the one and the other, neither able to give active support to measures for soil conservation nor to discourage Congress activities in their districts. But the rural areas rarely provided Congress with good publicity; and the hiatus following the implementation of Federation, extremely damaging to Congress prestige in the eyes of the general African public, meant that Congress activities had to be kept constantly before both Black and White. Hence Congress continued to organize boycotts and to lead attempts to break or reduce the incidence of discrimination in public places in the urban areas, for such action undoubtedly had the support of a wide section of the African public and was inevitably accompanied by intense publicity.

The culmination came in April 1956, when Congress ordered Africans in Lusaka to boycott certain Asian and European stores trading almost exclusively with African customers. The boycott was immediately successful, and business in the African trading area quickly came to an almost complete standstill. The boycott was introduced, explained Mr. Nkumbula, the President-General, in order to redress African consumers' complaints that they were being exploited by the shops in question. From Lusaka the boycott was gradually extended until almost all those shops dealing primarily with African customers in all the main urban centres were affected. It was so effective and of such a duration, that many of the store-keepers were brought to the brink of ruin.

A storm of protest broke over the Northern Rhodesian Government's head over their handling of the matter. Demands were voiced that Congress should be banned completely; the Government was accused of being too 'soft' with the African. Eventually the Northern Rhodesian Government did institute proceedings in the case of the boycott at Mufulira. Several members of Congress, including the president and deputy president of the organization in the Western Province and the chairman and secretary of the Mufulira district, were arrested on the grounds that the boycott was a malicious conspiracy in which Africans were counselled, exhorted, or induced to withhold custom from traders. All legitimate grievances of the African consumers could have been represented to traders through the auspices of the Mufulira African Urban Advisory Council or some other official channel; in particular, it was pointed out that three of the defendants were members of the Urban Advisory Council. During the trial it was shown that the Urban Advisory Council had been trying for some two and a half years to seek a meeting with the Mufulira Chamber of Commerce, but that no meeting had taken place. On 23 May 1956 the local branch of Congress sent a letter to the Chamber setting out African complaints in detail. But the Chamber refused to meet a Congress delegation, though agreeing to meet the local Urban Advisory Council, a meeting which occurred after the boycott had begun. Only two grievances raised by Congress were discussed at the meeting, and no progress was made. One of the principal African complaints was that bags of maize meal were delivered free to European but not African customers, although the price to both was the same. The Chamber of Commerce refused to do this for African customers unless there was an increase in price to them. Other complaints were the rudeness of European shop assistants; shopping through window hatches; short weight; and the low standard of the meat sold to Africans. Most of these complaints were substantiated at the trial. The magistrate reserved his decision for a week, and then discharged the accused, stating that he had no hesitation in saying that the boycotters had sufficient justification for their action. The evidence showed that the object of the boycott was to redress customers' grievances, and not to force recognition of Congress.

In addition to the Congress-inspired boycott of the shops, the Copperbelt had been wracked with strikes for months; numerous incidents of Africans stoning European-occupied cars had occurred, particularly after accidents involving Africans; and finally, a riot took place on the Nchanga mine after an African had been injured in an accident with a machine driven by a European. Eventually the Acting Governor was forced to declare a state of emergency in the whole of the Western Province, and to arrest numerous members of the Northern Rhodesian African Mine Workers' Union.

These developments silenced the anti-Federal and anti-Southern Rhodesian sentiments which had been expressed by certain sections of the European community in Northern Rhodesia subsequent to Federation, and which had their origin in the belief that Northern Rhodesia, rich from the high price of copper, was being 'milked' by her poor neighbour, since Southern Rhodesia was widely regarded as 'bankrupt' north of the Zambesi. Colour was given to these views by the dispute over the Kariba hydro-electric scheme. Prior to the inception of the Federation, the three Territorial Governments had signed an agreement acknowledging that the Kafue hydro-electric scheme in Northern Rhodesia was to have priority over the Kariba project. In the circumstances this was inevitable: the financing of the Kariba project was beyond the means of any of the individual states, while without Federation and the acceleration in the pace of economic development which was expected to result from it, there was no guarantee that the power output from the project could be absorbed. The Kafue project, on the other hand, could be financed by the Northern Rhodesian Government and would meet the territory's power needs, particularly those of the Copperbelt. Once Federation was achieved, the situation changed. In terms of the power needs of the Copperbelt and Southern Rhodesia, the larger Kariba project was more important; moreover, the new state had sufficient borrowing potential to make the financing of Kariba a possibility. In Northern Rhodesia, however, the Federal Government's decision to give Kariba priority over the Kafue project was widely regarded as yet another instance of the way Southern Rhodesians were dominating and influencing the Federal Government.

But with the boycott and industrial unrest on the Copperbelt there were demands that the powers of the Federal Government should be strengthened; that in particular the Federal authorities should be immediately made responsible for the maintenance of law and order. At the same time European pressure for the Federation to be granted independence mounted. Such expressions were supported in Southern Rhodesia. Mr. Garfield Todd, successor to Sir Godfrey Huggins as Southern Rhodesian Prime Minister, took the unusual step of publicly commenting on the situation in the northern Protectorates. 'I don't think we can be blamed if we stand aghast when confronted with certain political developments in the northern territories of the Federation,' he declared. 'If Dominion status is good for New Zealand and the Gold Coast . . . then I believe it is good for Africans, the Europeans, all in the Federation. I will be fully prepared to consult and work together to attain Dominion status.' [9]

European opinion in the Federation, inflamed by events in Northern Rhodesia and the constant and vociferous opposition to Federation expressed by African political leaders in Nyasaland, was further exacerbated when Lord Malvern (Sir Godfrey Huggins was raised to the peerage in 1955), the Federal Prime Minister announced that his request for a further advance in the constitutional status of the Federation had been rejected by the British Government. His demand had not been for complete independence, but for amendments to the existing constitution so that the Federal Government would be made

[9] Africa Digest, September–October 1956, Vol. IV, No. 2, p. 51.

completely independent in those spheres for which it was already responsible. The existing constitutions of the constituent territories within the Federation would remain unaltered.[10] Lord Malvern pointed out that since 'this part of the world' had long been represented at Commonwealth Prime Ministers' conferences—he had just returned from one—initially through the Prime Minister of Southern Rhodesia and latterly through the Prime Minister of the Federation, feeling among the electorate would run very high unless something were done.

African reaction to Lord Malvern's statement was sharp. Mr. W. M. Chirwa, an African M.P. from Nyasaland in the Federal Assembly, immediately cabled the Secretary of State for the Colonies praying that Britain would not betray African interests, as was the case when Federation was imposed, and pointing out that Africans in Nyasaland were opposed to the Federal Government and desired secession from the Federation. 'We are determined to achieve self-government by constitutional means as soon as possible,' Mr. Chirwa concluded.

Within the space of three years of Federation being implemented, therefore, the European communities were demanding the immediate strengthening of the Federal Government's powers and the granting of complete independence at the earliest possible opportunity. African leaders in Nyasaland not only continued vehemently to oppose the Federal Government: they were openly demanding that Nyasaland should be allowed to secede from the Federal state. And within a short space of time this demand was reiterated by the Northern Rhodesian African National Congress and eventually by the African Representative Council. Once again, therefore, the political demands of the African and European communities in the two Protectorates were diametrically opposed. From the point of view of racial harmony, this could hardly be described as encouraging; but neither was it surprising. For Federation had done little to bridge the gap between the views of the two races in the Protectorates about future constitutional development. The preamble to the Federation constitution stated that 'the association of the three Territories under Her Majesty's

[10] *East Africa and Rhodesia*, 9 August 1956, p. 1761.

sovereignty . . . would conduce to the security of, advancement, and welfare of all the inhabitants, and in particular
would foster partnership and co-operation between their inhabitants.' [11] In the circumstances, these words rang a little
hollow.

[11] Cmd. 8754, p. 5.

CHAPTER 14

CONCEPTS OF PARTNERSHIP

THE crux of the racial problem in Northern Rhodesia is the question of standards. Which of two widely different sets is to form the basis for national life? After the Victoria Falls conference convened by Mr. James Griffiths in 1951 the Northern Rhodesian Government published a draft definition of partnership to clarify the concept. Part of it read: 'The ultimate political objective for the people of Northern Rhodesia is self-government within the Commonwealth; self-government must take full account of the rights and interests of both Africans and Europeans and include proper provision for both. The only satisfactory basis on which such provision can be secured is economic and political partnership between the races. The application of such partnership in practice must ensure that Africans are helped forward along the path of social, economic and political progress on which their feet have already been set, so that they may take their full part with the rest of the community in the economic and political life of the Territory. Africans for their part must be willing to accept the responsibilities as well as the privileges which such advancement entails.

'There can be no question of the Government of Northern Rhodesia subordinating the interests of any section of the community to those of any other section. The application of partnership is not inconsistent with and does not in any way interfere with the Territory's Protectorate status. It imposes on each of the two sections, Europeans and Africans, an obligation to recognize the right of the other section to a permanent home in Northern Rhodesia.

'Partnership implies that any constitutional arrangement must include proper provision for both European and African and proper safeguards for their rights and interests. Generally, partnership implies that Europeans and Africans will pay due regard to each other's outlook, belief, customs and legitimate aspirations and anxieties. In the political sphere, Africans will be able to advance until ultimately (so long as representation on racial grounds remains) they have the same numbers as Europeans in both the Legislative and Executive Councils, when they are fit for this. In the economic field, every individual must be able to rise to the level that his energy, ability, qualifications and character permit. As regards discriminatory practices based on racial distinctions, these are incompatible with the policy of partnership, and the trend of public opinion is towards a clear recognition of this fact.' [1]

There are several important features to note in this definition. No attempt was made to define standards; but by implication, since Africans were to be helped along the paths of economic, social, and political progress, the Black man was regarded as different from and inferior to the White man. Representation in the political sphere was to be racial, therefore, the hypothesis that neither race should dominate the other finding expression in the concept of parity between African and European representatives. But the definition did state unequivocally that racial discrimination was contrary to the philosopy of racial partnership, and that, in the economic sphere, every person was to be allowed to reach a level based on ability and training.

Sir Roy Welensky [2] subsequently filled in some of the gaps in the Government's definition. During the first Federal election campaign he said: 'The Federal Party [3] was determined to see that there was no lowering of European standards, which meant that Africans must exert themselves if they wished to rise to a higher level. In the political field, the African could enjoy only such a share of political control as he was capable of earning by demonstrating that he had attained civilized standards of behaviour and culture.' [4]

A multitude of questions occur immediately. What, for instance, did Welensky mean by 'European standards'? As a trade unionist he would no doubt agree that the wages, salaries,

---

[1] *East Africa and Rhodesia*, 17 April 1952, p. 979.

[2] He was knighted in the Queen's Birthday Honours List in 1953.

[3] Sir Roy Welensky and Sir Godfrey Huggins formed the Federal Party, subsequent to the affirmative vote of the Southern Rhodesian referendum, to fight all the elected seats in the Federation.

[4] Reported in *East Africa and Rhodesia*, 22 October 1953, p. 198.

and general level of material well-being of the European community should be protected and preserved. Under what conditions can this be achieved? Only—in the long term—if a majority of the inhabitants of the country are raised to a level of material prosperity akin to that characteristic of the White community. And this can only occur if there is either massive European immigration, or a socio-economic revolution designed to transform African living standards and African concepts of living, or by some combination of the two. In 1953 the White population of Northern Rhodesia was 49,000 and the African 1,960,000. To preserve European material standards by large-scale White immigration therefore involves raising the European population to at least several hundred thousand. Moreover, by the very nature of the problem, this has to be done quickly. In the eight years from 1945 to 1953, eight years in which European immigration had been at an unprecedently high level, the White population increased by 28,000—an annual increase of 3,500. In the same period the African population had swelled by 330,000, or by 41,000 every year.

What, then, of a large scale socio-economic revolution designed to raise African standards? The country is held in the strait-jacket of racial land divisions, and the only way this can be overcome—unless British pledges regarding African reserves and Native Trust land are to be broken—is for Africans to be assured of security politically by means of parity of representation. This would, of course, be opposed most strongly by the settler community; even the Northern Rhodesian Government in its draft definition of partnership had said that Africans might achieve parity eventually, when they were fit for it. But leaving aside these questions for a moment, is a socio-economic revolution possible on the scale necessary? Europeans are outnumbered 2,000,000 to 50,000. And as Sir John Moffat, chairman of the African Affairs Board wrote: 'The average income of Africans in employment in 1956 was approximately £70 per annum. The average income of all adult Africans will . . . be far lower than this. The average European income for that same year was about £1,100.' [5] (Sir John was referring

[5] Contained in Sir J. Moffat's letter, as chairman of the African Affairs Board, to the Speaker of the Federal Assembly asking for the Federal Electoral Bill to be reserved. Quoted in *East Africa and Rhodesia*, 20 February 1958, p. 790.

to the Federation as a whole, and not to Northern Rhodesia.) Finance on a gigantic scale would be needed. Which government or international agency would provide it? And how is such a revolution—or massive European immigration—to be supported by economic expansion? In view of the nature of the Northern Rhodesian economy, economic expansion—at least initially—would have to be based on expanded primary production. But the possibilities for developing high-priced cash crops, such as coffee or cotton, are extremely limited, both by virtue of unsuitable soil and climatic conditions and the distance Northern Rhodesia lies from the sea. Indeed, the only region of agricultural potential is the Kafue Flats, the seasonally flooded plains astride the Kafue river. In a pamphlet [6] outlining these potentialities the Rhodesian Selection Trust group, one of the two major groups of mining companies with interests in the copper-mining industry (which has financed investigations into the problem of developing the Flats), suggested that 450,000 acres could be empoldered and some 3,000 European-type and 20,000 African-type farms established, absorbing in all 15,000 African and European farmers and their families. But no development was envisaged before 1967; and the cost would be an estimated £90,000,000 at 1955 prices. The net national income of Northern Rhodesia at factor cost in 1954 was only £93,900,000. The only other possible type of economic development would be the extensive exploitation of mineral deposits on the pattern of the Copperbelt. Mines could then be opened and the present thinly scattered population concentrated into limited zones which would provide markets for agricultural produce and for the development of secondary industry. But while extensive exploration work has been continuously undertaken, no such deposits have been found.

From these preliminary considerations it becomes clear that it is quite impossible to raise a majority of the inhabitants of Northern Rhodesia to a standard of material prosperity equal to that enjoyed by the existing European population. This being so, how then are the Europeans to protect their standards? This problem has occurred *par excellence* in the copper-mining industry. By virtue of his training, the European occupied all

[6] *Kafue Flats—The Granary of the Federation?*—a pamphlet issued by the Rhodesian Selection Trust group, 1959.

the skilled and semi-skilled positions in the industry. And while insisting that African advancement was not opposed, the only condition on which the European Union was prepared to accept it was on the basis of equal pay for equal work. Moreover, by virtue of the closed-shop clause in the agreement with the mining companies, the Union had been able to ensure that this was not infringed. The mining companies recognized that industrial peace on the Copperbelt depended on conceding African advancement, but insisted that it was not practical on the conditions laid down by the European Union, since Africans worked more slowly than Europeans and needed a greater degree of supervision. The first result of the principle of equal pay for equal work, therefore—and it is a principle at the very root of the Europeans' concept of partnership—was that African advancement in the copper-mining industry was effectively blocked. But African frustration had reached such a pitch by 1953 that the matter could no longer be safely disregarded. As an independent conciliator in a dispute between the African Union and the copper-mining companies wrote in 1953: 'Satisfactory and harmonious industrial relations on the Copperbelt will not be attained unless or until effective steps have been taken to enable the African workers to advance to positions of greater responsibility and importance than those which are now open to them.'.[7] Discussions between the companies and the unions were subsequently re-opened, and when these failed, a commission of inquiry was appointed by the Northern Rhodesian Government. It too pointed to the urgent need for a solution.[8]

Eventually one of the two major groups of copper-mining companies, the Rhodesian Selection Trust, announced its intention of giving the European Union six months' notice of terminating its contract with European daily paid labour, unless an agreement covering African advancement was reached within that period. The group was prepared to accept the dictum of equal basic pay for work of equal value, provided the European Union accepted the need to amend the schedules of

[7] Quoted in the *Report of the Board of Inquiry appointed to Inquire into the Advancement of Africans in the Copper Mining Industry in Northern Rhodesia* (Government Printer Lusaka, 1954), p. 9.
[8] *Board of Inquiry Report, 1954*, op. cit., see p. 29.

200   RACE AND POLITICS

occupations and minimum basic rates in such a way that work which could reasonably be considered to be within the capacity of African workers could be provided from within the European field at rates of pay which would have due regard for the value of each job. Of the job categories removed from the European schedule, the first series would be included in the African schedule, since they were considered to be within the immediate capacity of the African. The second, which would constitute an intermediate field of employment, would be simplified and subdivided, so that they could be performed by Africans after a period of training. Rates for such jobs would be fixed with reference to those of the European, by negotiation first with the European Union, and secondly with the African workers' organization. Where their value to the employer when performed by an African was equal to the value when performed by a European, the companies undertook to pay the same rate of pay and to guarantee equal facilities and amenities. The Rhodesian Selection Trust group estimated that 170 Europeans would be displaced at Mufulira and 147 at the Roan Antelope mine, and that 137 job categories for African advancement would be created at the former and 191 at the latter mines. The group guaranteed that no Europeans would be discharged as a result of these measures, and that every European displaced would be reabsorbed, either by promotion or through alternative employment at the same rate of pay.

Agreement between both the major mining groups and the European Mine Workers' Union was eventually reached over African advancement on the basis of these proposals. The Anglo-American group of companies first signed an agreement whereby these interim arrangements were to last for three years, following which the question would be reopened on the basis of a report produced by an independent firm of consultants who were to prepare an objective analysis of the responsibilities, skill, and training in every job category undertaken by members of the European Union. In an accompanying statement, however, the group announced that no Africans would be advanced without the prior consent of that organization. The Rhodesian Selection Trust refused to concede this, arguing that it virtually gave the European mine workers a veto over African advancement, and thereby tended to reproduce the South

African pattern of industrial employment in Northern Rhodesia. An agreement was eventually signed with the European Union on broadly the same lines, but without any stipulation that it would be consulted over African advancement. Mr. R. Prain, chairman of the Rhodesian Selection Trust group of companies, stated that the feature of their plan would be 'the completion of the intermediate field for Africans and agreement on a permanent field of employment open to all union members (of the European Union) as at present and open also to suitably qualified and experienced Africans at the same rates of pay and emoluments as enjoyed by Europeans similarly engaged'.[9] This was to occur after the completion of a job survey on similar lines to the one initiated by the Anglo-American group.

These agreements on African advancement were widely regarded as a positive and clear-cut demonstration that partnership in Northern Rhodesia and the Federation was something more than a convenient catch-phrase. Nevertheless, there followed a period of unprecedented unrest on the Copperbelt. Numerous stoppages were organized by the African Mine Workers' Union, both in relation to demands for increased pay and over the question of advancement. Such action aroused critical comment among all sections of the European community, because of the damage they did to the national economy, and because the unrest was interpreted as yet another instance of Africans demanding the impossible. Closer examination shows that the basic causes of the unrest were more fundamental.

When the Rhodesian Selection Trust group of companies announced its plan for limited African advancement it stated specifically that some of the advanced categories of work, since they were of a supervisory nature, would fall within the jurisdiction of the African Salaried Staff Association, an unofficial body representing the interests of senior African employees on the mines. In March 1955 the Chamber of Mines granted the African Staff Association official recognition, a decision opposed by the African Union. In April the latter announced that it was in dispute with the Companies over the recognition of the Staff Association, arguing that the decision had been taken before

[9] *East Africa and Rhodesia*, 15 September 1955, pp. 46–47.

the Union had been informed, and was therefore null and void. In the following month the Companies gave the Union six months' notice of terminating their agreement with African daily-paid labour, and subsequently the Chamber of Mines announced that it was withdrawing the option which had hitherto ruled whereby certain senior African employees could either belong to the newly created Salaried Staff Association or the Union. In future they would be compelled to belong to the former, since among other things, it was administratively inconvenient to have some members of the same grade paid by the ticket and others monthly.

This decision precipitated a series of strikes organized by the African Union, usually on flimsy excuses, such as wearing leg guards, which were in reality protests at members of the Union being forced into the Salaried Staff Association. The reasons generally propounded for the Union's action was that it objected to African solidarity being broken. Certainly the move created a split in the previously united front of the African mine employees; but whether this was a machination of the Companies or not was in the long-term irrelevant. The members of Salaried Staff Association had, or potentially had, a basically different attitude to the differences between the levels of remuneration of Europeans and the ordinary Africans employed on the mines. They constituted an intermediate category between the two; collectively their attitude was more conservative, more approaching that of the European mine worker, for they were scaling the ladder of promotion. The mass of lowly paid members of the African Union also constituted a threat to their living standards. Thus the leaders of the African Union were left to deal with the intractable problem of the least skilled of the mine employees, discontented not because there were no opportunities for advancement—for they were unlikely to be advanced—but because of the tremendous disparity between their wages and those of the European mine worker. In 1954, for instance, the average income of the daily paid European underground employee—and that of the surface worker was only slightly lower—varied between £105 per month in January and £112 in December, figures which included all paid allowances and overtime, but excluded the copper bonus, which at the year's end stood at no less than 66 per cent. of the basic salary. In all, therefore, the average annual income of the European mine worker was in excess of £2,000. Over the same period, the average monthly wage of all Africans had risen from £6 11s. 7d. to just over £7 per month, figures which excluded the cost of free housing and rations.

There were in fact two problems in the copper-mining industry: the first, that of African advancement, and the second, the differential between African and European salary scales. A beginning had been made in tackling the former. But the companies admitted that the limited African advancement agreed would not in itself solve the industrial problems of the Copperbelt, and consequently both groups had initiated job surveys which were to analyse each job and place them into a definite scale according to its skill, responsibilities, and value to the companies. All jobs would then be open to all employees, providing only that they had the necessary ability to undertake them, and each would carry a specific remuneration, based not on whether it was in the European or African schedule of employment but its intrinsic value. Initially both groups of companies promised that no European would be dismissed or his current level of income reduced, while the Anglo-American group went further and stipulated that no African advancement beyond that already agreed would be initiated without the consent of the European Mine Workers' Union. At that time conditions in the copper-mining industry were such that the mining companies could afford both to create jobs for Europeans not specifically needed for maintaining efficient production and to expand the overall size of the industry. Copper continued to be in short supply; hence the metal's price—and the mining companies' profits—were constantly reaching new heights. An extensive programme of exploration and expansion was undertaken. Plans were made to re-open the mine at Kansanshi: two new mines at Chibuluma and Bancroft were begun, and a scheme announced for raising output at Nchanga by 50 per cent. These developments would create many additional employment opportunities, so that there was no immediate danger, provided the economic boom continued, that difficulty would be experienced in absorbing existing European employees and expanding the numbers of advanced Africans.

But if there was to be open competition based on merit in the industry, then at some point, no matter how distant, the time would come when an African would pass a European on the industry's promotion ladder by virtue of greater ability, even if an arbitrary minimum standard was decreed below which the European could not fall. At this point the physical lay-out and pattern of race relations as they had previously existed in the mining towns would become anachronistic. The superiority of the housing and social amenities provided by the mining companies for their European employees was justified on the grounds of their greater responsibilities in the industry. But they were also strictly segregated on a racial basis; furthermore, all Africans were barred from the 'European' hotels, restaurants, and cinemas in the civil townships. What, then, was to happen when an African passed a European on the industry's ability scale? To provide separate and equal facilities was physically impossible, and was in itself a contradiction. Logically, once an African held a post which was open to either Africans or Europeans on the basis of ability, there could be no justification for discriminating against him. And this meant that an African would have to be given the right to live in the 'European' area and patronize its facilities if he so chose. But Sir Roy Welensky had also said that participation was dependent on the attainment of civilized standards of behaviour and culture. Many of the jobs undertaken by the European mine workers were semi-skilled, and could easily be learnt by Africans of comparatively low educational attainments. Even the skilled jobs did not present insuperable difficulties, provided adequate training facilities were available. But the family relationships and social customs of those Africans who attained these technical standards would naturally be slanted towards those characteristic of their tribal societies rather than towards those of the European.

This is the crux of the problem of African advancement. Any solution in the technical sphere depends on open competition and freedom of choice in the social field. But if the artificial barriers separating the European and African communities are removed, then the particular characteristics of the White community will inevitably be changed by the influx of 'socially different' Africans. Hence Welensky's insistence on Africans attaining 'civilized standards of behaviour and culture'. The only Africans who could reasonably be expected to enter this exclusive club, for 'civilized standards of behaviour and culture' implies speaking, dressing, and behaving like a member of the White community, are those Africans who, through education and residence in a European type of community, could be said to be westernized. In the circumstances they will be limited principally to the few who have attended universities, especially universities in the United Kingdom. Such men, a small minority group, could conceivably be absorbed by the White community without altering any of its salient characteristics. But in reality even this is impractical. How, for instance, are these Africans to be distinguished from their well-dressed but illiterate fellows? And is a 'civilized' African to be cut off from his friends and family unless they too have passed the 'civilization' test? Most important of all, does the White community really expect an African fitter or carpenter or bulldozer driver to pass through a university in order to attain 'civilized standards of culture and behaviour', when all White men, regardless of occupation, training, or education are automatically 'civilized' and able to patronize all facilities, provided only they have the necessary cash?

The influence of these factors can be discerned in the manner in which the first stages of the African advancement programme was implemented. Because no Africans were allowed to be apprenticed or even trained in semi-skilled work in the industry, no suitable technical training facilities existed. The simplest method of overcoming this was for Africans to be trained in the industry, and in the circumstances this could only be done by members of the European Union. But they refused. Indeed, the *Union News*, organ of the European mine workers' organization, claimed that it was unreasonable to ask them to co-operate in implementing a policy to which a considerable body of opinion was still totally opposed. Moreover, the Union insisted that each category of work had to be handed over to Africans in its entirety, since European mine workers refused to work alongside Africans who had been advanced, the ostensible reason for this being that the dictum of equal pay for equal work was being broken.

This action indicated the line of retreat being taken over

African advancement. Since it was not possible for Africans to do the same work as a European at the same pay principally for social and not technical reasons, the only way to preserve the segregated pattern in the social sphere was for all Europeans to keep ahead of advancing Africans, thereby maintaining the validity of separate and superior facilities on the basis of higher degrees of skill and responsibility. Significantly, shortly after African advancement was conceded, the four principal copper mines, with the consent of the Federal Government, which is responsible for higher and technical education, each donated £100,000 towards the establishment of a foundation to promote technical education on the Copperbelt. Such facilities were to be confined to apprentices, although not necessarily to apprentices working on the copper mines. At the time, African participation was debarred by the terms of the Apprenticeship Ordinance. Subsequently, however, the Ordinance was amended so as to allow Africans to become apprenticed on the same terms as Europeans. This immediately raised the question of Africans being allowed to use the technical foundation schools, but the possibility was quickly rejected by Europeans on the grounds that African participation had not been envisaged when the foundation was established. African participation would, of course, reduce the chances of European youths entering the industry keeping ahead of the African, for the provision of training facilities was the key enabling Europeans to maintain their privileged position in the social sphere.

With the mining companies having guaranteed that no Europeans would be displaced or their salaries reduced through the introduction of the first stage of African advancement; with the industry expanding; and with the new technical training facilities available for European youths entering the industry, a framework was created which would enable the European to continue at the head of the industry's income and responsibility scales for a number of years. This in turn would justify the provision of superior social amenities and the exclusion of the African from them. But these developments provided no long-term solution to the problem of African advancement, nor to the more acute problem of the vast disparity between the standards of living of the European and African communities as a whole. In the immediate future, Europeans in the industry could continue to retreat in the technical sphere as Africans advanced; but even here the White man would eventually be forced back to the wall, into a position where it was no longer possible for all Europeans to keep ahead of all Africans. And this plan did nothing to alleviate African frustration and bitterness in the social sphere. Rather was the opposite true, since Africans taking over a particular schedule of jobs in the technical sphere would realize that the Europeans performing them had been considered 'civilized' and able to patronize all the social amenities of the 'civilized' community, while they were excluded on the grounds that they were 'uncivilized'.

It becomes clear that 'maintaining European standards' is in fact basically incompatible with African advancement; the one can only be achieved at the expense of the other. It is easy, of course, to lay the entire blame for the racial problem at the door of White prejudice. The White community has a vested interest in maintaining the *status quo*—how many would willingly abandon a position where a God-given characteristic is an automatic passport to an aristocracy, no matter what the worth of the individual? In a highly competitive and very insecure world it is comforting beyond measure to know that there is someone underneath, that it is not possible to sink to the bottom. Hence the confidence and assurance of the Europeans in the Rhodesias; hence the extreme race prejudice of those Europeans closest to the bottom of White society, for theirs is the greatest stake in preserving the existing position. Similarly, while the incompatibility between African advancement and 'maintaining European standards' has retarded African progress, it is easy to exaggerate its effects on the African community as a whole. But 'maintaining European standards' involves something more than preserving a particular level of material well-being, no matter how important that is in itself.

Let us diverge for a moment and consider a hypothetical situation. Suppose 60,000 British people were settled in a region of Italy, not as a distinct unit in a specially constructed town, but working with and among the existing Italian population. The Britons would be a minority, and the differences of language, social habits, and allegiances would combine to act as a centripetal force holding them together as a cultural entity. Nevertheless, young men and women would marry into the

Italian community; even those seeking to perpetuate British traditions would be forced to modify them, to find a more harmonious relation with the new environment. As in all such cases, these adjustments would involve strife and friction, with individual British and Italian families seeking to prevent intermarriage and thereby maintain the *status quo*, despite the fact that there would be no absolute physical characteristics differentiating one community from the other; that the level of technical competence and therefore of living standards would be broadly similar; and that both national cultures would have been moulded within the traditions of Western European civilization. Eventually, however, the British minority would be absorbed by the Italian community.

When permanent White settlement was established in Northern Rhodesia the position was very different. The African tribes had not been moulded within the traditions of Western European civilization; there was no national African culture; and the African level of technical competence and standard of living was vastly inferior to that of the European. In these circumstances it was hardly surprising that Europeans considered themselves superior and civilized and that because of this, they thought of their culture, their standards, as forming the basis for national life in the Territory. Instead of the minority being absorbed by the majority, the European minority decreed that the majority should be raised in the White man's image. This, together with the economic developments begun by the technically advanced White community and the creation of a modern political state, set in motion forces which began to transform the tribal societies, to draw Africans from the tribal environment and raise their standard of living and level of technical competence to that current in the European's society. This metamorphosis was in fact creating a new African national consciousness, an awareness of being a Northern Rhodesian and not simply a Bemba or a Ngoni, an awareness developed most acutely in those Africans advanced in a Western sense. Even so, an African engineer, doctor, or plant pathologist will not be wholly raised in British cultural traditions; family ties will still associate him with his tribe. With Africans achieving less advanced technical standards, such as artisans or semi-skilled workers, their tribal ties will be stronger; and for the largest group of Africans, the illiterate and semi-literate un-skilled labourer and peasant cultivator, their standards, their customs—even if not their way of living—will continue to be related overwhelmingly to that of tribal life rather than to the standards and concepts of the European.

The European and the forces he has unleashed are creating a new national way of African life in which the technical competence of the White man is blended with tribal social traditions. Precisely when this emergent African culture will achieve a stable balance between the sectional interests of the tribes, on the one hand, and the technical needs of a modern unitary state, on the other, is impossible to say. But two things are certain. First, the institutions of the state must be moulded to its requirements; hence they must reflect in some measure its character and the aspirations of the people as a whole. Secondly, and because of this, conflict between this evolutionary process and its White mentors is inevitable, even if they are official representatives of a trustee nation and believe themselves to be acting altruistically, for the White man sees society, its shape, its needs, its direction and the pace of its development, through eyes conditioned by his own national culture. The standards of living he considers normal are those of his mother country; so are the standards he expects in the civil service and in the administration of justice. He models the institutions for exercising power on those which have evolved in his own society. Neither is it possible for the interests of the trustee nation, whether economic or strategic, not to influence its policies towards its wards. The trustee nation is responsible for the ward's security, internally and internationally. The ward is therefore included within the defensive network of the trustee nation—which inevitably has as its prime purpose the preservation of the trustee's own national security. Consequently a point is reached when the technical benefits which might accrue from additional years of White tutelage are first balanced and then negatived by resentment bred by tutelage. There is therefore a watershed of power: on the one side, the shaping of society and its direction of development are principally controlled by Europeans; on the other, control passes to Africans. Whether the level of technical competence has been raised adequately, or sectional tribal interests merged into a national consciousness, before this watershed is passed depends on a number of factors. Certainly once it is passed, the new nation has a greater need than ever for technical assistance, for with power to shape and control society in indigenous hands, many Europeans will choose to leave.

The incompatibility between 'maintaining European standards' and African advancement in Northern Rhodesia arises therefore from two irreconcilable concepts of society. It is pointless therefore to assert that 'the racial dilemma' would be solved if the European community abandoned all racial discrimination—it is like a non-swimmer securely on dry land assuring another battling for his life in a turbulent sea that there is no need to hang on to the piece of drift wood because everyone can float. If the European community wishes to preserve its traditions and cultural heritage, then it has to erect and preserve artificial barriers separating White from Black. This attitude also overlooks the responsibilities of the British Government to the White community. Northern Rhodesia was founded on the basis of permanent White settlement. Even after the British Government assumed direct responsibility for the Protectorate, British immigrants were encouraged to settle there; economic development was left to them; such funds as have been spent in the African areas and on African development have come overwhelmingly from the fruits of that enterprise, and not from the magnanimity of the British tax-payer. Moreover, there were few if any British protests when the royalties, dividends, and company tax of the mining companies flowed into Britain's coffers.

The settlers have always realized that the maintenance of their position depends on erecting artificial barriers and then securing them by exercising political power. Hence their struggle to oust the Colonial Office, for the modern concept of trusteeship, of helping technically backward peoples to bridge the gap between past and present and fashion a new national synthesis, is equally incompatible with the *sine qua non* of the European community. But the White community has been unable to seize power; moreover, economic development has undercut their panacea of the early days, separate racial development in geographically distant regions. There has consequently been a considerable narrowing between the views of the settlers and the officials, the former being forced to accept in part the ideals of trusteeship, the latter to realize that each concession to the ideals of trusteeship erodes away the foundations on which the European community's security rests. Take the barring of Africans from hotels, cinemas, and bars. Simple and outrageous prejudice. But by virtue of the overwhelming numerical strength of the African population, the maintaining of the White man's authority depends to a large degree on preserving his prestige, of creating and projecting a concept of complete superiority. If social facilities were open to all, it would be impossible to sustain this myth, and the European would have to rely on something else to maintain his position. How deeply this necessity is ingrained in the White community can be seen from the Archbishop of Canterbury's admission that he was rebuked by a 'public official' during a tour of the Rhodesias for daring to shake hands with an African.[10] Likewise the instinct of self-preservation can be detected in the policies pursued by the Northern Rhodesian Government, for the enthusiastic official support for the chiefs—or at least those supporting Government policies—and the encouraging of tribalism; the continuing of labour repatriation, despite the advantages—and indeed the necessity—for developing urban stability, all delayed the build-up of African pressure for social and economic advancement within the European's sphere.

But the pressures have continued to increase; for the White community—and the Northern Rhodesian Government—is seeking to dam the evolutionary tide. They distract attention from this by using high-sounding generalizations such as the 'ideals of partnership', 'equal rights for all civilized men', and the 'preservation of civilized standards of behaviour and culture'; equally they are forced to condemn manifestations of African political consciousness, for this can only come from a realization on the part of the African of the irreconcilability between White and Black concepts of society. To argue that Africans should forget politics and concentrate on economic development and the raising of technical standards is to misunderstand the nature of the basic conflict. Political consciousness has developed before there has been any substantial advance in

[10] House of Lords Debates, 29 July 1959, col. 795.

raising the level of African technical competence, and even before there has been any significant development of a true
national consciousness on the part of the African community
generally, because the nature of economic development in
Northern Rhodesia has drawn Black and White into the same
framework; because the Africans emerging from their tribal cultures have been brought up against the barriers erected to maintain the White community as a cultural entity; and because
they have been forced to realize that these can only be broken
down through a redistribution of power. The demand for universal suffrage, for the introduction of a '100 per cent. democracy' in Northern Rhodesia, is simply the African equivalent of
'preserving civilized standards of culture and behaviour': the
African looks to universal suffrage as a means of redistributing
power so that an African way of life can develop in the Protectorate. It logically follows that the present level of technical
achievements in Northern Rhodesia could not be sustained if
there was a radical redistribution of power such that an African state emerged, since the former has been built up by Europeans principally for Europeans and protected by the European's monopoly of political power. Thus the Copperbelt and
the line of rail dominate the level of technical achievement in
Northern Rhodesia as a whole, and since they provide the only
extensive opportunities for paid employment, Africans have
flooded to them. But there is not work to support them all;
indeed, because of European self-interest, many spheres into
which the African could advance have been reserved specifically
for the White man. Thus on the state-owned Rhodesia Railways
all jobs for engine-drivers, firemen, bus and lorry drivers, and
ticket clerks have been *reserved* for Europeans. If African advancement was conceded, as was done on the copper mines,
there would be European retreat. Northern Rhodesia thus faces
this dilemma: continued White control will force African frustration to turn to bitterness, bitterness to dislike, and dislike to
hatred; but if that control is removed, the Territory will suffer
economic collapse and political chaos.

Let us turn now to look briefly at Southern Rhodesia and
Nyasaland. In Nyasaland at 30 June, 1953 there were 5,000
Europeans and 2,420,000 Africans. In the previous seven years
the White population had increased by 2,800 and the African

by 330,000. There were no large-scale mining or industrial developments, and political power was vested absolutely in the Governor, there being official majorities in both the Legislative and Executive Councils. Nyasaland was an isolated and backward African country, sleeping under the benign but dead hand of the Colonial Office. It is immediately obvious that the few thousand Europeans could not hope to dominate the country and protect their standards and traditions by wresting political power from the Nyasaland Government. But the question of who was finally to exercise power was still unresolved, and though the facts of population and economic development pointed to it passing into African hands, the European community in the country felt no differently from their compatriots in the Rhodesias about being absorbed in an alien culture. Moreover, there were the same problems relating to the level of technical competence achieved by the African community. By leaving economic development to private enterprise for so many years, the Colonial Office has allowed Nyasaland, which does not possess the known mineral potential of the Rhodesias, to be economically by-passed. Indeed, the Nyasaland Government has regarded the Protectorate as a labour reserve satisfying the needs of the capital-attracting countries.[11] In 1957, for instance, 140,000 able-bodied Nyasa males were working outside the Protectorate; at 31 March in the same year the number of Africans in paid employment internally, based on annual returns of employers with five or more workers, was 92,005.[12] Of those absent, 100,000 were estimated to be in Southern Rhodesia, 26,000 in South Africa, and 13,000 in Northern Rhodesia. Moreover, the numbers of identity certificates issued—all Africans wishing to leave the country to work had to obtain one—rose sharply, from an annual average of 33,852 over the years 1946–50 to an average of 55,515 in 1951–55, to 72,304 in 1956 and 74,346 in the following year.

Membership of the Federation is hardly likely to solve these economic and technical problems. It is true that since Federation, Nyasaland has received a larger share of the financial benefits accruing from economic expansion in the Rhodesias than

[11] As occurred in the Northern, Eastern, and Barotse Provinces in Northern Rhodesia.
[12] *Nyasaland, 1957* (H.M.S.O.), p. 24.

she would have merely from the remittances of expatriate Nyasas working there. But Southern Rhodesia continues to receive the greater part of new investment capital flowing into the Federation. Thus in 1956 the gross output of manufacturing establishments in Southern Rhodesia was valued at £87,234,000, or 80 per cent. of the total value of output in the Federation. The figure for Nyasaland was £4,750,000. In 1957 the value of Southern Rhodesian output had risen to £105,096,000, an increase of 20·4 per cent. over the previous year's figure. In Nyasaland the value of output went up to £5,526,000, a 16·3 per cent. increase. Moreover, such development projects as have been initiated in the Protectorate have been sited in the small area of freehold and leasehold land, especially in the vicinity of Blantyre-Limbe. But if membership of the Federation is not likely to solve Nyasaland's economic and technical problems, it has had a profound political effect. Inclusion within the Federation jerked Nyasaland away from the expected direction of constitutional development and set her instead in a political sphere where the over-riding consideration is the 'maintaining of European standards'.

In Southern Rhodesia political power has been exercised by the White community since the attainment of internal self-government in 1923. Moreover, at 30 June 1953 there were 157,000 Europeans in the Colony, and the White to Black ratio was 1 : 13, compared with 1 : 40 in Northern Rhodesia and 1 : 484 in Nyasaland. Because of these factors, the White community in Southern Rhodesia was more confident in its outlook, especially with regard to the future and the relative positions of White and Black races in Southern Rhodesian society. Southern Rhodesian views on these topics were clearly set out in an officially published pamphlet issued in 1953 before the creation of the Federation. 'The whole policy of geographical segregation postulates by implication that there should not be a mixed society in Southern Rhodesia. This may run counter to the principle of certain political thinkers outside Africa who would deny the European the right to a separate permanent place in any African community. With those who hold such views the European, and indeed the African in Southern Rhodesia, have no common meeting ground. This pre-supposes the maintenance of the two races and the avoidance of a mixed

race. This in turn means that there is generally no social inter-
course between them because at present the races are not of an
equal intellectual level and have not a similar outlook and
social traditions. It is not the custom for Africans and Europeans
to visit one another's houses in a social way, to frequent the same
places of entertainment, to use the same restaurants and hotels.
It has to be accepted then that social distinctions associated
with colour are a recognizable feature of the Southern Rhodesian scene. They are likely to persist, though they may be modified as time goes on, until both races can accept their disappear-
ance without misgivings. No term can be set for the arrival of
this stage of development; indeed, no one can be certain that it
is likely to be reached.' [13]

As in Northern Rhodesia and Nyasaland, the philosophy of
the European community was irreconcilable with the evolutionary changes set in motion by its presence. Nevertheless,
there was a basic difference between the Colony and the two
Protectorates in respect of its economic development. White
settlement has not been confined to a narrow strip as in Northern Rhodesia but occurs throughout the Colony. Consequently
urban centres are scattered over most of the country, and road
and rail communications are more widely and extensively developed. In addition, the economy is more broadly based than
in Northern Rhodesia. Prior to the Second World War, the
Southern Rhodesian economy was dependent principally on
European agriculture and mining, flue-cured tobacco and gold
being of particular importance. In 1938, of the actual net income of £21,000,000, £3,000,000 accrued from European agriculture and £5,000,000 from mining, while of the exports in the
same year valued at £10,000,000, £9,000,000 came from
minerals and tobacco and under £1,000,000 from secondary
industry.[14] African labour during this period was regarded as
entirely migratory, the country being divided into strict zones
of European and African settlement. Because there was little industrial development and no mining enterprises on the scale of
the copper-mining industry in Northern Rhodesia, the size of
the urban African communities remained comparatively small.

[13] Reported in *East Africa and Rhodesia*, January 29 1953, p. 704.
[14] *Report of the Urban African Affairs Commission, 1958* (Government Printer
Salisbury), pp. 9–10.

This pattern was drastically changed subsequent to the Second World War, when heavy European immigration was accompanied by large-scale investment and a surge in the growth of secondary industry. By 1953, for instance, while the net income from European agriculture was £18,928,000 and that from the mining industry £12,669,000, the net income produced from manufacturing, construction, electricity, and water supply had soared to £31,700,000.[15] The numbers of Africans drawn into the urban areas increased correspondingly, particularly in Salisbury and Bulawayo, where a high proportion of the industrial development was sited. Though there was a rapid increase in the African population, between 1936 and 1957 it is estimated to have almost doubled, from 1,260,000 to 2,350,000 (including immigrants from other territories), there began to develop an acute labour shortage, so that Southern Rhodesia became more and more dependent on foreign migrants. This, coupled with a rapid deterioration in the soil fertility of the African-reserved areas, forced the Southern Rhodesian Government to implement measures to raise the standard of African skills and abilities in order to make maximum use of the indigenous human and natural resources.

In the Native reserves this entailed the implementation of a social and agronomic revolution forcing the African to abandon traditional tribal customs and to adopt stable intensive farming. The measure for implementing this revolution was the Native Land Husbandry Act, passed through the Southern Rhodesian Legislature in 1951. Under the Act the entire area of Native reserved land was to be surveyed, protected against erosion, provided with adequate water supplies, and allocated for specific uses on the basis of co-ordinated development. If need be, villages were to be re-sited, and, in consultation with Native councils and chiefs, the Government planned to allocate land on the basis of a modified form of individual tenure. Such land rights could be sold or bequeathed; but under no circumstances could the standard holdings be subdivided. Neither could they be pledged or attached for debt.[16] This rural revolution could only be contemplated because there was substantial local de-

[15] *Report of the Urban African Affairs Commission, 1958* (Government Printer Salisbury), p. 9.
[16] *East Africa and Rhodesia*, 3 May 1956, p. 1222.

mand for the agricultural products grown in the reserves, and because the pattern of European settlement had produced a fairly balanced development of communications and markets throughout the Colony. By 1956 it was estimated that the total value of African-produced agricultural products was of the order of £10,000,000 per annum, equivalent to approximately £32 per family holding of four to six acres, and it was confidently expected that when the Native Land Husbandry Act was implemented in full this would be increased considerably. Under the Act land rights were confined to those Africans who were actually farming in a given area at the time the Act was proclaimed.

By creating 'master' farmers throughout the African-reserved areas, the concept of migrant labour, at least as it concerned Southern Rhodesian Africans, was inevitably swept aside. Under the Land Husbandry Act it is not possible for an African to hold land in the rural areas unless he is a professional farmer. Consequently, those Africans deprived of the right to cultivate had to be absorbed in the towns, and this entailed permanent housing and the granting of social security. Recognizing this, the Southern Rhodesian Government embarked on an extended programme of housing construction in the urban areas. Several schemes were also initiated whereby for £350 an African could purchase a house on a ninety-nine-year lease by means of easy credit facilities. But it was also necessary to raise the level of African skills substantially and rapidly, since an unskilled labourer drawing a wage of a few pounds per month could not be expected to finance his own social-security arrangements and at the same time contribute to the cost of implementing rural reform and urban housing schemes. It was estimated, for instance, that the cost of the Land Husbandry Act for the five years from 1956 would be £6,750,000: and the initial cost of the urban housing schemes was £2,000,000, considerable sums in relation to the size of the Government's income and the demands on it in other spheres. As a necessary first step in raising African educational standards, the Southern Rhodesian Government embarked on a five-year education plan aimed at producing 5,000 trained African teachers by 1960 and substantially increasing educational facilities. It is expected to cost £12,000,000.

Thus Southern Rhodesia is in a position to attempt something quite impossible in either Northern Rhodesia or Nyasaland: the mounting of a socio-economic revolution designed to raise African living standards and force their pattern of life towards that accepted as normal in the European community. Moreover, the Colony is richly endowed with known mineral deposits, including all the necessary ingredients for establishing a large iron and steel industry. Indeed, the Southern Rhodesian Government initiated a pioneer steel works at Que Que. A vast expansion and extension of industry is possible in Southern Rhodesia, therefore, based on the exploitation of local mineral deposits and the production of a wide range of consumer goods previously imported into the Central African market. There will also be a commensurate expansion in the demand for agricultural products as the population expands and the standard of African living rises.

But the measures set in train to raise African living standards will have inevitable consequences. The Native Land Husbandry Act will deprive large numbers of Africans of 'free' rural security, and the provision of urban security, a costly undertaking, will fall principally on the shoulders of the European tax-payer. Furthermore, if the African is to be able to contribute to his own security he will have to be trained in skills traditionally within the European preserve. And while there is nothing equivalent to the copper-mining industry dominating the Southern Rhodesian economy, it will be equally impossible to treat Africans with the same technical training as social inferiors. Thus Southern Rhodesia, despite its greater potential for achieving balanced development between the urban and rural areas and for raising African material standards towards those of the European community, faces precisely the same problems as the White communities in the Protectorates.

The two vital questions for the White community as a whole are therefore: can they, through Federation, wrest power from the British Government? And if they succeed, can they effectively contain African pressure for advancement?

CHAPTER 15

THE FUTURE OF THE FEDERATION

I. THE MACHINERY TO CONTROL POLITICAL POWER

THE franchise problem was first investigated in Southern
Rhodesia, by a commission appointed by the Government in 1956. In its report [1] the Commission recommended a common roll on which all voters would be registered,
but for which there would be a number of alternative qualifications. Basically this involved the creation of two rolls, a higher
or ordinary roll, and a lower, special roll, the former having a
series of high qualifications based either on income, property,
or education, and the latter a series of lower qualifications of
the same type. The higher qualification roll would be permanent and predominantly European, and the lower primarily
African, though the Commission recommended certain safeguards to ensure that special voters exercised only a limited influence on elections. In describing the merits of the recommended franchise system, the Commission wrote: 'True responsible government implies that the legislature is responsible
not only for a narrow electorate, but to the people as a whole.
The roll can fairly be described as a common roll, admission to
which is gained by qualifications that are independent of race
and colour. We frankly accept the fact that for many years to
come the voters qualifying on the ordinary qualification would
be principally European, and those qualifying on the special
principally African. Nevertheless, the special qualification would
give the African immediate and substantial voting power. From
the outset, a certain number would be included among those
with the ordinary qualifications, and these would have reached
a standard at which only the most prejudiced Europeans could
grudge them full participation in the franchise.' [2] As subsequently amended, the Colony's franchise is based on a two-tier
common roll, with all registered voters voting for the same

[1] *Report of the Franchise Commission, 1957* (Government Printer Salisbury).
[2] *Franchise Report*, op. cit., p. 10.

candidate. The numbers of special voters who can register, however, is limited absolutely to 20 per cent. of the total registered on the upper roll, the lower roll being permanently closed as and when this occurs. And to obviate the risk of an African candidate being elected on a minority vote in a constituency where the upper roll votes are more or less equally divided between two European candidates, optional preferential voting has been introduced.[3]

The revision of the franchise in Southern Rhodesia thus ensured that political power would continue to be exercised 'for many years to come' by Europeans, for the qualifications for the ordinary vote were substantially raised compared with those governing the former common roll. Nevertheless, a liberal gesture was made: by extending the franchise to the more educated and prosperous Africans through the special vote, the new franchise ensured that European legislators could not ignore absolutely the aspirations and needs of the African community. But modifying the franchise in Southern Rhodesia was not of crucial importance: power had been, and was to remain, in the hands of Europeans. The creation of a Federal franchise was, for the Federal Government was to hold the umbrella protecting the European communities' interests, particularly in the two Protectorates. Moreover, the franchise question was inextricably linked with the review of the Federal Constitution and the gaining of independence. In April 1957 the Federal Prime Minister, Sir Roy Welensky [4] and the Federal Minister of Law, Mr. J. M. Greenfield, visited London and consulted the Secretaries of State for the Colonies and of Common Relations, respectively Mr. A. T. Lennox-Boyd and Lord Home. Afterwards a joint statement was issued on behalf of the two Governments announcing a series of agreements. The Federal Government was to be entrusted with external affairs to the fullest extent possible consistent with British responsibilities in international law dur-

---

[3] Second preference votes have to be counted in a three-cornered election where the winning candidate does not obtain an absolute majority of all the votes cast. This is done by eliminating the first preference votes of the candidate lowest in the poll and distributing his second preference votes between the remaining candidates. The process is continued until one candidate has an absolute majority of first and second preference votes over the total votes of the remaining candidates. See Appendix for full franchise qualifications, p. 262.
[4] He succeeded Lord Malvern in 1956.

ing the period the Federation was not a separate international entity. The Federal Prime Minister drew attention to doubts which had arisen 'in regard to the purpose and effect of Article 29 (7) [5] of the Federal Constitution and to the subject of legislation in the United Kingdom for the Federation. United Kingdom Ministers made it clear that the United Kingdom Government in practice would "not initiate any legislation to amend or to repeal any Federal Act or to deal with any matter included within the competence of the Federal Legislature, except at the request of the Federal Government."' Furthermore, United Kingdom Ministers accepted in principle that all civil services in the Federation, whether Federal or Territorial, would eventually be locally based and would look for their future in the Federal area. Finally, 'the Federal Prime Minister informed United Kingdom Ministers of the position reached in his discussions with the Prime Minister of Southern Rhodesia and the Governors of Northern Rhodesia and Nyasaland in regard to the enlargement of the Federal Assembly and to the Federal franchise. United Kingdom Ministers accepted in principle proposals for the enlargement of the Federal Assembly. The Federal Prime Minister stated that he would not be able to inform Her Majesty's Government of the Federal Government's definite proposals for the franchise, or to present a bill on this subject to the Federal Legislature, until further discussions had been held in Salisbury. Meanwhile, however, he could assure United Kingdom Ministers that a franchise bill would be introduced and would ensure that British Protected Persons otherwise qualified would not be required to change their status in order to be eligible for the Federal franchise, and that the qualifications for that franchise would permit a reasonable number of such persons acquiring the franchise. United Kingdom Ministers took note with satisfaction of these assurances.' The British and Federal Governments took the opportunity to reaffirm that they were opposed to any proposals which would lead to the amalgamation of the Territories of the Federation into a unitary state or for the secession of the states from the Federation. They decided that the conference to review the Federal constitution

---

[5] Article 29 (7) reads: '. . . nothing in this constitution shall effect any power to make laws for the Federation or any of the Territories conferred on Her Majesty by an Act of Parliament'.

should be convened in 1960, and that the purpose 'of this conference is to review the Constitution in the light of the experience gained since the inception of Federation and in addition to agree on the constitutional advances which may be made'. In this latter context the conference would 'consider a programme for the attainment of such status as would enable the Federation to become eligible for full membership of the Commonwealth'.

The franchise finally adopted [6] was based on a two-tier common roll with qualifications similar to those of the Southern Rhodesian franchise. Under the Constitutional Amendment Act enlarging the Federal Assembly, the ratios of racial representatives and territorial representatives were the same as in the 1953 Constitution. The position in the enlarged Federal Assembly is thus: forty-four ordinary constituency members elected by voters registered on the general roll; eight directly elected African members, two from Northern Rhodesia, two from Nyasaland, and four from Southern Rhodesia, elected by the combined votes of the general and special roll voters; the European representing African interests in Southern Rhodesia, elected by the same means; and the remaining Africans, two from each of the Protectorates, together with the two Europeans representing African interests in those territories, nominated as under the 1953 Constitution. By virtue of the qualifications governing enrolment, the general roll would be overwhelmingly European—the Federal Minister of Law during the second reading of the Electoral Bill estimated that 81,000 Europeans and slightly over 1,500 Africans would qualify.

The estimates of voters likely to register were only intelligent guesses.[7] But the consensus of opinion was that in 1958 there would be more Africans on the special roll than Europeans on the general roll in Nyasaland, roughly equal numbers in Northern Rhodesia, and a majority of Europeans over Africans in Southern Rhodesia. In terms of the second Federal general election,[8] therefore, forty-four—or 75 per cent. of the total membership of the Federal Assembly—would be elected by an

[6] See Appendix for full franchise qualifications, p. 261.
[7] The Under-Secretary of State for Commonwealth Relations told the House of Commons that while an estimated 37,000 Europeans were eligible to register on the common roll in Northern Rhodesia in 1957, actual registrations were in fact only 16,000.
[8] See Appendix for full election results, p. 271.

overwhelmingly European electorate. Of the fifteen African members or members representing African interests, three would be Europeans (one elected by a dominantly White electorate); the four Africans from Southern Rhodesia would also be elected by a dominantly European electorate; the two African members from Northern Rhodesia would be elected by an electorate in which White and Black voters were in equal numbers; the two from Nyasaland would be returned by an electorate in which Africans would be in the majority; and the two special African representatives from each of the Protectorates would continue to be nominated by an all-African electoral college.

In December 1956 the Northern Rhodesian Legislative Council passed a motion that constitutional talks should commence during the first quarter of 1957, and that an announcement of proposed constitutional changes should be made during the first quarter of the following year. Accordingly, the Governor began a series of discussions with individual members and with groups of members of the Legislature and with leaders of other political organizations, including the Northern Rhodesian African National Congress. But no agreement was reached. Subsequently the United Federal Party [9] published its constitutional proposals. The franchise proposed was similar to that in the Federal Electoral Act, a two-tier common roll with high qualifications governing entry to the ordinary roll and lower qualifications controlling enrolment on the special roll. The territory was to be divided into fourteen constituencies distributed along the line of rail and eight special constituencies covering the African reserves and rural areas. Commensurate with the increase in the elected ordinary members, the United Federal Party suggested that the numbers of Officials in the Legislature should be reduced from eight to six, and that the leader of the Legislature should be an ordinary elected member, who, as Chief Minister, would preside over the Executive Council. Official representation on the Executive Council would also be reduced, from five to three, and that of the Unofficials increased in like proportion. The United Federal Party

---

[9] An amalgamation of the Federal Party—from which the first and second Federal Governments have been formed and which has a majority of elected members in the Northern Rhodesian Legislature—and the United Rhodesia Party, then the governing party in Southern Rhodesia.

thus proposed that the franchise and electoral machinery in Northern Rhodesia should be brought into line with that existing in Southern Rhodesia and the Federal Assembly. There would be a numerical balance between the ordinary elected members and the Officials together with the specially elected members—which from previous experience certainly did not mean that on every occasion the latter two groups would combine to neutralize the former: moreover, the leader of the majority group of ordinary elected members was to be Chief Minister, and the Unofficials were to dominate the Executive Council. In these circumstances the Unofficials, provided they were not split between two parties, would completely dominate the Government. At the same time the party made liberal gestures. It agreed to the enfranchising of the British Protected Persons under the same conditions as in the Federal sphere; to give the special voters a maximum 20 per cent. influence on the election of ordinary candidates—the ordinary vote was to count in full in both special and ordinary elections; to increase the numbers of African members by 100 per cent., from four to eight; and finally to give a seat on the Executive Council to an African, provided one suitably qualified was elected.

When the Northern Rhodesian Government's proposals were published [10] they were based on broadly the same pattern as had been proposed by the United Federal Party. The two-tier common roll and the franchise qualifications were practically identical. So were the numbers of seats to be given Officials and ordinary and specially elected members in the Legislative Council, except that the Government proposed that there should be two seats covering the ordinary constituencies which would be reserved for Africans, two covering the special constituencies reserved for Europeans, and two nominated members. But the United Federal Party's suggestion that an Unofficial should be Chief Minister and president of the Executive Council was rejected. Instead, the official proposal was for an Executive Council presided over by the Governor and consisting of four ex-officio ministers and five others, of whom four would have to be ordinary elected members. In addition there were to be two assistant ministers who would not be members of the Executive

[10] *Proposals for Constitutional Change in Northern Rhodesia, 1958* (Government Printer Lusaka).

Council. Of the total of eleven ministers and assistant ministers, two were to be African, including one minister. At the same time, the Government proposed that the qualifications for the special vote should be raised to the ordinary level in five bi-annual increments—although all qualified voters would remain on the roll—and while cross voting was to be allowed, with special voters exercising a third influence on the election of ordinary members and vice versa, all special candidates would have to be approved by two-thirds of the chiefs recognized by the Government within a constituency.

In commending its proposals, the Federal Government wrote: 'In addressing itself to the problem of devising a sound and equitable franchise system for the Federation it has been the primary concern of the Federal Government to extend the common roll principle which, it believes, holds out the only real prospect of a complete and genuine multi-racial partnership and the hope that the political energies and aspirations of all races will be directed into party political channels rather than into racial cleavages.' It fully realized that 'on a determination of valid standards of civilization and responsibility only a comparatively small portion of the African inhabitants will, at the present stage of African development, initially be eligible for the franchise, and that recourse must be had to special devices to associate Africans with the process of government until they are equipped to play a full part on the same terms as Europeans. It is important in the Federal Government's view to regard these devices as . . . temporary expedients to bridge the gulf between widely disparate standards of evolution, and as a means of giving a strictly limited influence to the numerically large but politically immature section of the population.' [11] By its own definition, the Federal Government regarded the attainment of a standard of living and education common to the European community as the essential prerequisites for full political participation. That section of the community which had not reached those standards were regarded as minors, as wards who were to be controlled by the civilized and politically mature segment—though the wards were to be given special representation by means of 'temporary expedients'.

[11] A statement issued by the Federal Government in defence of its Constitution Amendment Bill, quoted in *East Africa and Rhodesia*, 14 November 1957, p. 335.

The Northern Rhodesian Government's arguments justifying its plan for constitutional reform were cast in a similar vein. Despite the fact that 'by the very nature of the Constitution (Federal), much of our work is concerned with Native Affairs'— the words are those of a Southern Rhodesian Prime Minister [12] —the Northern Rhodesian Government rejected the possibility of balanced numbers of seats reserved for elected Africans and Europeans as asked for by 'moderate' African opinion or balanced representation between Africans and all Europeans whether official or elected as asked for by the Northern Rhodesian African National Congress, thereby reversing the idea postulated in the 1951 draft definition of partnership, on the grounds that 'any form of parity . . . could not but consolidate and perpetuate a racial outlook' and that this was contrary to the 'first principle on which Government policy has always been based . . . that political parties should begin to develop on non-racial lines, and that politics should cut straight across race'.[13] The Northern Rhodesian Government also accepted that 'European standards' should govern full political participation. 'The crux of the problem . . . is that the majority of Europeans are still far ahead of the majority of Africans; and if the franchise were limited to Europeans and to the few Africans who have . . . achieved European standards, the African race would be seriously under-represented. The difficulty will persist for a number of years.' Hence the Constitution had to be so framed that 'European standards' were the accepted norm, this ensuring that the government of the country would 'continue to rest in the hands of responsible men'.

These arguments were, of course, a skilful attempt to camouflage self-interest by equating it with the national weal. In the twentieth century economic problems and political discontent have been closely allied; but the Northern Rhodesian Government were seriously arguing that in a country where there were 72,000 Whites and 2,220,000 Africans,[14] where the average wage of the Europeans was over £1,000 per annum and that of the African in employment was less than £100, where the White

[12] Mr. Garfield Todd addressing the annual conference of the United Rhodesia Party in September, 1957. Reported in *East Africa and Rhodesia*, 3 October 1957, p. 157.
[13] *Proposals for Constitutional Change in Northern Rhodesia*, op. cit., p. 4.
[14] At 30 June 1958.

community was privileged in all things and the Black under-privileged, that party politics should cut across race, and that the overwhelming majority of Africans who had not reached and could not reach 'European standards' should remain contentedly apolitical. In a strictly European context it was as though the 2 per cent. of the population having the highest income in the land should stipulate that no one could enjoy their privileges unless and until they had achieved their 'standards', and that in the meantime, political power and control over society should be vested exclusively in their persons.

The Labour Opposition in the House of Commons bitterly attacked the British Government for refusing to reject the Federal Electoral Act and the Constitutional Amendment Act after both measures had been declared differentiating in terms of the 1953 Constitution by the African Affairs Board. During the debate on the Constitutional Amendment Act, Mr. J. Callaghan, principal Labour speaker on colonial affairs, declared: 'We recognize the economic advancement that has taken place (in the Federation) . . . we also recognize that no minority group can for ever pretend to govern these Territories to the exclusion of the millions of inhabitants there. I believe . . . that it will be possible for us to work out a solution under which the economic benefits of the Federation will be united with the political advancement of the African people. If the Government drive this proposal through . . . they must get ahead as quickly as possible with internal reforms for self-government in Northern Rhodesia and Nyasaland to give Africans more opportunity of government in those territories.' [15] Mr. Callaghan further announced that the Labour Party would not support the agreements reached between the British and Federal Governments in April 1957 if they were returned to power. 'The Government may have bound their hands . . . but they have not bound ours. We do not recognize the existence of the convention. We rely upon and govern ourselves by the words laid down in Article 29 (7) (of the Federal Constitution).' [16]

But in reality neither the Conservative nor the Labour Parties were able to reach to the heart of the racial problem. The Conservatives, Empire-conscious, sensitive to the plight of

[15] Hansard (House of Commons), 25 November 1957, col. 827.
[16] Ibid., col. 826.

their fellow countrymen settled overseas, aware that the White communities had made the Federation of Rhodesia and Nyasaland and of the low standards of technical competence and material well-being of the African communities, felt that the British Government had a moral obligation to safeguard European interests and that in any case the White man's presence was essential if African standards were to be raised. The Conservatives consequently accepted the conditions laid down by the White communities; and logically they had to apply them both in the Federal and Territorial spheres, ignoring the incompatibility between 'maintaining European standards' and African advancement and the impossibility of ever achieving political stability in any of the three states on the basis of the former concept. Hence the British Government's dilemma in Nyasaland. The Nyasaland Constitution had been revised in 1955. The composition of the Executive Council had remained unchanged but the new Legislative Council consisted of twelve officials, including the Governor, six non-Africans elected on a non-African voters' roll, and five African unofficials elected by the African Provincial Councils. Subsequently the Governor announced that the Constitution was to remain in force for four years, during which time those concerned could work together and seek to agree on further measures of constitutional reform, which would then be introduced into the next Legislative Council. If these reforms were to be acceptable to the White community in Nyasaland and to the Federal and Southern Rhodesian Governments, they had to follow the broad lines laid down in the constitutional revisions already implemented in those spheres. Hence they would have to be framed so that 8,300 out of a total population of 2,690,000 could dominate the country. Inevitably, no agreement could be reached between the parties concerned.

But if the Conservatives ignored the incompatibility between African advancement and 'maintaining European standards', so did the Labour Party. They also failed to appreciate the reality of the local European communities' power; for it was naïve to suggest that legislation passed by a British Government in Westminster could have any effect whatsoever in the Federation unless a British Government were willing to see its provisions forcibly implemented. Thus the Conservatives hoped that political stability might emerge, despite the support accorded the concept of 'maintaining European standards', while the Labour Party hoped that the economic benefits arising from the presence of a permanent White community would continue, despite its intention to rapidly increase African political power in Northern Rhodesia and Nyasaland. Meanwhile, both parties supported one of the two irreconcilably different concepts of society which constitutes the Federation's racial dilemma.

II. EUROPEAN REACTIONS

While the Federal, Northern Rhodesian, Southern Rhodesian, and Nyasaland Governments have pledged themselves to support 'partnership', the European communities consider it largely in terms of raising African standards within the framework of separate racial development. Despite this, an interracial university was established in Salisbury—though the pattern of race relations therein was probably affected by the British Government's grant of £1,250,000 towards the cost of establishing it. The Federal Government created a civil service open to all races on the basis of merit; likewise it agreed to admit non-Europeans to the dining-cars in the state-owned railways. In Northern Rhodesia there was a marked diminution in discrimination in post offices and in shops; legislation prohibiting the sale of light wines and beers to Africans was repealed; African-owner housing schemes based on long-term leases were introduced into the urban areas; a number of multiracial clubs were established; and the obligation to carry night passes in urban centres abolished for a trial period. In Southern Rhodesia the Land Apportionment Act was modified so that among other things African professional men could establish offices in that part of an urban area previously designated European. In the eyes of the European communities these were substantial concessions; hence they were hurt when criticism by the Labour Party and demands by African political leaders continued unabated. In particular were the African Congress movements criticized. Mr. Garfield Todd, the Southern Rhodesian Prime Minister, told a Caledonian dinner in Bulawayo in November 1957 that unless leaders of the Southern Rhodesian African National Congress [17] co-operated in maintaining law, order, and

[17] Formed in 1957.

racial harmony, legislation would be necessary to restrict the freedom of the individual and of organizations. 'The Congress is endeavouring by its actions, and in conflict with its constitution, to discipline a mass machine whose powers would not be exerted through the vote but through some type of mass action. At recent Congress meetings the authority of the chiefs and the police have been flouted. European shopkeepers in the reserves have been threatened, and Africans who have joined the existing political parties have been victimized. What lies before us— co-operation or unrelenting racialism?' [18] This plea pin-pointed the dilemma of the White liberal. He too had to support a qualitative franchise to isolate the overwhelming mass of illiterate Africans, though he advocated the raising of the level of education and earning power of the mass and the entry of the African *evolué* into White society in the belief that this would solve the racial dilemma. Hence, like Mr. Todd, he talked of co-operation or racialism, forgetting that White 'racialism' was necessary to protect the European community's sectional interests.

But it was not only Congress activities and Labour Party outbursts which were affecting the White communities. The sharp fall in the price of copper during 1956 and 1957 had completely transformed the economic situation in the Federation, changed boom times to recession and brought to the surface once again the fear of White displacement by cheap African labour. At this time too the cost of providing facilities for Africans was beginning to make itself felt, especially in Southern Rhodesia. A new political party, the Dominion Party, was formed in Southern Rhodesia in 1956, reflecting White apprehension, for in a policy statement, the party rejected a policy of racial partnership, since it felt that this was unsuited to the conditions of Southern Rhodesia. And on 9 January 1958 Mr. Garfield Todd, returning from South Africa, was met at the airport in Salisbury by four of his Cabinet colleagues and a Parliamentary Under Secretary and informed that they had lost confidence in his leadership and in particular in his ability to lead the United Federal Party to victory in the forthcoming Southern Rhodesian general election. All insisted, however, that they had no criticism to make of the policies he had followed. There then

[18] Reported in *East Africa and Rhodesia*, 5 December 1957, p. 456.

followed a series of complex manoeuvres within the Southern Rhodesian division of the United Federal Party, which ended with Mr. Todd being rejected from the Party leadership and Sir Edgar Whitehead, a former Finance Minister in Lord Malvern's Administration, being recalled from his post as Federal Minister in Washington to become Party Leader and Prime Minister designate. Throughout the political crisis there were frequent protestations that the sole cause of the conflict had been Mr. Todd's leadership: that the party and the Southern Rhodesian Government did not intend to diverge from the policy of African advancement. Subsequently, however, Sir Edgar was defeated in a by-election, and shortly afterwards Parliament was dissolved and a general election called. This was quickly followed by Mr. Todd breaking away from the United Federal Party and re-establishing the United Rhodesia Party, claiming that Sir Edgar Whitehead was being unduly influenced by reactionary elements in the United Federal Party.

Despite protestations to the contrary, the issue had become clear cut. The Southern Rhodesian Government was virtually dependent on the support of a European electorate. If the United Federal Party was to be returned to power, therefore, European reaction had to be reflected in the party's policy. The Dominion Party, in its election manifesto, declared that the special voters' roll was unacceptable, and further that all applicants for registration on the common or upper roll would have, if it were returned to power, to be 'civilized'. Any persons whom registering officers did not feel lived in a civilized manner would be referred to a franchise board, which would then examine his or her 'franchise-worthiness'. The standards by which this would be judged would be: that they lived in a civilized manner, understood in general the notion of liberal democracy, and were of a good repute.[19] Earlier the African Affairs Committee of the Party had suggested that applicants for registration on the common roll would have to produce ten testimonials from persons already registered thereon, while Africans would have to submit a certificate from a Native Commissioner to the effect that they lived in a civilized manner and were of

[19] *The Dominion Party, Principles and Policies*, Revised Edition, April 1958—issued for the Southern Rhodesian general election of June, 1958.

good repute.[20] While conceding the necessity for fostering a spirit of mutual confidence and co-operation between the races, the over-riding consideration in the Dominion Party's view was that each racial group should maintain its separate identity. Racial association existed in the economic sphere and had to continue; but in the social and educational spheres there had to be a basic liberty of choice of association, and this must not be interfered with.

The result of the general election confirmed the correctness of the United Federal Party's assessment of the electorate's feelings, for while it was returned to power, its majority was reduced to four in a House of thirty. Mr. Todd, together with the other twenty-two United Rhodesia Party candidates, was defeated. But, on the contrary, the Dominion Party increased its representation from five seats at the dissolution to thirteen; indeed, it would have been returned to power had it not been for the operation of the optional alternative vote, four of its candidates having majorities of first preference votes but not when second preference votes were distributed. Of the total votes cast, the Dominion Party received 46 per cent., compared with 43·9 per cent. and 10 per cent. for the United Federal and the United Rhodesia Parties.

The United Federal Party subsequently demonstrated that it had learnt its lesson. The Bulawayo correspondent of *The Times* wrote of the Federal general election, held in November 1958: 'The United Federal Party candidates . . . in all their political utterances exercise exceeding care to say nothing to offend the predominantly European electorate. The eclipse of Mr. Garfield Todd is well remembered and its lessons well applied. To preach racial liberalism is to invite defeat. The two main parties (the Dominion Party and the United Federal Party) . . . are essentially, in spirit as well as in composition, European parties catering for European voters.'[21] The election proved to be a triumph for the United Federal Party, which won a sweeping victory[22] because its leaders demonstrated that they could be trusted in racial affairs, and also because the Dominion Party made a singularly poor showing during the election campaign,

[20] Reported in *Rhodesia Herald*, 28 March 1956.
[21] *The Times*, 11 November 1958.
[22] See Appendix, p. 271.

principally over the action it proposed taking in the event of the British Government refusing to grant the Federation independence in 1960 at the time of the constitutional review. During the election campaign the Dominion Party declared that if independence was not granted, the Federal Government should first hold a referendum on the issue, and then, if this went in favour of independence, it should place a resolution before the Federal Assembly praying the Queen to accept the Federation's declaration of independence. If this were not accepted, another general election would be held, and the task of the newly elected government would be to implement the declaration of independence. Barotseland and Nyasaland were to be given the opportunity of voting out of the 'Federation', but they would remain under the control of a joint condominium of the British and Federal Governments. Sir Roy Welensky and other Federal Ministers pointed out that the Dominion Party's plan would amount to a *coup d'état*; that it would entail a clash with the Governor of Northern Rhodesia and armed conflict between the military authorities under the control of the Federal Government and the territorial police force in Northern Rhodesia. But Sir Roy Welensky had himself expressed belligerent opinions regarding the constitutional review conference prior to the Federal general election. On one occasion, having declared that he hoped Federal independence could be obtained, with satisfactory safeguards for all concerned, by agreement rather than unilateral action, he went on: 'I don't want to talk about Boston tea parties and utter threats about what we will try to do in 1960. We shall go to the conference firmly believing that the achievements of Federation fully justify the granting of independence to us: and it is on that basis that our case rests. Should we fail to convince H.M. Government of that, then it will be time to take stock and decide what other action is necessary. I personally would never be prepared to accept that the Rhodesians have less guts than the American colonists had.' [23]

This increased stridency on the part of European political leaders in Southern Rhodesia and the Federation was a direct result of the franchise: with all-White electorates in the Southern Rhodesian and Federal spheres each party had to compete for the White man's vote, and this inevitably meant that each

[23] Reported in *East Africa and Rhodesia*, 22 May 1958, p. 1193.

vied with the other in seeking to allay his fears. But the stridency was also due to a greater appreciation of the problems facing the White communities. A cursory examination shows, for instance, that the high franchise does not ensure the maintenance of 'European standards'. If the Federal Assembly remains as presently constituted—and assuming that there will be normal economic development and African educational progress and that Africans will register as and when they are qualified—then in the foreseeable future there would be a majority of Africans registered on the general roll in Nyasaland. When this occurs there would also be a substantial number of African ordinary voters registered in Northern Rhodesia and Southern Rhodesia, so that, together with the African specially elected members, there could be an overall majority of Africans in the Federal Assembly. And an African majority cannot be expected to support the maintenance of the barriers which have been erected to preserve the European communities as cultural and social entities. In fact, the high franchise has been erected merely to gain time and *not* to preserve 'civilized standards of behaviour and culture'; it serves, in other words, to postpone the day when other means of protecting the White communities will have to be found.

Logically, therefore, any devices which prolong European dominance through the high franchise have to be used. In Southern Rhodesia the system of alternative voting was adopted so as to limit the chance of an African being returned in a constituency where the White vote was split between two candidates. In the Federal sphere, though the Federal Government decreed that party politics were to be the preserves of the politically adult section of the community—those elected on 'valid standards of civilization and responsibility'—and hoped that the political energies of all races would be directed into these channels, when an African was returned by the ordinary vote he was nevertheless to be treated on a racial and not on a party political basis, because, and despite the fact that the largest section of the community was only to have a limited political influence and restricted representation, that representation was to be automatically decreased if and when an African was returned as an ordinary elected member. If this was not done, of course, the number of African representatives would be increased in relation to those of the Europeans; conversely, this device ensured that the election of the first eight ordinary elected Africans would have no effect on the ratio of White and Black representatives. Likewise, it was necessary to silence those members of the community who refused to accept that 'maintaining European standards' should be the criteria for full participation in the life of the community. Thus the Federal Government arranged for ordinary and special voters to vote together for the election of the specially elected African candidates, thereby hoping to secure the election of 'moderate' Africans and not 'extremists'—those who, in the words of the Northern Rhodesian Government, would look to 'sectional interests alone'. The Northern Rhodesian Government suggested that the special vote should be eliminated in a decade by raising the qualifications of the special vote to those of the ordinary franchise, and that all special candidates would have to have their candidacies endorsed by two-thirds of the Government-supported chiefs in each constituency. Finally, both the Northern Rhodesian and the Nyasaland Governments changed the African electoral colleges for selecting the nominated African representatives in the Federal Assembly, the African Representative Council in Northern Rhodesia and the African Protectorate Council in Nyasaland being discarded in favour of new colleges consisting of all past and present African members of the Provincial Councils. Officially this was to increase the size of the electoral colleges; in reality, it was again an attempt to block the return of African 'extremists' by weighting the electoral colleges with the votes of older, more conservative men who were usually more closely connected with tribal affairs.

Since the franchise cannot protect White interests, it is vitally necessary to obtain independence and freedom of action at the earliest possible moment. The Rhodesian political parties are therefore trapped by a dilemma no less acute than those of the Conservative and Labour Parties. Independence in 1960 is vital; but because of the need to negotiate with the British Government it is not possible to categorically abandon the concept of racial 'partnership' before then. Thus the Dominion Party, while stating that it rejected partnership, merely offered a more conservative policy than the United Federal Party. In relation to the franchise, for instance, it promised to repeal the provisions for the special voters' rolls and to make it more difficult for an African to register on the ordinary roll. Nevertheless, by the time of the second Federal general election, the Dominion Party was aware, first, of the impracticability of asking the British Government to abandon its obligations to the African communities in the Protectorates, and, second, of insisting on a policy based on the concept of 'maintaining European standards' *throughout* the Federation. Thus Mr. Winston Field, leader of the Dominion Party, said, during a tour of Nyasaland shortly before the election, that while Nyasaland had to remain in the Federation for its own good, plans for its future should be based on the assumption that Nyasaland would be granted self-government within the Federation. During an interim period the Nyasa people would be trained for the tasks of government, and authority would be vested in a commission appointed by the British and Federal Governments. Eventually, when self-government was attained, the property and political rights of minority races in Nyasaland would be guaranteed in a treaty between the Territorial and Federal Governments. Later the Dominion Party included these proposals in their plan for a Central African Alliance in which Northern and Southern Rhodesia, as areas of major European interest and influence, would be united into one state and granted Dominion status, while Barotseland and Nyasaland, as areas primarily of African interest, would continue as Protectorates until such time as they became African states, at which point the three states would be linked together by treaty.

At the time of the Federal election Mr. Garfield Todd also said that an African Government was to be expected in Nyasaland, when Africans were ready for such responsibilities, while Lord Malvern, in a message published by the *African Weekly*, pointed out that in the normal course of events Nyasaland was likely to have the first African Minister and the first African Prime Minister in the Federation. None of these statements, however, really faced the fundamental issues. The Dominion Party was simply reducing the White/Black ratio in the central zone and guaranteeing to preserve the European community's interests in Nyasaland through the strength of the central White-dominated Rhodesian Government. Lord Malvern and Mr. Garfield Todd appeared to expect that in the course of time, through the operation of the high franchise and with European interests largely under the umbrella of the Federal Government, an African Government would emerge in Nyasaland which would be stable and which would support the concept of 'maintaining European standards'.

III. AFRICAN REACTIONS

Africans in the Federation face a simple alternative: they can either support or oppose the existing European-dominated Administrations. The implications of this choice, however, are far from simple; indeed, before Federation was implemented, Africans in the Protectorates were unaware of this fundamental alternative. The position was very different in Southern Rhodesia. Any thinking African seriously advancing proposals for constitutional development there had either to cast them in conformity with the basic tenet of the European's political philosophy—separate racial development—or accept that the only alternative to work for was the overthrow of the European Administration. Since Europeans dominated the state and controlled political and economic power, the latter alternative was hardly a practical proposition. Moreover, the more advanced members of the African community, those most sensitive to the indignities and insults of the colour bar, were more clearly aware of the disastrous consequences of attempting to overthrow the establishment, on the economy, the African community generally, and themselves in particular.

In Northern Rhodesia and Nyasaland the Protectorate status masked the basic alternative; nevertheless, there were fundamental differences between the Protectorates and Southern Rhodesia. The absence of urbanization and industrialization in Nyasaland on the scale of Northern and Southern Rhodesia meant that the African community there was more homogeneous and united, and this unity was enhanced by the experiences of generations of Nyasa migrant workers, who, looking back to their homeland from Southern Rhodesia or the Union, saw it as an oasis free from discrimination in a continent where a black skin was a stigma and everything African branded inferior. Thus, to Africans in Nyasaland, dignity, not economic advancement, was of over-riding importance. And dignity, they knew from experience, could only be secured through the advent of an African Government. The argument that the latter would deter investors and herald economic chaos had little force with Nyasas in any case: it could hardly be otherwise with a population of subsistence cultivators who had always been forced to migrate abroad to seek paid employment. In this context Northern Rhodesia was somewhere between Nyasaland and Southern Rhodesia: there was a larger White population and a greater degree of industrial development than in Nyasaland; but over 90 per cent. of the country constituted an essentially African state. Hence, while politically conscious Africans wished to rid the country of discriminatory practices, while they wished to see Northern Rhodesia become an African state, they were more conscious of the benefits arising from European-inspired enterprises.

The implementation of Federation first made the African communities in the Protectorates aware of the political realities of Central Africa. Fundamentally, their opposition to Federation was based on an appreciation that if it was implemented they would be forced to depend more on the local White communities and less on the Colonial Office, and this would make the attainment of independence as African states correspondingly more difficult. Hence the widespread support accorded to the Congress movements in the Protectorates; for Africans were also forced to realize that there were no constitutional channels available through which Africans could adequately influence the situation. The constitutional changes introduced by the Federal and Northern Rhodesian Governments after the creation of the Federation confirmed African fears, for it was plain that the British Government did not intend any of the constituent states to evolve as African states; that the overwhelming majority of Africans were to be condemned to second-class status; and that, perhaps most important of all, the transfer of power from the Colonial Office to the local White communities would occur within a comparatively short period. Hence all politically conscious Africans were brought face to face with the basic choice—as Southern Rhodesian Africans had seen it for many years. In these circumstances it is not surprising that a number of the more advanced Africans in Nyasaland and Northern Rhodesia expressed support for the existing regimes—as many of their compatriots had earlier done in Southern

Rhodesia—by joining the European-dominated political parties, especially the United Federal Party, so that in both the second Federal general election and the general election held in Northern Rhodesia in March 1959 Africans stood as special candidates on the United Federal Party's ticket. But it should be noted that their support was conditional, since fundamentally it was the choice of the lesser of two evils, an appreciation that co-operation might gain more for the African communities than direct, active opposition. Their continued support could only be secured, however, by a genuinely liberal racial policy which aimed at eliminating racial discrimination of the kind which prevented them eating a meal in a restaurant—by something in fact which the European communities could not concede.

But what of the remainder of the African communities in these circumstances? Their stake in the preservation of the *status quo* was smaller; the franchise excluded them from full participation. For them, the evolution of African states, the creation, safeguarding, and acceptance of an African way of life was of supreme importance. Their choice was in one sense less agonizing than that faced by the more educated and financially successful members of the African communities; they had less to lose and more to gain by opposing the existing Administrations. Since there were no constitutional channels available through which effective action could be taken—though all the Congress movements in the Protectorates presented programmes for constitutional change which would ensure that political power was effectively controlled by Africans—this opposition had to be channelled through what Mr. Todd had called 'a mass machine whose powers would not be exerted through the vote'. The only question of importance was: what actions were to be taken? As the machinery for controlling power was erected, so there were changes in the leadership of the Congress movements equivalent to the European reaction which had swept Mr. Todd from office, and which had forced European political leaders to declare that 1960 would see the Federation an independent Dominion. In Nyasaland these changes centred on the return of Dr. Hastings Banda, a doctor long resident outside Nyasaland, but who had for many years, and especially since the time Federation was first mooted, kept a watching brief on Nyasaland affairs. As early as November 1956 Mr. H. B. Chipembere, a member of Congress who had been elected to the Nyasaland Legislative Council in the election of 1955, had written to Dr. Banda expressing dissatisfaction about Congress leadership. What was needed was a man of about fifty or sixty, an intellectual, with a character combining nationalism with honesty, self-denial, and spirit of co-operativeness,[24] though he also admitted that if Dr. Banda returned his reputation would have to be built up in Nyasaland. He was not to be frightened if he was heralded as a political Messiah; it would cause great excitement, and could be used with advantage. While Dr. Banda was hesitant, the agreement between the British and Federal Governments in April 1957 brought his first decisive intervention in the affairs of the Nyasaland African National Congress.[25] And in July 1958 he returned to Nyasaland, to be elected president-general of Congress in the following month on his own terms, which were 'that there should be a new constitution which among other things gave him the sole power to nominate the other officers of Congress and the members of the executive committee'.[26]

In Northern Rhodesia too there was a split among Congress leaders. The cause was essentially the same: a demand, particularly among the younger men, for a more aggressive policy designed to break European domination and take the Protectorate out of the Federation. And in October 1958 Mr. Kenneth Kaunda, secretary-general of the Northern Rhodesian African National Congress, broke away—with many of its officials—to found the Zambia African National Congress: its policy, immediate self-government based on universal suffrage.

This new aggressiveness was accentuated when the Congress leaders returned from Ghana, where they had attended the Pan-African People's Congress convened by Dr. Nkrumah, the Prime Minister of Ghana. When Dr. Banda was driven to Salisbury airport—after staying the night in an African suburb—to catch his plane back to Nyasaland on his return from Accra, *The Times* reported that 'young women flung themselves on the

---

[24] *Report of the Nyasaland Commission of Inquiry, 1959* (H.M.S.O.), Cmd. 814, pp. 12–13. Hereafter called Devlin Commission.
[25] See *Devlin Commission Report*, op. cit., pp. 13–14.
[26] Ibid., p. 26.

vehicle and covered it with kisses, men took off their hats, and youths fought to touch the car'.[27] On his arrival at Chileka airport near Blantyre, Dr. Banda declared that his policy was one of 'non-violence, passive resistance, and civil disobedience'. Shortly afterwards he asserted that he wanted to get Nyasaland out of Federation without Communism; but if Communism was the only way of achieving this, he was prepared to have it.[28]

Illegal political meetings began to be organized by Congress leaders, who deliberately courted arrest. And on 19 February 1959 the Governor of Nyasaland requested the Northern Rhodesian and Federal Governments to send military and police reinforcements to the Protectorate because of the deteriorating situation, especially in the Northern Province, where the Nyasaland African Congress was especially well organized and supported. In addition to the dispatch of units of the King's African Rifles, 120 White territorials of the 2nd Battalion, Royal Rhodesia Regiment, were flown from Southern Rhodesia to Chileka airport. And because of the continuing unrest, the Federal Prime Minister, Sir Roy Welensky, acting in his capacity as Defence Minister, called up additional units of the all European territorial force in Southern Rhodesia. Sir Roy said he had not taken the step lightly, and that he was sure that only through personal sacrifice would the object of maintaining peace and essential respect for law and order throughout the Federation be attained.

Early in the morning of 26 February the Southern Rhodesian Prime Minister, Sir Edgar Whitehead, declared a state of emergency in the Colony. European police reserves were called up, all the leaders of the Southern Rhodesian African National Congress were arrested and detained, and all four Congress movements in the Federation declared to be illegal organizations and banned. Subsequently, spokesmen for both the Nyasaland and Northern Rhodesian Governments announced that it was unnecessary to declare a state of emergency in either Protectorate. But shortly after midnight on 2 March 1959 the Governor of Nyasaland did declare a state of emergency. The Nyasaland African National Congress was declared an illegal organization, and its leaders, including Dr. H. Banda, arrested during wide-

[27] *The Times*, 23 December 1958.   [28] *The Times*, 27 December 1958.

spread sweeps by members of the security forces. Riots occurred, particularly in the Northern Province, as Congress leaders were rounded up, and in several places troops and police opened fire on African crowds seeking to release them. On the first day of the Nyasaland emergency twenty-three Africans were killed.

In Northern Rhodesia meantime a general election [29] was due to be held under a new Constitution which gave Unofficial members—including two Africans—a majority on the Executive Council.[30] At 11 p.m. on 11 March the Governor of Northern Rhodesia declared the Zambia African National Congress and all its branches illegal societies under the Societies Ordinance, and through regulations under the Emergency Powers Ordinance served restriction notices on leaders of the Zambia Congress, who were rusticated to the rural areas. The Governor, in a subsequent broadcast, was at pains to emphasize that he had not declared a state of emergency, and that the Northern Rhodesian African National Congress was not affected by the regulations he had made.

Different reasons were given by the authorities for taking these actions. The Southern Rhodesian Prime Minister announced that the emergency had been declared 'in view of the general security situation in the Federation and the grave situation which has occurred in Nyasaland following the policy of violence pursued by the Nyasaland African National Congress. The fact that this policy . . . is supported by the African National Congress in this Colony has given rise to the reasonable fear that a similar grave situation may occur here unless immediate steps are taken. . . . The growing tendency of the movement (the African National Congress) to incite people in the rural as well as urban areas to defy law; the persistent attempt to suborn African employees of the Government from their loyalty, and the campaign of intimidation and boycott against moderate Africans who supported racial co-operation . . . was becoming intolerable. Most of the leaders were young men who had never established themselves in a reputable busi-

[29] See Appendix for composition of the Legislative and Executive Councils and for detailed results of the general election.

[30] The Colonial Secretary had to 'impose' a Constitution after Officials and Unofficials had failed to agree. Details of his decision were published in the *Government Gazette* of 11 September 1958, Vol. XLVIII, No. 43.

ness or trade, and a considerable number had criminal records involving crimes of dishonesty.' [31]

The Governor of Nyasaland, in a dispatch to the Secretary of State for the Colonies,[32] gave details of two meetings convened by the Nyasaland African National Congress. At the first, held in Blantyre on 24 January and attended by at least 150 delegates from all parts of the Protectorate and by representatives from Northern and Southern Rhodesia, plans were laid for staging a general strike, including stoppages by civil servants, and railway and road transport workers, in the event of Congress's constitutional demands being rejected. In the afternoon of the following day some 140 delegates were conveyed by lorries to 'another and secret meeting' at which everyone was sworn to secrecy. There plans were laid for arranging unlawful public meetings and processions, while four persons—who were named—were nominated to run the Congress organization in the event of Dr. Banda being arrested. Moreover, they were to fix a day when a campaign of violence was to begin, if Dr. Banda was arrested. This would include the sabotage of communications and power installations, the murder of administrative officers and other Europeans, including missionaries, certain Africans labelled as quislings, and finally, the assassination of the Governor and other senior British officers.

The Governor of Northern Rhodesia blamed indirectly the Pan-African Conference in Accra, and especially the resolution passed there which supported non-violence and 'all those who are compelled to retaliate against violence to attain material independence and freedom'. In the Governor's view, this encouragement of violence was the cause of the split between Mr. H. Nkumbula, president-general of the Northern Rhodesian African National Congress, and Mr. K. Kaunda, and the reason for the formation of the Zambia National Congress. For, according to the Governor, Zambia had 'been threatening violence to other Africans . . . making violent speeches . . . declaring that Africa is for Africans alone . . . organizing disobedience to just laws, and in particular had been making plans and preparations to prevent, by violence and intimidation, any African voter from

[31] Broadcast by Sir Edgar Whitehead, quoted in *East Africa and Rhodesia*, 5 March 1959, p. 786.
[32] *Nyasaland, State of Emergency*, March 1959, Cmd. 707.

casting his vote at the elections on 20 March'. Zambia was 'a subversive and seditious organization' associated with the Nyasaland African National Congress and its 'murder plot', for the Governor declared that there had been a meeting between officials of the two organizations at which attempts were made to plan disturbances in Northern Rhodesia to coincide with the campaign in Nyasaland, and so prevent security forces being released.

The actions of all the Governments in the Federation—and the British Government for supporting them—were widely criticized in the United Kingdom. The crux of the controversy was whether the Congress movements had decided on a policy of violence, and in particular whether there had been a 'murder plot' in Nyasaland, where fifty-one Africans were killed and seventy-nine injured during the disturbances, as had been suggested by the Governor of Nyasaland and the Secretary of State for the Colonies, Mr. A. Lennox-Boyd. On 6 April 1959 the Colonial Secretary appointed a Commission of Inquiry under the Chairmanship of Mr. Justice Devlin to inquire into the disturbances in the Protectorate and events leading up to them. The principal conclusions reached by the Commissioners were that 'by the beginning of 1959 the extremists (in the Congress) had made up their minds that they would get Congress to adopt a policy of violence';[33] that at the secret meeting of 25 January a policy of violence was adopted;[34] that while Congress leadership generally was a party to it, Dr. Banda, who was absent, 'would never have approved a policy of murder . . . but that he had come to regard some degree of violence as inevitable';[35] that there had been 'talk of beating and killing Europeans, but not of cold blooded assassination or massacre';[36] that there was no 'murder plot', nor, except in a very loose sense of the word, a plan;[37] that on 3 March 1959 the Government 'had either to act or to abdicate';[38] and that if the Government 'had had no information about a murder plot . . . they would still have declared a state of emergency on or about 3 March'.[39]

In Northern Rhodesia Mr. N. C. A. Ridley was appointed by the Governor to inquire into all the circumstances giving rise to

[33] *Devlin Commission Report*, op. cit., p. 47.   [34] Ibid., p. 82.
[35] Ibid., p. 82.   [36] Ibid., p. 84.   [37] Ibid., p. 88.
[38] Ibid., p. 74.   [39] Ibid., p. 88.

the making of the Safeguard of Elections and Public Safety Regulations, 1959, in accordance with Section 4B (1) of the Emergency Powers Ordinance. The commissioner concluded that members of the Zambia African National Congress intended to use intimidation, force and violence in carrying out a boycott of the Northern Rhodesian general election; that Zambia also planned to obtain self-government by other violent means; that many public speeches were made containing statements calculated to stir up strife between the races and to bring the Government departments, police, and public officers into 'hatred and disrepute'; that in private, such matters as arson, causing malicious damage to property and death and injury to persons opposed to them were discussed and planned, some in connexion with the election, but some of more general application; that during this period, Zambia leaders were working towards joint action with Congress leaders in Nyasaland and Southern Rhodesia; and that proposals for discussion at a conference between the three organizations 'did include a suggestion that if one territory were to start a civil disobedience movement resulting in disorders the other two territories should start a similar movement'.[40] Commissioner Ridley came to the conclusion that the 'Government had to take steps to prevent the continuance of wrongful interference by the Zambia organization with the election . . . and thus ensure that it was held in a calm atmosphere in which every voter, in particular the African, could exercise his right to vote. . . . In addition . . . a general challenge to the maintenance of law and order was being made by Zambia, and the Government had knowledge that its leaders were pressing on towards the completion of their plans for widespread disorders to occur as soon as they had been arrested.' [41]

In Southern Rhodesia the Minister of Justice and Internal Affairs subsequently stated that 'the activities of the Southern Rhodesian African National Congress . . . led to the state of emergency',[42] and that in particular, these activities were: 'to

[40] *Report of an Inquiry Into All the Circumstances Which Gave Rise to the Making of the Safeguarding of Elections and Public Safety Regulations, 1959* (Government Printer, Lusaka), p. 31. Hereafter called the Ridley Report.

[41] *Ridley Report*, op. cit., p. 32.

[42] *Report of the Review Tribunal (Preventive Detention, [Temporary Provisions] Act, 1959,* C.S.R. 27—1959, p. 7—hereafter called the *Beadle Report*.

excite disaffection towards the constitution with the object of altering the constitution by unlawful means; to excite disobedience and hostility to the laws and lawful authorities; to excite racial hostility; to coerce the Government by demonstrations, processions, and strikes; to ridicule and undermine the authority of Native Commissioners, land development officers, chiefs, police, African Members of Parliament; to organize boycotts, to misinterpret and falsify facts with a view to bringing the Government and Europeans in disrepute; to intimidate people to join Congress by threats of boycotting business and threats to life; to give out that Congress was more powerful than the Government; to co-operate with the Nyasaland African Congress, the Zambia African Congress, and the Northern Rhodesian African Congress, and to co-ordinate its activities with those organizations'.[43] In the first general report of the Review Tribunal, set up under the Preventive Detention Act, 1959, the tribunal found 'that all the allegations contained in the Minister's statement of particulars in the general case against the Southern Rhodesian African National Congress are proved'.[44] Earlier, however, the Southern Rhodesian Prime Minister had made it clear that the state of emergency had been declared at that particular juncture because of security needs in Nyasaland. 'When our own round-up on Thursday last was an obvious success and security risks in Southern Rhodesia had been immensely reduced, full discussions were held between the Federal Prime Minister and myself . . . to decide what additional security forces could be moved to Nyasaland without taking any risks in Southern Rhodesia.' Lord Malvern, the first Prime Minister of the Federation, put the matter more succinctly when he said in the House of Lords: 'It was decided that the Southern Rhodesian African Congress must be put behind wire so that they could not create a diversion and prevent the sending of necessary police to Nyasaland.' [45] This was not to imply that similar action would not have been taken at some other time; indeed, the Southern Rhodesian Prime Minister told Parliament that his Government had watched the rise of extremism in the African National Congresses for the past few

[43] *Beadle Report*, op. cit., p. 9.
[44] Ibid., p. 24.
[45] House of Lords Debates, 24 March, 1959, col. 258.

months, and that as soon as the Government had realized that its existing powers were inadequate to curb this trend 'preparations were under way for the measures that are being taken today' (the declaration of the state of emergency).

But was the adoption of a policy of coercion and violence surprising? Terrorism and revolution are time-honoured means of achieving independence from despotism. And the Administrations in the Federation—as far as African affairs were concerned —were essentially despotic. Once a policy of violence had been embraced, bloodshed was inevitable. To distinguish between talk of beating and killing Europeans and cold-blooded assassination and massacre, as the Devlin Commission had, might be meaningful in a strictly legalistic sense. But as Sir Robert Armitage, the Governor of Nyasaland wrote: 'If it was the intention of the Commission to seek to differentiate in this respect between different types of murder, then I must confess myself unable to appreciate the distinction. Massacre may be a matter of numbers, but murder is murder whether you call it killing or assassination. What was important from my point of view was not whether there was just talk of killing Europeans or talk of cold blooded or for that matter hot blooded, assassination or massacre, but whether there was a real threat to the lives of Europeans and Africans as a result of the adoption by Congress of a policy of violence.'[46] While the aims of the Southern Rhodesian, Zambia, and Nyasaland Congresses were emancipation and the achievement of self-government and independence, their plans for achieving them appear to have been loosely framed, contradictory, and even naïve, their foundations principally passionate conviction, violent intention, and mob oratory. Perhaps co-ordination and joint planning were in an early stage and were never completed because of the declarations of the states of emergency in Southern Rhodesia and Nyasaland—although Congress leaders believed 1960 to be the fateful year, and so they had left themselves little time to work out and organize deliberately planned campaigns. What is perhaps more likely is that Congress plans reflected the low standard of technical competence which characterizes all the African communities in the Federation, and that in any case they

[46] Nyasaland Despatch by the Governor, relating to the Report of the Nyasaland Commission of Inquiry, July 1959, Cmd. 815, p. 7.

were based on a serious miscalculation. Congress leaders seem
to have been convinced that an extensive defiance of authority
in all three territories would force the British Government to
accede to the demands of the Congress movements in Nyasaland
and Northern Rhodesia and would topple over the European
Administration in Southern Rhodesia. Thus Dr. Banda expressed the view that notwithstanding the declared aim of self-
government for the people of a British Colonial territory, the
bogey of immaturity or the desire to uphold the vested interest
of the European always prevailed until some great pressure was
put on the British Government. And so, in the words of the
Devlin Commission, Dr. Banda 'conceived his task as being that
of organizing the people of Nyasaland behind him to bring
about the degree of pressure required to right the basic wrong
regarding political rights'.[47] The same kind of sentiments,
though expressed in a more violent form, can be detected in a
speech made by Mr. Chipembere which was recorded and
taken to Northern Rhodesia for propaganda purposes. 'We are
no longer playing as we used to do in the days of the rotten
Manoah Chirwa[48] and in the days of the rotten T. D. T.
Banda[49] and their filth-ridden hearts. We are now doing serious
business. We mean to die for this country or win liberation. . . .
So much so that from Port Herald to Karonga, you will find
everybody in a state of mental revolt against the imperialists.
. . . Away in Fort Manning, in Dowa, people have become so
infuriated against imperialism that they have gone so far as to
lay their hands on the dirty body of a white-skinned fellow. And
away in Karonga you will hear people have stood in open revolt
against British authority. . . . They are defying death, they are
defying all the diabolical instruments of death in the face of the
imperialist. They are defying prison bars of the Central Prison
Zomba and exposing themselves deliberately for arrest.'[50] At the
secret meeting in January when policy decisions of vital importance to the campaign were taken, there appears to have been
considerable confusion. Some notes, prepared after the meeting,
reported that: 'If our doctor were caught word will issue from

[47] *Devlin Commission Report*, op. cit., p. 28.
[48] A former member of the Federal Assembly, subsequently expelled from Congress.
[49] President-general of Congress before Dr. Banda.
[50] *Devlin Commission Report*, op. cit., p. 70.

the Central Body telling all people to start war after two days, to dig up roads, to destroy everything belonging to Europeans', and 'to hit Europeans and cut throat'. But, 'if a person is arrested because of Congress the case must be taken to senior Europeans'. In the midst of these considerations there was a note to the effect that 'our African police must not wear puttees as putties make the legs thin!' Simon Kapwepwe, General-Treasurer of Zambia, told a public meeting at Kasama in the Northern Province that Africans should drive fear from their minds into the minds of Europeans, and they would then be in a better position to obtain independence. The Belgian Congo, he declared, had obtained self-government after only a three-day 'strike' [51]—a reference to rioting which had taken place in the Congo early in 1959, but which certainly did not produce self-government. Cornelius Mwanza, Zambia Vice-Secretary of Lusaka district, told an illegal meeting in Lusaka on 8 March 1959 that 'independence cannot come without suffering unless you fight for it. That means you must be prepared to be arrested or to be killed, and if you do not fear these things it is *very easy* (italics mine) to get self-government either today or tomorrow.' [52] In Southern Rhodesia Congress plans appear to have been even more vaguely outlined. The Secretary-General, G. Nyandero, was reported to have told a meeting at Harare on 8 September 1958 that the British Government must grant the Protectorates self-government, and that while Southern Rhodesia had self-government, it was in White hands. 'This is to change over.' [53] But the more detailed evidence in the Beadle Report relating to the organization of strikes and disturbances was largely obtained from secret witnesses, who were 'considered reliable'.[54] Nevertheless, the impression given is one of Congress over-confidence. Congress plans appear in fact to have assumed that the kind of pressure which had brought self-government to other British Colonies could be applied equally successfully in the Federation. But in their hour of crisis the Nyasaland Government appealed for help to the Federal and Southern Rhodesian Governments; and they were controlled

[51] *Ridley Report*, op. cit., p. 23.
[52] *Ridley Report*, op. cit., p. 24.
[53] *Beadle Report*, op. cit., p. 22.
[54] See for instance *Beadle Report*, op. cit., pp. 23–24.

by men having an infinitely greater interest in crushing opposition than transient British officials.

IV. PATHWAYS TO INDEPENDENCE

With the militant Congress movements smashed, the path was finally cleared for the European communities, the Administrations in the Federation, and the Conservative Government, to translate into practice the ideals of 'partnership' based on 'maintaining European standards'. And in March 1959 Sir Roy Welensky, the Federal Prime Minister, announced that Mr. J. Z. Savanhu, an African M.P. from Southern Rhodesia, was to be appointed Parliamentary Secretary to the Ministry of Home Affairs, with special responsibilities for race relations— the first African minister to be appointed by a Government in the Federation. In the following month Sir Roy announced that new post offices built in Southern Rhodesia—posts and telegraphs being a Federal subject—would not have separate entrances for Africans and Europeans; that existing signs and partitions would be taken down; and that the 'pinpricks' suffered by the more educationally advanced members of the African communities would have to go. The Southern Rhodesian Government accepted a Government back-bencher's motion that Africans should be allowed to join the civil service; [55] the Land Apportionment Act was amended to allow hotels valued at more than £50,000 to register as multiracial, while the Liquor Amendment Act enabled Africans to be served therein with hard liquor, a privilege previously limited to a small group of African *evolués*.

On 21 July 1959 Mr. H. Macmillan, the British Prime Minister, announced the appointment of an advisory commission 'to advise the five Governments, in preparation for the 1960 review, on the constitutional programme and framework best suited to the achievement of the objects contained in the Constitution of 1953, including the Preamble'.[56] The Commission was to consist of a chairman from the United Kingdom, six Privy Councillors from the United Kingdom Parliament, including three from the Opposition, six independent members, of whom four would be from the United Kingdom and two from

[55] Previously they had been legally debarred.
[56] Hansard (House of Commons), 21 July 1959, col. 1072.

other Commonwealth countries having federal constitutions, four from the Federation as a whole, to be proposed by the Federal Government, three from Southern Rhodesia, to be proposed by the Southern Rhodesian Government, and three each from Northern Rhodesia and Nyasaland, appointed by the respective Governors. Of the thirteen members from Central Africa, five were to be Africans; none were to be members of the Legislatures. Mr. Macmillan subsequently declared that 'our paramount object . . . has been to try and create . . . a common mind on the next stages of the political evolution of the Federation', and though he later admitted that 'if questions were put about the possibility of secession being within the purview of the Advisory Commission I would say . . . that the Commission would be free . . . to hear all points of view from whatever quarter on whatever subject', [57] the Commission's terms of reference and its composition meant there could be no questioning the continuance of the Federation. Indeed, Sir Roy Welensky told the Federal Assembly forthrightly that as far as the Advisory Commission was concerned the Federal Government would not 'have associated itself with anything which called into question the continuance of the Federation itself'.[58] In general, Mr. Macmillan defined the attitude of his Administration to the constitutional future of the Federation as one of 'increasing the constitutional responsibilities of the Territorial Governments, as distinct from the Federal Government, so that the position of each component Government can gradually approximate to that of the Federation itself. The purpose of our policy is . . . as rapidly as possible to move towards self-government in Northern Rhodesia and Nyasaland. We therefore hope to see a broadening of the electorate and the functions of self-government on normal party lines. When all the units are in a position to agree . . . that British Protection is no longer needed, then . . . can the whole Federation go forward to . . . full Commonwealth membership. Meanwhile, for practical purposes, there can be independence . . . in respect of the Federal functions transferred to the Federal Government.'

The question of transferring the power to the Northern Rhodesian and Nyasaland Legislatures brought the Conserva-

[57] Hansard (House of Commons), 21 July 1959, col 1079.
[58] Federal Assembly Debates, 21 July 1959, col. 1679.

tive Government face to face with the question of representation. Who were the powers to be transferred to, especially in Nyasaland? On 22 July 1959 the Secretary of State for the Colonies announced in the House of Commons that, although it was impossible to hold elections in Nyasaland under the existing conditions, significant steps could still be taken in the constitutional field. To this end, African representation in the Nyasaland Legislature was to be increased by providing two additional seats, making a total of seven, giving African Un-officials a majority of one over Unofficials of other races. Two African members were also to be appointed to the Executive Council. To give the new Legislative Council the opportunity to function satisfactorily, and for a reasonable length of time, its life was to be extended beyond May 1960, though it was hoped that the period of extension would not greatly exceed one year. But, the Colonial Secretary announced, any member of the Legislature subject to a Governor's detention order would have to vacate his seat at the Governor's direction; moreover, the Governor was empowered to appoint Africans to occupy the seats of any African members which might become vacant, and these would be appointed 'during Her Majesty's pleasure'. Finally, there was to be an increase of Official representation in the Legislature of two. These new arrangements were introduced by Additional Royal Instructions published on 24 August 1959. The Governor of Nyasaland immediately declared the seat of Mr. Chipembere vacant; that of Mr. M. W. K. Chiume, another Congress leader who had been abroad at the time of the declaration of the state of emergency, was also declared vacant in terms of the Legislative Council Ordinance, 1955. The Governor announced that these were interim measures 'to tide over the difficult period that lies ahead during which normal conditions must be restored' and 'a situation . . . created in which there will be the opportunity to resume consideration of the constitutional advancement of the peoples of the Protectorate, including the provision of a non-racial qualitative franchise'.

What of Northern Rhodesia? Speaking in the House of Lords, Lord Home, Secretary of State for Commonwealth Relations, said that power would be transferred to the 'Governments of the two Northern Territories, which will progressively become more and more representative of Africans until they have African majorities'.[59] Mr. H. J. Roberts, Northern Rhodesian Minister of Mines and chairman of the Northern Rhodesian division of the United Federal Party, immediately pointed out that there was a contradiction between Lord Home's concept and that outlined by the Prime Minister, who had looked forward to a 'broadening of the electorate and the functions of self-government on normal party political lines'. Mr. Roberts declared that Lord Home's interpretation was 'a blast at the very foundations on which the present Northern Rhodesian Constitution has been built'. If it were accepted it would be the death knell of non-racial party politics in the Territory. Subsequently Lord Home issued a statement saying that he was in full agreement with the policy of developing non-racial politics on party lines in Northern Rhodesia. 'The point I meant to make was that as more and more Africans qualify for the franchise the time will come when the Africans will numerically be a majority on the voters' roll, though of course, when that time comes, they should be voting entirely on party lines.'[60]

Let us turn now to the relations of the Labour Party with the Federation. Mr. Hugh Gaitskell, the leader of the Opposition, outlined his Party's position frankly and at length during a debate in the House of Commons on Central Africa in July 1959. Mr. Gaitskell admitted that 'we are principally concerned not with Southern Rhodesia . . . but with Northern Rhodesia and Nyasaland, and at least to an extent with the Federation. I do not think there is any doubt what our objective should be. It must be to look after the interests of those peoples who were entrusted to us . . . to benefit all Africans, who are the overwhelming majority of the population.' [61] While he did not believe there was necessarily a clash of interests between Africans and Europeans, while economic development could not be achieved without European investment, techniques, and personnel, economic development was 'neither enough in itself, nor would it be regarded by the African peoples as in any way a substitute for political freedom'. Mr. Gaitskell therefore

[59] House of Lords Debates, 27 July 1959, col. 596.
[60] Quoted in *Press Communiqué No. 392*, Information Department, Northern Rhodesian Government, 18 August 1959.
[61] Hansard (House of Commons), 22 July 1959, col. 1291.

declared that 'our second objective must be the establishment of political democracy and self-government'. Thirdly, 'partnership must be based on equal rights and equal status, and it must not be regarded or treated as a device to justify *de facto* white supremacy'. And finally he declared that if partnership meant equal rights, then 'the only ultimate principle which is possible in the political field . . . must rest upon . . . one man one vote'. Mr. Gaitskell admitted that there was a scarcity of Africans capable of carrying out the necessary political and administrative work; but he felt that in Nyasaland there should be a majority of elected Africans in the Legislature and at least the same number of African ministers as those of other races. In Northern Rhodesia there should be parity of representation between Africans and other races in the Legislature and the Executive Council. 'These we hold to be the immediate minimum steps necessary if African opinion is once again to have any confidence in our ultimate intentions.' [62]

Much to the relief of the European communities in the Federation, the Conservative Party won the United Kingdom election of October 1959—although in reality their relief was scarcely justified, for time was sharpening the dilemma of the Conservatives as much as it was that of the local Administrations, particularly the Federal and Southern Rhodesian Governments. Mr. Savanhu, for instance, was offered a Federal Government house in a European suburb of Salisbury after his ministerial appointment. But the Southern Rhodesian Land Apportionment Act stipulated that only African employees could reside permanently in a European scheduled zone—and while Mr. Savanhu might have been acceptable, 'there was doubt about his family'.[63] The Federal Government subsequently decided to build a house for the African Parliamentary Under-Secretary in an African suburb. In 1959 there was still no 'European' hotel in Southern Rhodesia where visiting non-Europeans could stay—except by special dispensation from the Minister of Native Affairs (a facility not extended to indigenous Africans). The Land Apportionment Act was amended, however, so that hotels wishing to do so could apply to cater for a multiracial clientele. But despite official pressure, none applied.

[62] Hansard (House of Commons), 22 July 1959, col. 1294.
[63] *The Rhodesia Herald*, 6 January 1960.

Indeed, rumours that the Salisbury hotel accepting non-European visitors, and thereby saving the Federal and Southern Rhodesian Governments a great deal of embarrassment, was to apply induced such a sharp drop in White patronage that the management changed its mind. Moreover, the Salisbury City Council announced that a municipal by-law made the provision of separate 'sanitary facilities' compulsory for each racial group using a public building—and that the by-law would be enforced.[64] When Mr. Macmillan, the British Premier, toured the Federation in January 1960 he spoke at a Salisbury cinema normally barred to non-Europeans, though on this occasion representatives of the Coloured communities were invited—and told they could use the cinema's African staff lavatories.[65]

Late in 1959 the Federal Minister of Transport published a plan for African advancement on the Rhodesia Railways which proposed that a number of existing job categories should be fragmented and made available to Africans at salaries between the accepted European and African rates. The two European Unions concerned categorically rejected the proposals, and the plan was subsequently abandoned in favour of another which suggested that all jobs reserved for members of the White Unions should be opened to competition on the basis of the rate for the job. Selected Africans would, after training, be placed on probation for four years—to see if they 'maintained European standards'—at a salary £10 less than the accepted rate; if accepted, they would then be given the full rate, 'together with the normal conditions of service that go with it'. The plan was accepted in principle by the executive of the European Railway Workers' Union but rejected by the Amalgamated Engineering Union because it infringed the rate for the job principle. At compulsory arbitration in Southern Rhodesia, the latter's objections were overruled—though the probationary period was reduced to two years—and subsequently the Amalgamated Engineering Union called a twenty-four-hour protest strike, while several branches of the Railway Workers' Union in Southern Rhodesia repudiated their executive's decision. Since Europeans refuse to accept social integration, advanced Africans would have to live in African areas where it would be impractical to provide

[64] *The Rhodesia Herald*, 7 August 1959.
[65] *The Guardian*, 15 January 1960.

'equal' social amenities. Hence the total cost of an advanced African to the Railway Authorities would probably be less than for an equivalently trained European, and so, theoretically at least, European living standards could be undercut. In reality, however, White workers have exploited the social implications of 'the rate for the job' deliberately to retard African advancement, for they are no more willing than the White communities generally to accept social integration.

The need for independence, for freedom of action, was, from the European point of view, becoming more than ever vital; but the old stalemate continued, for the British Government was pledged to maintain British protection over Northern Rhodesia and Nyasaland so long as the peoples thereof desired it—and by virtue of the central incompatibility, Africans in the Protectorates were adamanant that it should continue. Nevertheless, the balance of power underlying the stalemate was shifting—because of changes in the wider, continental context. European support for the federation of the Rhodesias and Nyasaland has rested primarily on their belief that it would protect them from the consequences of African political advancement by enabling the three territories to achieve independence while political power was still vested in their hands. The reasons for their confidence in the efficacy of this were various. Contact with a technically backward people breeds a conscious superiority. This has imbued Europeans in Central Africa with a false confidence in their own abilities and power, which in turn has led them to make equally false assessments of their political position. Thus the majority of Europeans were convinced that White domination was not only necessary but just; that African national consciousness in the Federation was confined to a few irresponsible urban dwelling politicians and so could be dealt with finally and completely by detaining the troublemakers in the general good; and that African national consciousness generally was being deliberately created and encouraged by the Colonial Office and the political left wing in the United Kingdom. In 1953, moreover, the Federation was geographically isolated, securely positioned between the Union of South Africa to the south and the Belgian Congo to the north, the former, the most powerful state on the continent, pledged to maintaining White supremacy, the latter, a vast, politically inert—or so it seemed—buffer state between the Federation and the main-springs of African national consciousness on the West Coast. In these circumstances, with the local White communities effectively controlling political power within the Federation, with the British Government able to do little more than delay matters, there was every reason to expect—provided there was evidence of some European good faith in African advancement—that independence would be gained, particularly if the Conservative Party continued in office.

Subsequently, however, there has been a surging growth in African political and national consciousness, inspired fundamentally by the European's presence, and a scarcely less rapid appreciation by the European Colonial Powers that because 'maintaining European standards'—whether of a European Power or of a settled White community—is fundamentally incompatible with African advancement, the cost of attempting to repress and contain African 'nationalism' would be both prohibitive and futile. Consequently the frontier of independent African states has swept south, and indeed has reached the northern border of the Central African Federation, for the Belgian Congo becomes an independent African state on 30 June 1960. In this new situation, no British Government could break the pledge to maintain British protection over Northern Rhodesia and Nyasaland without gravely damaging its reputation and its relations not only with the independent African states, but with all the Afro-Asian group of countries. Not unsurprisingly, Mr. Macmillan reaffirmed the pledge in Salisbury during his tour of the Federation.

There was a sharp, unfavourable reaction from the European communities, for the Prime Minister's statement, by finally dispelling all hopes that the Federation would attain independence as an effective White-dominated state, brought the European communities' long period of self-deception to an end. There were naturally protests that the Conservative Party was abandoning the White man in Africa; in fact, European disillusionment could be attributed to a fundamental difference of aim, for while the Conservative Party broadly supported the concept of maintaining high standards in certain spheres in the Federation, they also supported equality of opportunity and opposed discrimination, particularly against 'civilized' men, something quite different from what the White communities meant by 'maintaining European standards'. The Conservative concept was theoretically attractive but quite impractical in the conditions and circumstances of Central Africa—ironically, it was largely based on ideas propagated by leaders of the European communities, and they, unable to state their real intentions openly, had consequently never analysed the fallacies in their own propaganda. European disillusionment sprang from their own self-deception.

A policy based on 'maintaining European standards' can be contemplated by a European community in Africa only if the ratio of White to Black is such that Europeans can dominate the economy by filling every technical and administrative post except the least skilled and at the same time staff an Army and police force of sufficient strength to control the African population. Only in Southern Rhodesia are these conditions met, so that even if the Federal Government had succeeded in winning independence at an earlier stage, it would not have been able to implement a policy based on 'maintaining European standards' in either Northern Rhodesia or Nyasaland. The idea that European interests could be safeguarded by a White-dominated Federal Government and African aspirations met by African-dominated Governments in Nyasaland and perhaps Northern Rhodesia would have reproduced the central incompatibility at Government level. Logically, if the Federation is not able to arrest African political advance and ensure that European standards will be maintained, its *raison d'être*—from the European point of view—ceases. There is a dawning awareness of this among Europeans in Central Africa. After hearing Mr. Macmillan reaffirm the British Government's pledge about the Protectorates, the Southern Rhodesian division of the Dominion Party announced that in these circumstances Southern Rhodesia might have to consider seceding from the Federation,[66] while Sir Edgar Whitehead, Prime Minister of Southern Rhodesia and leader of the Southern Rhodesian division of the United Federal Party, declared that he would feel obliged to resubmit the question of the Colony's continued participation in the Federation to Southern Rhodesian electors unless the remaining reservations on the Colony's constitution were removed and there were

[66] *The Times*, 21 January 1960.

guarantees that the Federal Government would remain in 'civilized hands'. Moreover, Sir Edgar expressed the view that the Southern Rhodesian electorate would not remain federated with the Protectorates if their Governments were operated on a 'nationalist' basis by African 'nationalists'.[67]

It is indeed merely a question of time before the Federation of Rhodesia and Nyasaland splits asunder, breaks down because of the incompatibility between 'maintaining European standards' and African advancement, and because the White community in Southern Rhodesia, through determination *and* its inherent strength, can attempt to pursue a policy of 'maintaining European standards'. When the Federation splits, Northern Rhodesia and Nyasaland will become independent African states; Southern Rhodesia will become the most northerly state of the southern bloc dominated by the strength and power of the settled White communities living therein; the Zambesi will thus become a divide between White and Black Africa; and a majority of the White communities at present living in Northern Rhodesia and Nyasaland will migrate south of this frontier of racial power. This is not to imply that Northern Rhodesia and Nyasaland will thereby become thriving, democratic states—though the copper-mining companies, in view of their enormous investments in Northern Rhodesia, can be expected to come to terms with the social and political revolution which will follow independence. Neither will the position in Southern Rhodesia be any easier. The economic consequences of the break-up will be just as profound as in the Protectorates. Moreover, there will inevitably be a sharp increase in African political consciousness, for Southern Rhodesia will no longer be able to pursue an ambiguous African policy; either African advancement is conceded, and the emergence of African state accepted, or it has to be repressed.

In the long perspective of history, the break-up of the Federation will be seen as a step in the direction of establishing a new political equilibrium in central-south Africa, a step towards righting the unbalance caused when the African tribes were conquered and European-dominated states based on the concept of 'maintaining European standards' created. As such, it will be neither the last nor the most painful and bitter adjust-

[67] *The Times*, 30 January 1960.

ment. Because of the very nature of the conflict in this stark Sophoclean tragedy, the White communities, hemmed ever more tightly into the toe of the continent, will one day stand and fight to defend the countries they have fashioned, to defend their way of life, the existence of a European society on the African continent.

APPENDIXES

A. FRANCHISE QUALIFICATIONS
(as at January 1959)

(1) Federal franchise.
(2) Southern Rhodesian franchise (territorial).
(3) Northern Rhodesian franchise.
(4) Nyasaland franchise.

1. FEDERAL FRANCHISE (FEDERAL ELECTORAL ACT, 1958)

A person may be registered as a *General Voter* if he:

(A) is a citizen of Rhodesia and Nyasaland or a British Protected Person;
(B) is over 21 years of age;
(C) (i) has resided continuously for a period of three months in a general electoral district or a sub-electoral district, and
   (ii) has resided in the Federation for any continuous period of two years;
(D) has an adequate knowledge of the English language and is capable of completing and signing, in his own handwriting, the claim form, and in addition

   (a) is in receipt of income, salary, or wages of not less than £720 during each of the two years immediately preceding date of claim, or owns immovable property in the Federation valued at not less than £1,500, *or*
   (b) (i) is in receipt of income, salary, or wages of not less than £480 during each of the preceding two years, or owns immovable property in the Federation valued at not less than £1,000, and
      (ii) has completed a course of primary education, *or*
   (c) (i) is in receipt of income, salary, or wages of not less than £300 during each of the preceding two years, or owns immovable property in the Federation valued at not less than £500, and
      (ii) has completed a course of not less than four years of secondary education.

(A person shall be deemed to have the necessary means qualification if he:

(i) has obtained a university degree in Divinity;
(ii) has undergone a period of not less than five years' full-time training in Divinity in a theological college or seminary, or
(iii) has undergone a period of not less than two years' full-time training in Divinity in a theological college or seminary followed by a period of service as a minister of religion, if the aggregate of training and service was not less than five years,

and is ordained or appointed as a minister of religion and receives no earned income other than that received by him directly as a minister of religion.)

(A chief shall be deemed to have the means qualifications specified.)

(A married woman of 21 years or over, other than a woman married under a system permitting of polygamy, shall be deemed to have the same means qualification as her husband.)

(E) has signed the Declaration of Allegiance to Her Majesty.

A person may be registered as a Special Voter if he holds qualifications (A), (B), (C) and (E) as for General Voters, and

(D) if he has an adequate knowledge of the English language and is capable of completing and signing, in his own handwriting, the claim form, and in addition

(a) is in receipt of income, salary, or wages of not less than £150 during each of the two years immediately preceding date of claim, or owns immovable property in the Federation valued at not less than £500, or

(b) (i) is in receipt of income, salary, or wages of not less than £120 during each of the preceding two years, and
(ii) has completed a course of two years of secondary education.

2. SOUTHERN RHODESIA FRANCHISE (ELECTORAL ACT, 1951 AND AMENDMENTS)

A person may be registered as a Voter if he:

(A) is a citizen of Rhodesia and Nyasaland;
(B) is over 21 years of age;
(C) (i) has resided in the Federation for any continuous period of two years, and

(ii) has resided in the electoral district for a continuous period of three months preceding the date on which application is made;

(D) has an adequate knowledge of the English language and is capable of completing and signing, in his own handwriting, the claim form, and in addition

    (*a*) is in receipt of income, salary, or wages of not less than £720 during each of the two years immediately preceding date of claim, or owns immovable property in the Colony valued at not less than £1,500, *or*

    (*b*) (i) is in receipt of income, salary, or wages of not less than £480 during each of the two years immediately preceding date of claim, or owns immovable property in the Colony valued at not less than £1,000, and

        (ii) has completed a course of primary education, *or*

    (*c*) (i) is in receipt of income, salary, or wages of not less than £300 during each of the two years immediately preceding date of claim, or owns immovable property in the Colony valued at not less than £500, and

        (ii) has completed a course of not less than four years' secondary education.

(A married woman of 21 years or over, other than a woman married under a system permitting of polygamy, shall be deemed to have the same means qualification as her husband.)

Limited enrolment of persons having certain lower qualifications (20 per cent. of the total number of other voters registered in the Colony: this roll will be closed to further enrolment when the 20 per cent. limit has been reached).

A person may be registered on this roll if he holds qualifications (A), (B), and (C) as above;

(D) and has an adequate knowledge of English and is capable of completing and signing, in his own handwriting, the claim form, and in addition:

    (*a*) is in receipt of income, salary, or wages of not less than £240 during each of the two years immediately preceding date of claim, *or*

    (*b*) (i) has completed a course of not less than two years of secondary education, and

        (ii) is in receipt of income, salary, or wages of not less than £120 during each of the two years immediately preceding date of claim.

3. NORTHERN RHODESIA FRANCHISE (N.R. LEGIS-LATIVE COUNCIL ORDINANCE 1958—NO. 36)

A person may be registered as a voter if he

(A) is a Citizen of the United Kingdom and Colonies or a Citizen of Rhodesia and Nyasaland or a British Protected Person by virtue of his connexion with Northern Rhodesia;
(B) has attained the age of 21 years;
(C) (i) has resided in the Federation for any continuous period of two years, and
   (ii) has resided in the constituency for a continuous period of three months immediately preceding date of application for registration as a voter;
(D) is able to complete, in English and without assistance, the application for registration as a voter, and have an adequate knowledge of the English language.

Further qualifications required: *For an Ordinary Voter:*

(E) an income of not less than £720 per annum; *or*
property to the value of not less than £1,500, *or*
(in the case of a person who has completed a course of primary education) either an income of not less than £480 or a property qualification of not less than £1,000, *or*
(in the case of a person who has attended at the first four years of a course of secondary education) either an income of not less than £300 or a property qualification of not less than £500, *or*
a Minister of Religion; (every person shall be deemed to have this qualification who:

(i) (*a*) has obtained a university degree in divinity; or
   (*b*) has undergone a period of not less than three years' full-time training in divinity in a theological training college or seminary; or
   (*c*) has undergone a period of not less than two years' full-time training in divinity followed by a period of not less than one year's service as a minister of religion, and is ordained or appointed as a minister of religion and receives no earned income other than that received by him directly as a minister of religion;
(ii) has undergone a period of not less than two years' full-time secondary education followed by a period of not less than four years' full-time service as a member of a pre-

scribed religious body and who follows no other profession, trade, or calling and receives no earned income other than that received by him directly as a member of such body or order); *or*

A chief shall be deemed to have the requisite means qualification, or

A wife of a person who possesses any of the requisite qualifications.

For a Special Voter:

(E) an income qualification of not less than £150, *or*
a property qualification of not less than £500, *or*
(in the case of a person who has attended at the first two years of a course of secondary education) an income qualification of not less than £120, *or*
(*a*) a hereditary councillor, or
(*b*) a headman, recognized by his chief, of a village which (i) has an unbroken existence since 1924, or (ii) consists of more than twenty-five registered tax-payers, and who is performing unpaid service in such office or (iii) a wife of a person who possesses any of the requisite qualifications.

4. NYASALAND FRANCHISE (NYASALAND LEGIS-LATIVE COUNCIL ORDINANCE, 1955—NO. 25)

Election of non-African members:

Every non-African with the following qualifications is entitled to be registered as a voter if he

(A) is a British subject:
(B) is over 21 years of age;
(C) has been born in the Protectorate or has resided in the Protectorate for a continuous period of two years immediately preceding the date of registration;
(D) during the whole of the period of three months immediately preceding the claim for registration,

(*a*) has occupied either solely or jointly with others a house, warehouse, shop, or other building in the Protectorate, which either separately or jointly with any land occupied therewith is of the value of £250 (provided that in the case of joint occupation the share of each occupier shall be of value of not less than £250), *or*

(E) (i) has an adequate knowledge of the English language, and
(ii) is able, unassisted, to complete and sign the prescribed
claim for registration as a voter.

(Note regarding (D): every married woman of 21 years or over,
other than a woman married under a system permitting of polygamy, shall be deemed to have the same means qualification as her
husband.)

Election of African members:

No person shall be entitled to vote at an election unless he is a
member of the African Provincial Council at a meeting of which he
seeks to vote unless he

(A) is a British subject or a British protected person;
(B) is a resident in the Protectorate on the day fixed for the
nomination of candidates;
(C) is in possession of a certificate signed by the Director of Education of the Protectorate certifying that the candidate is able
to speak, write, and comprehend the English language sufficiently to enable him to take an active part in the proceedings
of the Council.

(5) COMPOSITION OF THE VOTERS' ROLLS

(a) *Federal General Election (Held on 12 November 1958)*

Southern Rhodesia

Voters' Roll	Population	European	African	Other	Total Votes
Ordinary .	2,640,000 *	Not available			65,092
Special. .		125	635	44	804

Northern Rhodesia

Voters' Roll	Population	European	African	Other	Total Votes
Ordinary .	2,300,000 *	Not available	39	Not available	20,249
Special. .		4	53	6	63

Nyasaland

Voters' Roll	Population	Euro-pean	African	Other	Total Votes
Ordinary .	2,710,000*	2,112	5	389	2,501
Special. .		1	11	1	13

* Provisional figure at 30 June 1958.

In Northern Rhodesia and Nyasaland the respective Congress movements (the Nyasaland African National Congress and the Northern Rhodesian African National Congress) campaigned for a boycott of the Federal election, and this affected the numbers of Africans registering as voters.

(b) *Southern Rhodesian General Election (Held on 5 June 1958)*

Because there was insufficient time to revise the electoral rolls on the basis of the amended franchise introduced by Mr. G. Todd's Administration, the election was fought on the existing roll. Qualifications for this were broadly the same as in A, B, C, D, in the amended franchise (see above). But the means qualification was radically different—an income of at least £240 per annum, taking into account the value of clothing, food, housing, provided in kind; or occupation of property valued at not less than £500; or ownership of a registered mining location. At the time of the general election there were 55,158 voters registered on the common roll, of whom 1,696 were Africans.

(c) *Northern Rhodesian General Election (Held on 20 March 1959)*

At the time of the election there were 23,358 ordinary voters and 6,846 special voters. Of the ordinary voters, 20,546 were Europeans and 796 Africans. Twenty of the special voters were Europeans and 6,821 Africans. The Northern Rhodesian African National Congress had, prior to the election, encouraged Africans to register; the Zambia African National Congress had boycotted the election. In the Northern Rhodesian Government's White Paper outlining their constitutional proposals it was estimated that there would be 20,012 ordinary voters and 24,648 special voters—supposing all who were qualified, registered. (The franchise proposals in the White Paper were not significantly different from those finally adopted.) In 1954, at the time of the previous general election, there were 15,505 voters registered on the common roll, of whom eleven were African.

(d) *Nyasaland Election* (*Held on 15 March 1956*)

This was the first direct elections in Nyasaland, and is not strictly comparable with the elections previously described in the sense that a common voters' roll did not exist. Election of the non-African members of the Legislative Council was by voters registered on the non-African voters' roll. The African members were elected from the African Provincial Councils by members of the Councils, two from the Southern and Central Provinces, and one from the Northern Province.

B. COMPOSITION OF THE LEGISLATURES

(1) *Federal Assembly*

Under the Constitution Amendment Act, 1957, the Federal Assembly was enlarged from 35 to 59 members.

Composition 1954		*Composition 1959*	
Speaker		Speaker	
Ordinary Members . . .	26	*Ordinary Members* . . .	44
14 from Southern Rhodesia		24 from Southern Rhodesia	
8 from Northern Rhodesia		14 from Northern Rhodesia	
4 from Nyasaland		6 from Nyasaland	
Directly Elected African Members	2	*Directly Elected African Members*	8
2 from Southern Rhodesia		4 from Southern Rhodesia	
(Elected by voters on the common voters' roll.)		2 from Northern Rhodesia	
		2 from Nyasaland	
		(All elected by voters on the general and special rolls voting together.)	
Indirectly Elected African Members	4	*Indirectly Elected African Members*	4
2 from Northern Rhodesia		2 from Northern Rhodesia	
2 from Nyasaland		2 from Nyasaland	
(Elected from and by the African Representative Council in Northern Rhodesia and nominated by the Governor. Similar procedure in Nyasaland.)		On 3 October 1958 the Governor of Northern Rhodesia announced that the African Representative Council was no longer considered to be a body representative of Africans for the purpose of the election, as was required by the Federal Constitution. A new electoral college was created consisting of the members of the African	

Provincial Councils, 19 members of the Superior Native Authority in Barotseland Protectorate, and all Africans registered on the Federal electoral rolls (both general and special). Similar changes were made in Nyasaland, where the Governor designated all past and present members of the Provincial Councils to be the electoral college.

Europeans Nominated to Represent African Interests . . . 3
1 from Southern Rhodesia (Elected by voters on common voters' roll.)
1 from Northern Rhodesia (Nominated by the Governor.)
1 from Nyasaland (Nominated by the Governor.)

35

Europeans Nominated to Represent African Interests . . . 3
1 from Southern Rhodesia (Elected by voters on general and special rolls voting together.)
1 from Northern Rhodesia (Nominated by the Governor.)
1 from Nyasaland (Nominated by the Governor.)

59

(2) *Southern Rhodesian Assembly*

Speaker and 30 elected members.

(3) *Northern Rhodesian Legislative Council*

1954
Speaker (Unofficial)
Ex-officio Members (Officials) . 4
Nominated Officials . . 4
Elected Members (Unofficials) 12

Europeans Nominated to Represent African Interests . 2

1959
Speaker (Unofficial)
Ex-officio Members (Unofficials) 4
Nominated Officials . . 2
Ordinary 12
(Ordinary constituencies stretch along the line of rail in generally urban areas. Special voters registered therein are allowed to exert a maximum influence of one-third upon the elections.)
Nominated Unofficials . . 2
'Retained as an insurance that the increased requirement for Ministers who are

1954 (contd.)

Africans Elected by the African
Representative Council from
among its members and
nominated by the Governor   4

              26

1959 (contd.)

not Officials . . . can be
met in the conceivable circumstances that the elec-
tions fail to return a sufficient number of candidates
who are willing and able
to devote their full time to
Ministerial duties.'

Specially Elected Africans   .   6
(Special constituencies cover
the African rural areas
generally. All votes, special
and ordinary, count in
full.)

Reserved European seats   .   2
(Two composite constituencies covering the special
constituencies.   Special
voters allowed a maximum
one-third influence.)

Reserved African Seats .   .   2
(Two composite constituencies covering the ordinary
constituencies.   All   votes
count in full.)

              30

Composition of the Northern Rhodesian Executive Council

1954

Governor as President
Official Members .   .   .   5
Unofficial Members   .   .   4
(One of the Unofficials to be
a European nominated to
represent African interests.)

1959

Governor as President
Official Members .   .   .   4
Unofficial Members   .   .   6
(Under the Secretary of
State's instructions, 4 of
the Unofficials are to be
Europeans and 2 Africans.
The choice of Ministers is
in the Governor's discre-
tion; but before selecting
the Unofficials whom he will
recommend for appoint-
ment, the Governor has to
consult with and pay due
regard to the advice of the
member of the Legislature
who as party leader 'is in

1954 *(contd.)*

1959 *(contd.)*
the Governor's opinion most likely to command the support of the majority of the elected members of the Legislative Council'. And in making his selection, the Governor must first consider the elected members.

(4) *Nyasaland Legislative Council*

1956

Governor as President

Ex-officio Members (Officials) .	3
Nominated Officials . .	8
Unofficial Members .	11

(6 non-Africans elected on the non-African electoral roll, and 5 Africans elected by the African Provincial Councils.)

23

1959

Governor as President
Speaker (Vice-President)

Ex-officio Members (Officials) .	3
Nominated Officials . .	10
Unofficial Members .	13

(6 non-Africans elected on the non-African electoral roll, and 7 Africans. Five were originally elected by the African Provincial Councils, but 2 were unseated subsequent to the state of emergency being declared and 4 were nominated in their stead.)

27

Nyasaland Executive Council

1956

Governor as President

Ex-officio Members (Officials) .	3
Nominated Official Members .	2
Nominated Unofficial Members	3

1959

Governor as President

Ex-officio Members (Officials) .	3
Nominated Official Members .	2
Nominated Unofficial Members (3 European, 2 African) .	5

C. STRENGTH OF THE POLITICAL PARTIES

(1) *Federal Assembly (After the General Election Held on 12 November 1958)*

Abbreviations: U.F.P.—United Federal Party; D.P.—Dominion Party; Ind.—Independent; C.A.P.—Central Africa Party. (The Central Africa Party was formed shortly before the holding of the Northern Rhodesian general election, and is lead jointly by Mr. G.

Todd and Sir John Moffat, a former chairman of the African Affairs Board in the Federal Assembly.)

	Southern Rhodesia			Northern Rhodesia			Nyasaland		
	U.F.P.	D.P.	Ind.	U.F.P.	D.P.	Ind.	U.F.P.	D.P.	Ind.
Ordinary (European)	18	6	—	12	1	1	6	—	—
Directly elected African	3	1	—	2	—	—	2	—	—
Indirectly elected African	—	—	—	—	—	2	2	—	—
European elected to represent African interests	1	—	—	—	—	—	—	—	—
Europeans nominated to represent Africans	—	—	—	—	—	1	—	—	1
	22	7	—	14	1	4	10	—	1

Of the 59 seats in the Federal Assembly, the U.F.P. won 46, the D.P. 8, and the remaining 5 seats were filled by Independents.

In Northern Rhodesia there were 326 votes cast for the indirectly elected African representatives; the two successful candidates received 56 and 54 votes respectively. There were 15 candidates.

In Nyasaland there were only 2 candidates for the directly elected and 2 for the indirectly elected seats. All were elected unopposed. They were all members of the U.F.P.

(2) Southern Rhodesian Assembly

In the general election held on 5 June 1958 17 U.F.P. candidates were returned and 13 Dominion Party candidates. All were Europeans.

(3) Northern Rhodesian Legislative Council

In the general election held on 10 March 1959 the U.F.P. won 11 of the ordinary seats and the D.P. 1. In the special constituencies the C.A.P. won 2 seats, the Northern Rhodesian African National Congress 1, and 1 was held by an Independent. Two special seats were not contested because no valid nominations were received in time. In the 2 seats reserved for Europeans, 2 C.A.P. candidates were returned; in the 2 African reserved seats, 2 U.F.P. candidates were successful. Thus the U.F.P. won 13 seats, the C.A.P. 4, the D.P. 1, the N.R. African National Congress 1, and there was 1 Independent.

Subsequently the Governor appointed 5 members of the United Federal Party to the Executive Council, 4 of whom were European and 1 African. The second African Minister was nominated to the Legislative Council (the Governor also nominated an Asian to the Legislature.) The Executive Council thus consisted of 4 Officials and 6 Unofficials, of whom 5 were members of the United Federal Party.

INDEX

NORTHERN RHODESIA

Territorial boundaries ― ― ― ―
Federal boundaries ....
Native reserves (LUBA)   Mission stations +
Railways ―┼―┼―   Roads ―――
Towns ○   Hilly country
Rivers ―――   Swamps

BELGIAN

CONGO

ANGOLA

NORTHERN

TABWA

LUNGU (ZOMBE)

Abercorn

MAMBWE (FWAMBO)

MAMBWE (NSOKOLO)

Tunduma

Mporokoso

BEMBA (MPOROKOSO)

LUNGU (TAFUNA)

LUNGU (MUKUPA)

Kawambwa

Kalungwishi R.

Chambesi R.

BEMBA (MAKASA)

MAMBANGA

LUNGU (MUKUPA)

Kasama

BEMBA (MUWANGA)

IWA (KAFWIMBI)

TAM (BO-PUNGWE KAMANGA)

Chinsali

Mwinilunga

Zambezi R.

Kansanshi Mine

Solwezi

Ft. Rosebery

L. Kampolombo

Bangweulu Swamps

Livingstone Memorial

Mazimba

Bancroft

Mokambo

Mufulira

Chingola

ELISABETHVILLE

Kalaushi

Kitwe

Kafue R.

Ndola   SWAHILI

Lundazi

EASTERN

Luanshya

Mana M'Kubwa

Kabompo

Kasempa

Luena R.

LAMBA-LIMA

WESTERN

N. SWAKA

Lukulu R.

LUSANDWA

Ft. Jameson

Kapiri Mposhi

S. SWAKA

Luangwa R.

PEMAUKI

Petauki

HOOK

Ft. Manning

Katete

CHEWA

Busango Swamp

Lukanga Swamp

LENJE

Broken Hill

WAMBO

HSENGA

BAROTSELAND

Mankoya

Kafue Hook

C E N T R A L

LUANO-LALA

CHILINGA

MOZAMBIQUE

Mongu

LUBA

Chisamba

LUSAKA

SOLI

SHAMIFWE

Zambesi R.

PROTECTORATE

Zambezi R.

TONGA (SIGONGE)

Kafue R.

Kafue

TONGA (SIGONGE)

ILA

TONGA

Mazabuka

NKOYA

Monze

Pemba

TONGA (MAGOYE)

Kariba Gorge

SOUTHERN

Choma

SOUTHERN

Kalomo

RHODESIA

ANGOLA

TOKA

Sesheke

TONGA (CHOMA)

BALEYA

Kabulabula

Caprivi Strip

LIVINGSTONE

R.W. FORD

MILES
20 0 20 40 60 80 100 120 140